The Mau Mau War in Perspective

EASTERN AFRICAN STUDIES

The Mau Mau War in Perspective

Frank Furedi

Chairman, Development Studies
University of Kent at Canterbury

James Currey
LONDON

Heinemann Kenya
NAIROBI

Ohio University Press
ATHENS

James Currey Ltd
54b Thornhill Square
Islington
London N1 1BE, England

Heinemann Kenya
Kijabe Street, PO Box 45314
Nairobi, Kenya

Ohio University Press
Scott Quadrangle
Athens, Ohio 45701, USA

British Library Cataloguing in Publication Data

Furedi, Frank
The Mau Mau war in perspective.
1. Kenya. Revolutionary movements: Mau Mau, 1905–1963
I. Title
338.9669

ISBN 0-85255-051-0 (cased)
ISBN 0-85255-052-9 (paper)

Library of Congress Cataloging-in-Pulication Data

Furedi, Frank. 1948–
The Mau Mau war in perspective / Frank Furedi.
p.   cm.—(Eastern African studies)
Bibliography: p.
Includes index.
ISBN 0-8214-0940-9.—ISBN 0-8214-0941-7 (pbk.)
1. Migrant agricultural laborers—Kenya—History—20th century.
2. Squatters—Kenya—History—20th century.
3. Mau Mau—History.   4. Kikuyi (African people)—History.
I. Title.   II. Series: Eastern African studies (London, England)
HD 1538.K4F87   1989
307.3′96—dc20   89-32962
CIP

Typeset in 10/11 pt Baskerville by Colset Private Limited, Singapore
Printed and bound in Great Britain

Contents

Contents

Contents

PART II

Contents

Eight
The Consolidation of Reaction

Tables

Maps

Acknowledgements

There are many debts to acknowledge. During the research for this work, I was fortunate to have, in Dr Richard Rathbone, a supervisor who gave me invaluable guidance and enough rope to hang myself. John Lonsdale and Colin Leys were generous with their time and always gave valuable advice. At various times, I have benefited from discussions with Chris Leo, Susanne Mueller, John Spencer and Sharon Stichter. Roselle Warshaw, who worked alongside me in various Kenyan archives, is responsible for discovering much material that would otherwise have escaped my attention.

A grant from the Canada Council allowed me the luxury of carrying out three years' research. During the year 1973–74, a Junior Fellowship from the Institute of Commonwealth Studies, London, provided a stimulating environment for discussion.

In Kenya many former Mau Mau activists took me into their confidence. I hope that their trust has not been in vain and that in this book they will find an analysis that corresponds to their experience. Special thanks to Njoroge, who has never ceased to fight and who remains convinced that Mau Mau is a dress rehearsal for greater things to come.

During the writing stage I have enjoyed the support and comradeship of a number of demanding friends. Sabene Jansen provided a model of precision. Mick Hume has fought unsuccesfully to teach me how to write. Helen Simons always discovered the uncomfortable. Andy Clarkson, Mike Freeman, Alan Harding, Kennon Malik and Joan Phillips have all conspired to ensure that I could not take anything for granted. My greatest debt is to my partner Ann, who always knows what has to be done.

Carol Wilmshurst has typed and corrected this manuscript and has stoically put up with my terrible handwriting. Many thanks.

Abbreviations

AIM	Africa Inland Mission
ANC	African National Congress
CNC	Chief Native Commissioner
CO	Colonial Office
CP	Central Province
DC	District Commissioner
DEC	District Emergency Committee
DO	District Officer
EAS	*East African Standard* (newspaper)
FH	Fort Hall
For.	Forestry Department
GAWU	General Agricultural Workers' Union
KADU	Kenya African Democratic Union
KANU	Kenya African National Union
KASU	Kenya African Studies Union
KAU	Kenya African Union
KBU	Kiambu
KHSLA	Kikuyu Highlands Squatters' Landlords Association
KCA	Kikuyu Central Association
KISA	Kikuyu Independent Schools Association
KLFA	Kenya Land Freedom Army
KMGA	Kakamega
KNA	Kenya National Archives
KPU	Kenya Peoples' Union
Lab.	Labour
LBEA	*Leader of British East Africa* (newspaper)
LG	Local Government
LO	Land Office

Abbreviations

L&S	Land and Settlement
MAA	Member for African Affairs
NKU	Nakuru
NLO	Nakuru Labour Office
PC	Provincial Commissioner
PO	President's Office
PRO	Public Record Office
RLO	Resident Labourers Ordinance
RVP	Rift Valley Province
SLO	Senior Labour Officer
TN	Trans Nzoia
UG	Uasin Gishu

Glossary of Kikuyu & Swahili Terms

ahoi	landless tenants, plural of *muhoi*
arathi	prophet, plural of *murathi*
askari	soldier, or policeman
baraza	meeting
batuni	platoon, used to mean a soldier's oath
Dini	a revivalist or dreamers' church
Dini ya Jesu Kristo	Church of Jesus Christ
Dini ya Msambwa	Church of Msambwa
Dini ya Roho	The Red Church
duka	shop
githaka	land owned by a Kikuyu clan or landowner
karani	clerk
kiama	council
Kiama Kio Bara	council of fighters
Kiama Kia Muingi	Land Freedom Army
kipande	identity card
nyapara	foreman
posho	maize meal
shamba	plot of land
Watu wa Mungu	Men of God
Uhuru	independence

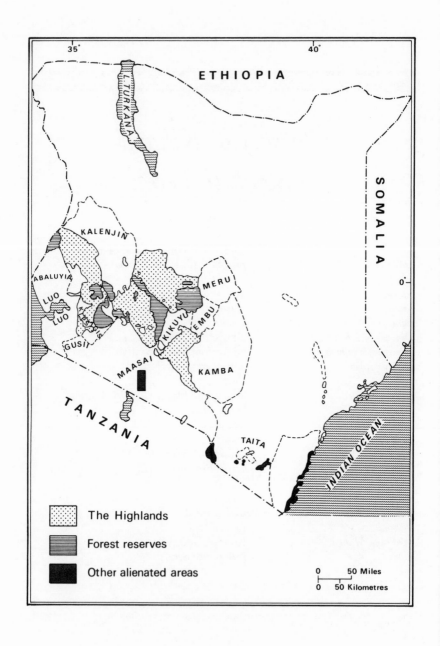

Map 1   Location of the White Highlands

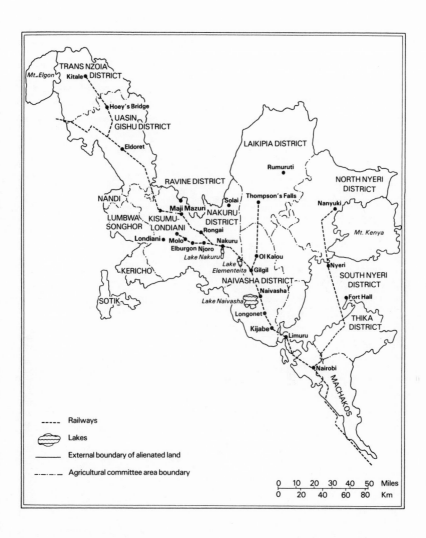

Map 2   The White Highlands

Part I

Introduction

The aim of this work is twofold. It is, first of all, an attempt to analyse the dynamic and social basis of the Mau Mau revolt. Secondly, through a discussion of Mau Mau it seeks to throw light on the subsequent process of decolonization and the consolidation of post-colonial domination in Africa.

Mystery still shrouds the Mau Mau revolt. Existing literature on the subject has a provisional character and cautiously stresses 'that more work needs to be done'. In this vein, R. Buijtenhuijs, the author of a recent essay on Mau Mau historiography argues that 'it is my impression that although we *know* much more about Mau Mau today than we did ten years ago, we do not *understand* the phenomenon any better; indeed, perhaps we understand it less well.'[1] To anticipate one of our arguments, this problem of 'understanding' is in no small part due to the fact that students of Mau Mau are often looking for something that isn't there.

There are a number of other reasons for the mystery that still surrounds Mau Mau. Unlike other liberation movements, such as those in Algeria or Zimbabwe, it was defeated almost a decade before the formal transfer of power to an African government. By the end of 1954 the British colonial authorities had the situation more or less under control – nine years before Kenya achieved formal independence. During the interregnum the colonial administration was able to construct what it considered to be a legitimate African leadership. The British administration and its moderate African allies had a common interest in mystifying the Mau Mau revolt.

The colonial regime had every reason to obscure the issue. Although the Declaration of Emergency in Kenya occurred in October 1952, the colonial government had been on the offensive for some time before. Throughout 1952 it had used exceptional measures to provoke and crush its militant opponents.[2] Parallel to this police offensive was the public relations campaign aimed at presenting Mau Mau as a criminal

3

organization. The colonial government went to great lengths to portray Mau Mau as an irrational force of evil, dominated by bestial impulses and influenced by world communism.[3]

An illustration of this ideological campaign can be seen in the response of the colonial state machinery to an attempt by Granville Roberts to publish in Kenya an article on Mau Mau, just a few weeks before the Declaration of Emergency. Counter-insurgency experts were disturbed by his economic analysis of the roots of Mau Mau.[4] One argued that an emphasis on economic causes would 'mislead' readers and complained that Roberts made 'no mention of the main cause i.e. perverted tribalism.'[5] The Chief Native Commissioner gave his verdict:

> The article stresses far too much the agrarian problems as being the cause of Mau Mau. To the Kikuyu the agrarian problem is no doubt uppermost in his mind; but the Mau Mau organization has been set up by Kikuyu demagogues imbued with tribal nationalism, encouraged by world movements, and with a particular eye upon their own personal advancement.[6]

The editor of the publication under consideration was duly informed that Roberts ought to change his line.

The sensitivity of the colonial administration to publications that made even a minimal attempt to investigate the social causes of the Mau Mau revolt is understandable. As far as it was concerned the world had to see Mau Mau as an illegitimate, perverted force. It is a testimony to the effectiveness of this campaign of criminalization that the irrational image of Mau Mau still endures. Even the European left, generally inclined to support anti-imperialist movements, looked upon Mau Mau as an unfortunate distorted product of colonialism. The post-independence governments of Kenya have also sought to bury Mau Mau. The Kenyatta regime, composed of politicians hostile to Mau Mau, tried to portray the revolt as a relatively minor episode. Kenyatta himself took the lead by emphasizing the theme 'forgive and forget'. As we shall argue, this historical amnesia is entirely understandable: if the issues surrounding Mau Mau are clarified, then the nationalist claims of the present Kenyan establishment stand open to question.

The argument

Kenya, like every African colony that experienced large-scale European settlement, suffered from white domination in a particularly acute form. This, in turn, provoked militant resistance. Not surprisingly, the impetus behind Mau Mau is most discernible in those parts of Kenya where the impact of European settler interests was most manifest: in the so-called White Highlands of the Rift Valley and in Nairobi.

Introduction

Of all the peoples of Kenya, it was the Kikuyu whose way of life was most disrupted by colonial rule. Many of them were dispossessed of their land and were forced to work for European enterprises at a relatively early stage of the colonial era. But the impact of colonialism on the Kikuyu was more comprehensive than the simple loss of land. Central Province, the area where the Kikuyu lived, was swiftly drawn into the capitalist market and underwent a major social transformation.[7] While many Kikuyu suffered the full brunt of this change, others became involved in the new colonial system. Indeed, it was precisely because the Kikuyu people were so involved in the new system that such a high proportion of educated and entrepreneurial Africans came from this ethnic group. Ironically, some of the colonial regime's most loyal African supporters as well as its fiercest opponents were Kikuyu.

Since they were the most affected by the colonial system and the most educated about its ways, the Kikuyu emerged as the most politicized African community in Kenya. Politicization does not necessarily lead on to armed revolt. There were many reasons for African radicalization and this point is discussed in Chapter 3 and Chapter 4. But one of the main dynamics behind Mau Mau was the agrarian revolution that was taking place at the time. Those most affected by this revolution were the squatters, more specifically labourers and their families who resided on European farms in the White Highlands. Threatened with a loss of land and grazing rights the Kikuyu squatters fought back. Their resistance provoked considerable support in Central Province, where in any case Kikuyu peasants were also facing the prospect of economic insecurity. This agrarian movement provided the energy for the revolt, but it could not have attained the political coherence it did without the intervention and leadership of radicalized nationalist elements from Nairobi. It was the convergence of interests between the movement of squatters, the Central Province peasantry and Nairobi activists that gave Mau Mau such coherence and force.

That Mau Mau was largely a Kikuyu affair has served as a justification for the thesis that the revolt was a tribalist one. Such an approach confuses cause and effect. It was the special character of the colonial impact that stimulated the politicization of the Kikuyu and not tribal traditions. Other African communities were also politicized, though not to the same degree. The inability of Mau Mau to acquire a more national dimension is due not only to the special Kikuyu experience but also to the colonial policy of divide and rule which explicitly sought to marginalise nationwide political movements. In any case it is not at all unusual for nationalist and other political movements to have a restricted regional base. The nineteenth-century role of Prussia and Piedmont in German and Italian unification is well known and no serious historian has yet suggested that Bismarck and Cavour were tribalist leaders. From a sociological point of

5

view the non-tribalist dimension of Mau Mau is shown by the different responses it provoked in Kikuyu society. Mau Mau was directed against the Kikuyu establishment as well as against colonial rule, and to a limited extent had the character of a civil war. In Chapter 5 we outline the social basis of Mau Mau.

But if Mau Mau was not tribalist it also was not a conventional nationalist movement. It is one of the central arguments of this book that it was precisely the underdeveloped character of the nationalist movement that led to the emergence of Mau Mau. The colonial administration did its best to thwart the early nationalist movement since within the framework of a white settler society African nationalism could not be considered as a legitimate point of view. It was the ineffectiveness of the nationalist politicians and the lack of prospects for political reform that drove thousands of Kikuyu outside the framework of what was considered legitimate protest. As a result, African politicians became isolated from the mass movement and Mau Mau developed outside their control. Indeed it is because the nationalist politicians lacked influence that a movement without the usual restraints could arise. It is important to stress this point, for ultimately the defeat of Mau Mau was conditional on the emergence of African nationalist politicians who possessed authority and credibility. Above all, this role fell on Jomo Kenyatta, a man with nationalist credentials who could play a restraining role on the mass movement while acting as a responsible negotiating partner with the colonial authorities.

Let us explore this point in more detail. In a recently published study, *Peasant Consciousness and Guerrilla War in Zimbabwe*, Terence Ranger asks why a revolt like Mau Mau broke out in Kenya but not in Zimbabwe. Ranger shows that there were considerable similarities between Kenya and Zimbabwe, and if anything the scale of the eviction of squatters in Zimbabwe in the post-war period was greater than in Kenya. Ranger argues that one of the main reasons for the absence of a revolt in Zimbabwe was the lack of differentiation among the Ndebele people compared to that of the Kikuyu,[8] and his argument corresponds to the results of our research and analysis.

By the late 1930s social differentiation in Central Province had begun to express itself in class tension. The growth of commercial farming had led to an active market in land and created social polarization. In 1941, the District Commissioner of the Kiambu District of Central Province noted that 'hundreds possibly even thousands of acres have changed hands by "irredeemable sale" during the past 10 or 15 years', and most of this had 'gone into the hands of a very few people'. He warned that the traditional system of land tenure 'is bent or broken as occasion arises, to suit the will of the influential, and the landless class is springing up in the reserve at a far greater pace than is healthy.'[9] Nine years later, in 1950, the Provincial Commissioner of Central Province pointed to the dramatic rise in the consolidation of land holdings, which he characterized as 'the local equivalent of the enclosures in England'. As in England, the enclosure movement implied the growth of the landless population. The warning of the Provincial Commissioner was prophetic. He argued that work had to be found for the landless 'if they are not to degenerate into an idle and feckless mob with no stake in the country – a ready instrument to the hand of every agitator.'[10]

The growth of social differentiation within the Kikuyu areas had important consequences. Tension between landowners and landless gave way to conflict, and when thousands of squatters were forced off European farms violence erupted. The strength of feeling against members of the Kikuyu establishment was evident in the early phase of the revolt when they constituted its main targets. In turn, the Kikuyu landowners and their allies unleashed a wave of repression against the rest of the community. One European farmer at the time noted that the discipline of the Kikuyu Home Guards broke down, forcing 'women and children to live in the bush or forest not daring to go near their homes except in day light.'[11] To Ranger's important observations we would add that the intensity of social polarization prevented the inclusion of the squatter revolt in mainstream nationalism. Social differences thus also acquired an important political dimension.

Social differentiation and class conflict found a clear expression in the political sphere. Social polarization prevented the emergence of a united nationalist movement. The educated political activists of the Kikuyu establishment had little influence among the landless and the squatters. The growing divergence between militant activists and those attracted to the option of moderate reform is one of the decisive themes of the period. It meant that the process of political radicalization could not be reconciled with the objectives of mainstream nationalism.

Mau Mau stands in sharp contrast to the experience of squatter movements in Southern Rhodesia and even in South Africa. In these areas squatter and rural protest was more readily reconciled with mainstream nationalist aspirations.[12] Political radicalism which is usually curbed or suppressed in the interest of an all-class nationalist alliance found considerable room for development in post-war Kenya. Mau Mau expressed the irreconcilable nature of social tensions. Its destruction was the precondition for the evolution of a more acceptable reforming nationalist movement and the consummation of the process of decolonization. But even the defeat of Mau Mau was insufficient to resolve the underlying social tensions. As we argue in Chapters 6, 7 and 8, the story continues well after Mau Mau's defeat.

The coincidence of the agrarian revolution, general radicalization and the ineffectiveness of nationalist politicians explains the Mau Mau explosion. The colonial authorities also made their contribution. Fearing a further escalation of unrest, the colonial administration unleashed a campaign of pre-emptive repression that forced militants to take up arms. The story of this explosion is documented in Chapter 4.

Books on Mau Mau are often distracted by the more exotic features of the movement. In particular there appears to be an enduring fascination with rituals and oaths. It is often forgotten that in colonial Kenya protest necessarily had to be secret. This was due not to any natural secretiveness but to a sense of survival. The issue of Kikuyu traditional oaths, which is often taken to be one of the distinctive features of Mau Mau, is in fact characteristic of rural protest in general. British and Irish eighteenth- and nineteenth-century history is full of examples of state authorities unleashing repression against the use of oaths by protesting peasants and craftsmen. Oaths for the Kikuyu, as for European rebels, had the straightforward role of forging consensus and unity.

Studies of Mau Mau have often isolated the movement from the unfolding of history. Too often it is treated as a formal organization and analysed as an institution. Thus Buijtenhuijs begins his essay by asking 'how do we exactly define "Mau Mau" and whom do we consider to be Mau Mau members?'[13] In reality agrarian revolts are not organized along formal institutional lines. Instead of defining Mau Mau, we ask at what point did agrarian protest turn into the explosion known as Mau Mau. As we argue in Chapters 3, 4 and 5, Mau Mau cannot be neatly compartmentalized and isolated from previous trends. Our research has shown that many of the practices associated with Mau Mau, such as oathing, had begun some time before it is generally thought.[14] Although Mau Mau cannot be reduced to the inevitable culmination of a pro- tracted period of agrarian struggle, it is this conflict that provided the main impetus behind the revolt.

In line with the approach of historical materialism, we believe that a social phenomenon like Mau Mau is best understood from the vantage point of what happened afterwards.[15] The three chapters that explore the post-Mau Mau period are in no sense secondary; they are essential for understanding the revolt. Through analysing the trends of development leading up to the revolt and its aftermath we hope to show what is distinct about the Mau Mau period. From this perspective, Mau Mau represents a phase in the development of Kenyan nationalism in which many of the questions facing society stand manifestly unresolved. The defeat of Mau Mau marks the beginning of the resolution from the point of view of the colonial authorities and the newly emerging African capitalist class. However, as we argue in Chapters 7 and 8, it was not until the late 1960s that the issues raised in their most acute form during the Mau Mau era finally find this temporary resolution. To complete the picture it was felt important to work out the mechanisms of the transfer of power in Kenya.

It is hoped that this development, which is fully documented, helps us understand not just Mau Mau but the patterns of decolonization throughout much of Africa.

The Kikuyu squatter

The main actor in our drama is the Kikuyu squatter. Squatting or labour tenancy was a creation of white settler colonialism in Africa. In the white settler colonies of Kenya, Southern Rhodesia (now Zimbabwe) and South Africa the life of the African population was reorganized around the interests of settlers. As J.K. Rennie argues, 'labour tenancy was a relation of serfdom which emerged wherever white farmers with limited capital took land from agricultural peoples'.[16] White settlement was synonymous with the appropriation of the land of the African people. In Kenya colonial land policy was dictated by the objective of establishing a prosperous European managed agricultural sector.

The major prize given to European settlers in Kenya was the White Highlands. These covered approximately 7½ million acres (3-million ha) (compared to nearly 33 million acres (13.3 million ha) in the African Reserves). But the scale of the land appropriation only tells part of the story. The land reserved for Europeans contained the richest soil of Kenya – the area most suitable for commercial farming. Since less than 10 per cent of Kenya's total land area was suitable for cultivation, European-owned land constituted 50 per cent of the arable land and 20 per cent of highly productive areas. By 1960, 4,000 European farms accounted for 83 per cent of the total agricultural exports of the country.[17]

The White Highlands were cleared for European occupation by the removal of the pastoral Maasai people. In addition land was alienated from the Kikuyu, Nandi and Kipsigis. Not only did the colonial state expropriate land from African cultivators, it also redefined the rights that Africans had to the land that was left to them. The Crown Lands Ordinance of 1902 'was drafted on the assumption that Africans had no title to waste or unoccupied and uncultivated land, and that . . . the Crown could assume a title to such land and allocate it' to Europeans.[18] Moreover, the Ordinance even considered African rights to the occupation of land to be temporary, for once occupation lapsed, the land could be expropriated. In practice, the colonial administration made little distinction between occupied and unoccupied land. Settlers had freedom to select their landholdings, and areas under African occupation were often expropriated. In one case in 1910, Governor Girouard suggested that the rights of those Kikuyu who lost their land this way could be bought for £5,000.[19]

The insecurity of African land tenure had a purpose; European settlers not only required land but also cheap labourers. As in South Africa and

Southern Rhodesia, the expropriation of land was only one of the means utilized to force Africans to work on European farms. Forced recruitment and taxation were other devices used to compel Africans to work for European enterprises. South Africa provided the model. Thus in Kenya we find the Colonists Association, a settler pressure group, demanding in July 1905 the institution 'of the pass system and the compulsory registration of all natives living amongst European settlements, such as prevails in South Africa.'[20]

Despite the availability of cheap fertile land, the European settlers were unable to develop their estates along the lines of efficient capitalist farming. Many European settlers lacked capital and agricultural experience. In many cases European settlers could not even compete with African cultivators. As a result steps were taken to prevent the emergence of African commercial agriculture. As R. Horowitz's study of South Africa suggests:

> It was indeed the awareness, or perhaps more accurately the fear, of the South African Native Commission . . . [of 1905] . . . that in a growing number of instances Africans . . . were being motivated by the market more than whites. The awareness and fear led the commission to make the epochal and decisive recommendation against the 'free traffic in land' as between white and black.[21]

Land expropriation and the prevention of African commercial agriculture were designed to force Africans to labour for European settlers.

While European settlers had little capital and labour, they had plenty of land. They used their monopoly over land to draw Africans on to their estates as quasi-tenants. This form of semi-feudal arrangement was already flourishing in the Cape in the late 1860s. It spread to the rest of South Africa in the 1880s and to Southern Rhodesia in the 1890s. It emerged in the Shire Highlands of Nyasaland (now Malawi) during the first decade of this century. In Kenya, the influx of European settlers around the turn of the century was coincidental with the emergence of squatting.

The squatter system was ideal for European settlers. In return for a plot of land, African producers had to pay a rent in labour or kind and sometimes both. Giovanni Arrighi argues that squatting was essential for the take-off of European agriculture in Southern Rhodesia:

> The exaction of labour services remedied the labour shortage, rent and fees were an important source of finance for capital accumulation. It also became customary for European landowners to market their tenants' produce, and often that of neighbouring peasants as well, a practice that must have effectively prevented Africans, or traders on their behalf from underselling European producers.[22]

For the European settler the squatter was a necessity. Without labour, land could not be brought under cultivation. Evidence to the 1912–13

Kenyan Native Labour Commission showed that African squatters performed a wide variety of roles. In some cases Africans living on European land paid rent in cash while in others they had to give up part of their produce.[23] One settler newspaper, the *Leader of British East Africa*, explained that in some districts Africans were invited to break in virgin or forest soil, the settler 'charging no rent and even guaranteeing the purchase of the crops, so long as the secondary use of the broken soil reverts to the owner of the land.'[24]

Initially, the colonial administration and European settlers were enthusiastic supporters of the squatter system. In July 1905 the Colonists Association wrote to the Secretary of State for the Colonies, arguing that the 'system of settling natives on farms in return for which they gave a certain amount of labour is one which should be encouraged by the Government under the present chaotic conditions of affairs, native labour is not only difficult to get, but impossible to keep where obtained.'[25]

During the first decade of this century the colonial administration fully backed the settlers' quest for squatters. As its head, Governor Sir James Sadler wrote in 1908, the 'settlement of natives on the farms under agreement with the settlers is for every reason to be encouraged.'[26]

Nevertheless there was an awareness that the squatter system was only a temporary solution to the short-term problems facing European settlers. European settlers were too weak economically and politically to control fully African squatters residing on their land and it was feared they would seek to acquire rights to the land they cultivated and that the integrity of the White Highlands would be undermined. Throughout the 1920s and 1930s, sections of the more efficient European settlers agitated for the termination of squatting contracts and their replacement with a system of wage labour. It was only the economic weakness of the settler community that prevented the realization of this objective. However by the end of the Second World War the dominant sections of settler interests were ready to rid the White Highlands of squatters. According to W.F.O. Trench, a leading settler spokesman, the squatter had become 'a real menace to the integrity and security of the White Highlands' and he warned that 'if we don't do something about it now we are absolutely sunk'.[27] It was this concerted campaign directed at squatters that provoked a protracted period of squatter unrest. This culminated in the Mau Mau revolt.

The squatter systems that had evolved in a makeshift fashion between 1903 and 1905 was under mortal threat four decades later. It was the experience of these four decades that shaped the outlook of the participants in the squatter revolt.

The squatter system took shape between 1903 and 1907, a period that coincides with the alienation of land from the Kikuyu. Many who lost this

Introduction

land to Europeans stayed on as others moved on. Thus we find the Church of Scotland Missionary Society kicking the Kikuyu inhabitants off its land in 1908 when they refused to sign a squatting agreement. According to a missionary, J.W. Arthur, the Kikuyu 'were given the option either to sign the agreement or not, if they did not sign they went.'[28] This original group of squatters who lost their land were joined by others as the pressure on land increased in Kikuyuland. Forty years later, in the mid-1940s, Kikuyu squatters and their families numbered around a quarter of a million and constituted around a quarter of the Kikuyu population.[29]

During the four decades before 1945 the way of life of Kikuyu squatters went through a succession of changes. Ironically, in economic terms life for squatters was often better than for their brethren in the reserves. There was plenty of available land and they could pursue their activities relatively unrestricted. At least initially, many squatters could look upon their lives as tenants as not very different to the ones they had led before.

Until around 1919-20 life on the European farms was relatively unregulated. Around 1918, a squatter on average worked three to four months a year for the settler. In turn squatters could cultivate as much land as they wished, though in practice it seldom exceeded 6-7 acres (2.5-2.8 ha). On most farms squatters were allowed to graze their sheep and goats. During the time the squatter worked for the settler, he received a wage of four shillings a month and a ration of *posho* (maize meal). This wage was insufficient for subsistence and squatters supplemented it with the proceeds of produce they sold.

From 1918 onwards the pressure for close regulation of squatters intensified. During the years 1922-25 the settlers, with the assistance of the colonial government, tried to turn squatters into servants under a Master and Servants Ordinance. Because of legal objections from the Colonial Office this aim was not realized. In 1925, however, the Kenya Government passed the Resident Native Labourers Ordinance. This forced all male members of the squatter's family over 16 years of age to 'enter into a contract on their own behalf or cease to reside on the farm'.[30] The enactment of this Ordinance was followed up with a general move to restrict existing squatters' rights. On many farms squatter livestock was eliminated or drastically reduced and the land available for cultivation was also limited. Squatters were also obliged to increase their labour obligations to the European landowners – at least according to the law, the Kikuyu squatter was obliged to perform 180 days of labour service by 1925.

Squatters today remember the years 1925-29 with bitterness. They call it the time when settlers 'started shooting our animals'. From this period the way of life of the squatters steadily deteriorated. Worse still, the reduction of tenant rights created a sense of insecurity and an awareness

12

of the overwhelming power of European settlers over the squatters' lives. The erosion of the squatters' way of life continued throughout the 1930s. By 1945 the transformation of the squatter from a tenant to a wage labourer was well under way. Compared with an earlier situation in which a tenant provided labour services of around three months a year and had on average 6 acres (2.5 ha) of land and 25–30 sheep and goats, the Kikuyu squatter in 1945 was obliged by law to work 240–270 days and was limited to five sheep and 1 ½ acres (0.6 ha) of land.

This steady encroachment on the rights of squatters met with resistance. From 1929 onwards there is a growing process of politicization which provides the prehistory of the Mau Mau revolt. As the Kikuyu squatters saw it, what was under threat was a whole way of life. Loss of rights to land implied not just economic insecurity but an inferior status. The growth of landlessness in Kikuyuland meant that squatters living on European farms could not go back to the reserves but had to stay and resist further attacks on their rights.

As we argue in Chapter 4, the squatter movement was politicized through a group of traders, artisans and skilled workers who were connected to the Kikuyu community on the European farms. This ambitious and highly mobile group, which had close links with activists in Nairobi and Kikuyuland, was able to articulate squatter grievances and provide the coherence that an agrarian movement might otherwise have lacked. Many of these squatter leaders were born or grew up on the European farms. They looked upon the Highlands as their home and bitterly resented threats to the integrity of their communities. In contrast to the reserves, where this entrepreneurial and educated stratum might have been absorbed into the Kikuyu establishment, there were real restrictions on social mobility in the Highlands. It was for this reason that this stratum was drawn towards the militant activists in Nairobi and why its members set about constructing a radical alternative to mainstream nationalism.

Despite the revolt, the Kikuyu squatters were never able to win back the rights they had lost. Nevertheless their actions had major effects on subsequent developments, creating a major split in the nationalist movement and undermining the process of orderly decolonization. This was particularly evident between 1960 and 1963 when the struggle of landless Kikuyu for rights to European farms constituted the major political challenge to the withdrawing colonial power.

In the end, despite the military repression of Mau Mau and of the subsequent land agitation movements, it was not until 1969 that the situation became truly stable.

Historical specification

The last two decades have seen a veritable flowering of discussion on peasant movements and the role of peasants in social change. One consequence of this debate has been the attempt to develop an analytic framework or models for explaining peasant action. While efforts in this direction are a useful antidote to the narrow focus of empiricist case studies, there are severe limits to the comparative method adopted in the literature.

Comparisons are useful for throwing light on specific instances of peasant actions. They also provide general insights into the nature of rural communities. However, comparisons are in danger of becoming too schematic if they seek to evolve general concepts and a ready-made framework of analysis. A comparison of peasant resistance represents a photograph of one moment in historical development outside of time. The main weakness of the comparative approach in both its Marxist and non-Marxist forms is that it tends to dehistoricize specific features of the peasant movement. Taken out of the historical process, models of peasants tend to become abstract frameworks of comparison. As a result comparative studies begin with ready-made concepts rather than a critical examination of historical development. This tendency is evident, for example, in the debate concerning the revolutionary potential of different sections of the peasantry. Is this to be found among the middle peasants, consisting of independent cultivators producing for the market, or among the landless semi-proletarian peasants?[31]

The weakness of this debate lies in the fact that it looks for revolutionary potential from within this or that group of peasants rather than as emerging from specific historically determined conditions. Peasants, especially in the post-war period, do not exist in isolation from other social groups, and the way they are likely to act cannot be determined *a priori*, outside the complex of relations they inhabit. Protest, resistance and revolt are the historical products of interaction between the peasantry and other classes, and between the peasantry and the state. These relations are mediated through communicators, public leaders, social and political associations and subjective perceptions about the viability of action. This is why, for example, impoverishment does not necessarily force peasants to revolt, any more than it pushes them towards inaction. In terms of comparative socio-economic facts, the Bukusu squatters resembled their Kikuyu counterparts in significant respects. Yet, as we argue in Chapter 3, despite this striking similarity, the Bukusu squatters did not revolt while the Kikuyu did. Both communities had an internal potential revolt. But whether this potential is realized depends not on the internal characteristics of these communities but on historical determinants which cannot be conceptualized in advance.

14

Introduction

From the perspective of historical materialism, analytic models tend to obscure that which is central to understanding, the relations within which objects interact. The comparative approach one-sidedly abstracts a moment in the process of change and dehistoricizes its object of study. This defect is manifest in the comparative study of motives and objectives of peasant revolts. Charles Tilly's model of the development of collective action contains insights into the Western European experience.[32] His argument that such actions tend to become more national than local, more proactive (pursuing new demands) and less reactive (defending traditional rights) and more associational and less communal makes general sense. And yet adopting such a model can easily confuse what is in fact a dialectic process of interaction rather than an evolutionary one. It is necessary to distinguish between the forces that create the determination to take collective action and the manner of its articulation. Movements do not evolve in a unilinear direction, and in Africa as elsewhere widespread national mobilizations may be succeeded by manifestations of parochial and regional sentiments. More to the point, the distinctions between proactive and reactive demands may be more apparent than real. Reactive demands in the context of intense conflict often give rise to the formulation of new objectives. Thus squatters defending their 'traditional rights' ended up as the most fervent supporters of national freedom during the Mau Mau revolt. A decade later the more proactive demand, *Uhuru* (national independence), would to many mean simply access to land or the repossession of lost rights.

Peasants protest, rebel, revolt and sometimes participate in revolutions. The range of possible forms of peasant collective action is wide. But the question that is worth pursuing considers the stage at which a particular form of peasant action constitutes itself into a political factor. The answer to this question cannot be established on the basis of examining factors internal to the peasant communities. As most studies of peasant mobilizations show, external forces play a decisive role in the shaping of rural revolt.[33] It is through the relations of protesting peasants and other social groups that rural movements are transformed into a force for change. One of the main failures of the comparative approach is its reluctance to come to terms with this process of transformation. The focus on models and institutions tends to analyse historical process in terms of continuity and breaks. In the case of Kenya this has led to the portrayal of Mau Mau as either the natural successor of previous political organizations such as the Kikuyu Central Association or as something of a historical break with the past. From both points of view the historically specific features of the movement become obscured as the movement is taken out of the process of evolution and change. Mechanistic counterpositions of the past and the present can only abstractly account for the process of change.

It is the equation of knowledge with the classification and definition of social phenomena that underlies the comparative approach. From our perspective social phenomena have no fixed or eternal elements or character but are subject to constant change. As H. Grossman has argued: 'a definition fixes the superficial attributes of a thing at any given moment or period, and thus transforms these attributes into something permanent and unchanging'.[34] Thus from the point of view of dialectic logic the relationship between the peasantry and external forces cannot be determined in advance. The relation between the two forces changes both. It is only in an abstract scheme that the process of interaction leaves untouched the parties within the relation. The relation between subject and object in history changes what is interacting.[35] It is through the study of the relationship that the process of transformation from protest to more politicized forms of resistance becomes understandable.

In nineteenth-century Ireland, for example, it was the interaction between rival secret societies like the Ribbonmen and the National Land League that turned peasant protest into a political force which the British government could not ignore. For the middle-class leaders of the Land League, peasant resistance provided the mass force necessary for the pursuit of their political claims. Although the Land League constituted the leadership of this movement it could not control the activities of the secret peasant societies and the two forces existed in an uneasy relation with each other.[36] Moreover, the forms of organization of the peasant movements influenced the subsequent development of Irish nationalist politics. According to C. Townshend, Fenianism and specifically the Irish Republican Brotherhood, the forerunner of the modern republican movement, 'borrowed both political ideas and organizational methods from the secret insurrectionist societies'.[37] Clearly the peasant secret societies had an impact on the subsequent development of the nationalist movement, just as the rural communities came under the influence of Irish nationalism.

The comparative approach has predominated in the analysis of Mau Mau. It has been particularly concerned with classification and in answering the question of how this movement is to be defined. Unfortunately social movements cannot be reduced to definitions, and such a procedure risks tearing the subject of the analysis away from the historical process within which it developed. According to E.J. Keller, Mau Mau represents a form of social banditry.[38] W.R. Ochieng emphasizes the Kikuyu or tribalist dimension while R. Yankwich believes that Mau Mau was a civil war among the Kikuyu.[39] These definitions do not exhaust the various characterizations of Mau Mau. There can be little doubt that elements of the Mau Mau revolt could be characterized as civil war or as forms of actions akin to social banditry. But to insist that certain elements of the movement can be equated with the revolt is to confuse local grievances that push peasants into action with a social movement that is the product of broader complex historical forces.

The local factors that spark off collective peasant action are often arbitrary and even contradictory. To return to nineteenth-century Ireland, many of the actions undertaken by secret societies were fights between contending family factions or private retributive acts against those who appeared to prosper at the community's expense.[40] No doubt many who joined Mau Mau had their own private scores to settle, others hoped to profit from the success of the movement, while some saw an opportunity for criminal gain. As noted in our article on Mau Mau in Nairobi there was often only a fine line between criminal and activist.[41]

But how relevant are the private personal motives of participants in social revolt? It is certainly useful to grasp the concerns that provoke people to rebel. However, it is rarely the case that there is a direct relation between private motive and the collective act of revolt. Individuals with their personal concerns are also part of a community and of broader relations with society. And it is the social not the individual forces that affect local communities that transform a collection of individuals into a social movement. This transformation is seldom a conscious process. Peasants who are angered by loss of rights to land do not say one morning: 'I have become impoverished and therefore I will join the struggle for national liberation'. Rather, the collective awareness of the implications of the threat to a community's way of life may dispose peasants to act. At a certain point this disposition to act converges with the awareness that the objectives of the peasants can only be realized through political change such as the attainment of national independence.

Too strong an emphasis on the ideology of a social movement can often be misleading. No more so than with the terms nationalist or national. Self-proclaimed nationalists with explicit nationalist ideologies tell us little about the dimensions of the movement and explain little about its social character or its dynamic. In Kenya, many African public figures given to the promotion of nationalist rhetoric were also often those most dissociated from the struggle for independence and were themselves fervent advocates of a regional/ethnic outlook. In contrast, Mau Mau, which was less explicit in its nationalist vocabulary, expressed a dynamic which placed the question of national freedom firmly on the political agenda. In his interesting analysis of Mau Mau as a historical phenomenon, D. Maughan-Brown backs away from drawing out the implications of his argument that this was a national liberation movement because it does not appear to approximate to the model. He remarks:

Analysis of the . . . [Mau Mau] . . . phenomenon is complicated by the fact that most of the peasants who participated had received a

17

rudimentary politicization in the context of a goal which happened, almost accidentally, to coincide in a large measure with what actually transpired: an actual revolt which led ultimately to 'independence'.[42]

Maughan-Brown concludes that as a result of this accidental coincidence 'there is not enough evidence to suggest that the move to the forest [of Mau Mau fighters] can be read as an index of widespread nationalism' and that it was 'instead, a largely defensive action on the part of the peasantry'.[43] As a description of individual motives, Maughan-Brown is probably on the right track. However, such a dynamic is hardly unique to Mau Mau. The links that bind peasants to a wider movement need not always be formal and explicit. The very revolt itself questioned the legitimacy of European rule in Kenya and invited the solution of independence, the individual motives of some of its participants notwithstanding.

To gain an all-round understanding of Mau Mau it is essential to situate it within the process of change. From the vantage point of the post-Mau Mau period, the specific features of this social movement become clear. Unlike subsequent political movements, it put to question the existing socio-economic structures of society. Despite its restricted regional constituency it provided the most extensive foundation for collective action and participation that had existed in Kenya hitherto. Subsequent nationalist parties like the Kenya African National Union, or the more populist Kenya People's Union, were formally more 'national' than Mau Mau. But these parties were essentially the restricted organizations of middle-class or capitalist politicians rather than movements for collective mobilization and action. The hunger for land and related concerns that provoked squatters to revolt are motives that still preocccupy millions in Kenya. But with a balance of classes, and in particular with the strengthening of the African capitalist class, such grievances have the character of purely local affairs. Consequently, at least for the time being, the landless and the rural and urban proletariat do not count as a political factor. The brief entry for these groups into the centre of the political stage in Kenya was the historical significance of Mau Mau.

Research method and scope of the study

The Mau Mau revolt affected the whole of Kikuyu society. In focusing on one region there is the danger that a study may confuse specific local phenomena with a national pattern. It is certainly the case that there are important regional variations in the intensity of support and in the motives for resistance. Regional variations notwithstanding, it appears to us that the Nairobi–Rift Valley nexus provides the critical relationship behind the revolt. Nairobi was the organizational centre and the Rift

Valley squatters provided the mass support. The important organizational innovations associated with Mau Mau originated either in the Rift Valley or in Nairobi. And it was the spillover of resistance from these regions into the Kikuyu reserves that brought to a head the underlying tensions that were evident there. While regional in detail, it is hoped that this study provides a vantage point to grasp the general impulse behind Mau Mau. Although we have examined a limited range of material for the Kikuyu districts of Kiambu, Nyeri and Fort Hall, and looked at the roots of the revolt in Nairobi in detail, the focus of this study is the squatters residing on European farms. Archival research was carried out during the early stages of the study on five districts of the White Highlands: Laikipia, Naivasha, Nakuru, Trans Nzoia and Uasin Gishu. During this stage it became evident that the Elburgon–Njoro–Molo regions of Nakuru district were central to the development of the squatter movement and subsequent field work was concentrated in this area. During field work carried out in 1971–72, 45 in-depth interviews were conducted with participants in the Mau Mau movement. Shorter discussions occurred with 74 ex-squatters about life in the White Highlands.[44]

The following procedure was adopted. From correspondence and intelligence reports I worked out a list of activists during the 1945–55 period. It was possible to track down 27 from this list, and this provided an opportunity to verify the oral information with archival sources. My work was facilitated by the existence of an informal network of ex-activists who often knew each others' whereabouts.

Most of the general archival material was obtained from the Kenya National Archives (KNA). Unfortunately, crucial information on Mau Mau and the period afterwards is not available through the KNA. However, local files on this period were located at the office of the Rift Valley Provincial Commissioner and especially at the office of the Nakuru District Commissioner. The district intelligence reports on Nakuru, Naivasha and Nyandarua, which go up to 1969, were invaluable in throwing light on the subject under study. An additional valuable source of information was the archives of the Labour Office in Nakuru. This office had a collection of files on every farm in the district, often going back as far as 1930. This collection is probably the best source on the social history of the area. Files were also consulted in the District Commissioner's office in Thomson's Falls (now Nyahururu) and the Labour Office in Molo. Useful information, particularly on developments in Nairobi, was obtained from the office of the Provincial Commissioner in Nyeri. Other archival and secondary sources are referred to in the Bibliography.

Notes

1. Buijtenhuijs (1982), p. 1.
2. See the discussion, 'The state counter-offensive', in Chapter 4 below.
3. See Carothers (1954), United Kingdom, 1960 Cmd. 1030, *Historical Survey of the Origins and Growth of Mau Mau*, and Leakey (1954) for illustrations of this approach. A useful overview critical of this approach is provided by Maugham-Brown (1985).
4. The file on Robert's proposed article 'The Mau Mau Secret Society' is available in Kenya National Archives (KNA), PO 3/129, 'Unrest General', nos. 12–21.
5. *ibid.*, no. 19, 21 October 1952.
6. *ibid.*, no. 21, 26 October 1952.
7. Kitching (1980).
8. Ranger (1985), p. 130.
9. KNA, Kiambu District Annual Report, 1941, p. 4.
10. KNA, Central Province Annual Report, 1950, p. 3.
11. KNA, PO 3/129, 'Unrest General', I.M. Nightingale to Chief Secretary, Nairobi, 24 January 1953.
12. C. Bundy shows the ineffectiveness of nationalist support for rural protest in South Africa. Nevertheless he notes that the 'peasant committees of the Transkei were parochial and small-scale, but they also displayed a readiness to accept tactical links with and leadership from other classes and movements.' See Bundy (1985), p. 28.
13. Buijtenhuijs (1982), p. 4.
14. Furedi (1973, 1974a).
15. Marx explained his approach to history thus: 'Bourgeois society is the most developed and the most complex historic organization of production. The categories which express its relations, the comprehension of its structure, thereby also allows insights into the structure and the relations of production of all the vanished social formations and out of whose ruins and elements it built itself up, whose partly still unconquered remnants are carried along within it, whose mere nuances have developed explicit significance within it, etc. *Human anatomy contains a key to the anatomy of the ape.*' (Our emphasis). See Marx (1973), p. 105.
16. Rennie (1978), p. 86.
17. Odingo (1971), p. xix.
18. Sorrenson (1968), p. 17.
19. Public Record Office (PRO), CO 533/71, Girouard to Crewe, 12 February 1910.
20. *East African Standard (EAS)*, 8 July 1905.
21. Horowitz (1967), p. 96.
22. Arrighi (1970), p. 209.
23. Kenya Government, *Native Labour Commission 1912–1913; Evidence and Report*, witness no. 101.
24. *Leader of British East Africa (LBEA)*, 18 October 1916.
25. *EAS*, 28 March 1908.
26. *EAS*, 28 March 1908.
27. *EAS*, 23 February 1945.
28. United Kingdom, 1934 Cmd. 4556, *Report of the Kenya Land Commission: Evidence*, Volume 1, p. 465.
29. The number of Kikuyu squatters in the 1940s can only be approximated. In addition to those who signed contracts approved by the Labour Department, many squatters lived illegally on the farms and in the forests.
30. PRO, CO 533/328 no. 8164, 'Resident Natives Labourers Bill' Croydon to Secretary of State 24 June 1925.
31. Ferguson (1976), Gough (1968–69), Alavi (1965), Landsberger (1974), Wolf (1969).
32. Tilly (1978), pp. 143–71.

33. Chesneaux (1973), Ferguson (1976), Shanin (1971), Skocpol (1979), Wolf (1969).
34. Grossman (1943), p. 517.
35. See Lukacs (1971), p. 3.
36. Clark (1979), p. 324.
37. Townshend (1983), pp. 26-7.
38. Keller (1973).
39. Ochieng (1976), Yankwich (1977).
40. Townshend (1983) pp. 11, 22-3.
41. Furedi (1973a).
42. Maughan-Brown (1985), pp. 217-18.
43. *ibid.*, p. 48.
44. Of the 74 ex-squatters interviewed in Nakuru, Naivasha and Nyandarua Districts, 30 originated from Kiambu, 30 from Nyeri and 14 from Fort Hall.

One

The Squatter Time Bomb

The policy to be pursued with regard to natives in European settlement and towns is a more difficult subject to deal with, and its solution is one of the most important tasks before us. . . . We forget that by bringing the native into contact with civilisation his mind may be rudely awakened.[1]

Governor Sir E. Percy Girouard, 1911

The only real anxiety now arises from the activities and ambitions of detribalised Kikuyu living outside the Reserve.[2]

Governor Edward Grigg, 1930

The problem of the squatter is going to be one of the most serious problems of this country and it has already assumed in certain areas almost unmanageable proportions.[3]

P. Wyn Harris, Acting Labour Commissioner, 1945

The enduring concern of European settlers and colonial administrators in Kenya with Kikuyu squatters is understandable. Compared to European settlers in Southern Rhodesia or South Africa they were a weak minority lacking in confidence. European settlers in Kenya did not have the weight to guarantee decisively their claims to predominate over African and even Asian interests. Throughout the inter-war period a key objective of settler politics was the wresting of guarantees of European rights from the colonial government.[4]

For Kikuyu squatters the assertion of European interests ultimately implied impoverishment and virtual enslavement. It was evident by the end of the 1920s that their role was to be nothing more than that of serfs to the European farmers. Even the Colonial Office was taken aback by the far-reaching subjugation of squatters proposed in the Masters and Servants (Amendment) Ordinance which was passed in the Nairobi Legislative Council on 4 January 1924. It took the unusually firm step of disallowing the Ordinance.[5] Fortunately for the squatters there were severe obstacles to assertion of European domination which are examined

22

below. But it was the impossibility of reconciling the conflicting interests that was to lead to the explosion of the squatter time bomb.

The consolidation of the White Highlands

As the dominant interests in the Highlands, the European settlers were able to dictate terms to the squatters. With the backing of the administration, the settlers treated squatters as a necessary evil. In 1913 Governor Sir Henry Belfield authorized this approach:

> It is undoubtedly to the advantage of the farmer that a native settle-ment should be located upon his property, provided that the people are there for the purpose of working on the estate. I do not therefore propose that such settlement should be prohibited or discouraged, but that it should be permitted only upon terms which will preclude the relationship of landlord and tenant . . . and will relegate the native to the position of hired labourers.[6]

Belfield's attempt to reconcile the defence of European land rights with the squatter system did not mean that Africans would indeed become 'hired labourers'. Rather, an informal system of tenancy emerged that gave European farmers the power to expel their squatters if they wished in the future.

The *de jure* denial of rights to the squatters rested on the political motive of the assertion of European claims to the Highlands. Although there was a succession of ever more coercive laws directed at squatters in general between 1918 and 1945, they were seldom implemented. This ideological use of legislation corresponds to developments in South Africa and Southern Rhodesia. Thus J.K. Rennie notes in his study of landlord legislation in Southern Rhodesia that the 'attack on rent tenancy and share-cropping had been an ideological one, using legislation as an instrument of control'.[7] For European settlers in Kenya the question of control was crucial. They had neither economic, nor despite their links with the colonial machinery, political means for controlling the squatter population.

European settlers lacked the economic clout to force Kikuyu squatters to become pure labourers. It was indeed the inability of the European settlers to use their land productively in the years leading up to 1918 that enabled the squatters to become independent producers in their own right.[8] Competition for labour among European settlers and lack of capi-tal led to a system of tenancy based on rent in kind called 'Kaffir farm-ing'.[9] Kaffir farming, which in practice endowed the squatter with the status of a tenant, potentially represented a claim to land rights. It was for this reason that leading sections of settler society agitated against it and why laws were passed to make it illegal. Nevertheless at least on a minority of less prosperous farms this form of tenancy persisted all the way through the colonial period.

Even in areas where Kaffir farming was rare, the economic activities of squatters were considerable. Thus the District Commissioner of Naivasha reported in 1917 that agriculture had 'made little progress except at the hands of native squatters'.[10] By 1928, squatters and their families numbered 111,682 and were utilizing 20 per cent of the land under European occupation.[11] The scale of this economic activity is thrown into relief by the fact that at this time European settlers themselves only cultivated around 10 per cent of the land they occupied.

European settlers were disturbed by the competition they faced from their squatters. The theme of 'native competition' was a regular topic of discussion at meetings of settlers.[12] Through such devices as a Masters' Union and wage and price fixing, the European farmers tried to limit the emergence of the African squatter as an independent producer. However, they were greatly constrained by the lack of capital, by their inability to obtain a supply of labour on terms other than some form of tenancy arrangement and by their dependence on the rent they obtained from their squatters.

Nevertheless the relationship between settler and squatter was far from static. Whenever possible Europeans sought to encroach on the squatters' rights, only to stop because of economic difficulties. The general trend during the period 1918–45 is a slow erosion of the status of the squatter as a tenant. The first serious crackdown on squatters occurred between 1923 and 1929 when a degree of stabilization of European agriculture allowed the settlers to impose severe restrictions on the land and grazing rights of Kikuyu squatters. It was only the collapse of international prices of agricultural produce in 1929, precipitating a crisis in European agriculture, that gave the squatters a temporary reprieve.

The early 1930s saw the continuation of the settler campaign against squatters. In the settler press major articles appeared with such headlines as 'Squatter System a Menace to White Settlement'.[13] The settlers sought to obtain legal rights for Europeans exclusively in the Highlands and to restrict the status of squatters to that of labourers. This goal was realized thanks to the ruling of the Kenya Land Commission, whose task was to define the White Highlands and thereby the rights of squatters in the settled areas. The report of the Commission dealt with squatters rather briefly, but explicitly rejected any notion that Africans had any rights to land in the White Highlands. It concluded 'squatters . . . have no right to the land . . . But they have a temporary right to use land while in employment. In our view care should be taken to ensure that the essence of the contract is a labour contract . . .'[14]

On the basis of this recommendation the colonial government enacted the Resident Labour Ordinance in 1937, which specifically defined squatters as labourers. From this point on, at least legally, squatters ceased to be regarded as tenants.

Despite the anti-squatter campaign led by the press, and the legal victories of the settlers, culminating in the 1937 Ordinance, the assault on the squatters' way of life tapered off after 1930. The beginning of the Great Depression in 1930 cut short any hopes of further European agricultural expansion and the motivation of the anti-squatter campaign was long-term and political. The number of squatters in the White Highlands fell, on paper, from 113,176 in 1931 to 93,112 in 1936.[15] However these figures are misleading, for they include only those who were squatters on legal contracts. To be sure, in some cases 'progressive' European farmers replaced squatters with wage labour, and some squatters were thrown off the land when plantations closed down and farms were abandoned. But in fact the system of squatting reasserted itself in the early 1930s. For the debt-ridden settler with few market opportunities, a tenancy arrangement became attractive once again. This trend is clearly illustrated by a report of the Principal Labour Inspector in 1935:

> For some years now the prevailing tendency in the evolution of the squatter system has been the increasing recession in importance of the labour aspect of the matter and the increasing dominance of the stock. The question has not been that of getting labour at any cost but of getting labour at under market rates and of getting free or at nominal cost such squatter products as manure, milk and actual stock. This is of course illegal but there is a widespread conspiracy between occupiers and squatters to circumvent the law in this respect and from the nature of the case such a conspiracy is difficult to detect and impossible to control.[16]

Thus by 1935 Kaffir farming had again become widespread.

Squatter competition again became an issue as European settlers turned to the internal market to compensate for the fall in agricultural export prices. Settler agitation turned to calls for restrictions on the freedom of squatters to market their produce and demands that squatters should sell their produce to them.[17] The government took steps to control the squatter produce trade. In 1936 the Native Produce and Marketing Ordinance was applied in Nakuru District. A marketing and inspection organization was set up to control the 200,000 bags of maize sold by squatters annually[18] and a year later the inspection of African-grown potatoes was made compulsory.

The land-use system established between 1920 and 1930 was based on the production of maize and wheat. Overdependence on these crops meant that the less-capitalized among the European farmers could not survive the economic depression of the early 1930s.[19] However, state support prevented the complete collapse of settler agriculture. With considerable government assistance European agriculture was restructured on a more scientific pattern and the uneconomic aspects of the early agricultural sector were discarded.[20] The introduction of new crops, particularly pyrethrum, revived labour demand in the late 1930s.

Pyrethrum was a crop that yielded high returns but required only a small initial capital investment. Its cultivation was labour-intensive and the squatter system was ideally suited to it since the squatters' wives and children could help in cultivation. Pyrethrum gave the African squatter a new lease of life. The P.C. of Rift Valley reported in 1938:

> The infiltration of Kikuyu squatters into the Nakuru District continued unabated and was stimulated by the demand for the labour of the women and children as pyrethrum pickers . . . Pyrethrum growers in particular are anxious to secure resident labour; it is regrettable that they seem to be competing in some areas to attract what are really squatters by offering liberal grazing for stock and even forest land for cultivation.[21]

The shortage of agricultural labour in the late 1930s enabled squatters to assert their position against the settler strategy of reducing them to cheap agricultural labourers. One government report complained in 1937 that in Nakuru District: 'The demand for native labour has increased considerably, wages have risen slightly and the native labourer is much more independent and offhand.'[22]

The Second World War greatly stimulated European farming activity in the White Highlands. The need for increased produciton to meet the new wartime demand led the colonial government actively to assist and direct European agriculture. Long-term and medium-term credit for European farmers was made available and, through the Increased Production of Crops Ordinance (1942), subsidies facilitated the expansion of agriculture.

The need to increase production for the war effort led to a correspondingly increased demand for labour. The labour shortage that consequently developed gave African squatters new room for manoeuvre. Settlers were reluctant to use the powers that the 1937 Resident Labour Ordinance provided to control squatters for fear of losing their labour force. In his Annual Report for 1940, the District Commissioner of Nakuru noted that the Ordinance was not welcomed by employers.[23] Resolutions to the effect that its enforcement be postponed until after the war in order to prevent labour discontent were passed by a number of European Farmers' Associations during this period.[24] The Provincial Commissioner of Rift Valley Province warned the Governor:

> My present information is that in the Trans Nzoia, Nakuru and Laikipia districts there is considerable danger that the application of the Ordinance will unsettle labour which hitherto has been working quite peacefully . . . Bearing these consideratons in mind, and

remembering how very important it is at this time to retain the good-will of native labour, I suggest that His Excellency might consider suspending the operation of the ordinance in so far as Trans Nzoia, Nakuru and Laikipia are concerned.[25]

European settlers tried to solve their labour problems by demanding the introduction of compulsory labour.[26] They were successful in their demand and, on 2 March 1942, compulsory labour for essential agricultural production was introduced. This had the desired effect, as labour supply was substantially increased by compulsion. By November 1944, conscript labour accounted for 7 per cent of the work force in pyrethrum and mixed farming, and 26 per cent and 50 per cent on sugar and sisal estates respectively.[27] Famine-level food shortages in the Reserves in 1942–43 led to further increases in the labour force.

In 1944 the settler-dominated district councils decided that the time had come to enforce the Resident Labour Ordinance. The Nakuru District Council implemented a 1942 order limiting squatter stock to 15 sheep and cultivation to two acres (0.8 hectares) per resident labourer, with an acre for each wife after the first one.[28] The squatters reacted by refusing to accept the new terms. At the request of the Agricultural Production and Settlement Board, the government implemented a Standstill Order. This Order put a 'standstill' on the engagement of squatters and aimed to force resident labourers to remain on the farms where they were, on the new terms. It took the unprecedented economic stimulus of the Second World War to give the European settler the confidence to finally take on the squatter. During 1945 the colonial administration launched a campaign of inspection of farm labourers.

The closer inspection of squatters was intimately connected to the declared strategy of the settler community of turning their tenants into wage labourers. Restrictions on livestock held by squatters was followed by increases in the number of days squatters worked for their landlords to 240, and sometimes 270 days a year.[29] Local orders passed by the district councils put new ceilings on area of cultivation and the number of livestock that squatters could hold. These moves tended to erode the distinction between squatters and monthly contract labour.[30] Many farmers preferred to reduce the importance of squatters, and turned to employing Africans as wage labourers. Thus, while the number of squatters remained stable, monthly paid and casual labour increased as a proportion of the labour force in the 1940s. Reliable statistics are not available, but according to those published by the Labour Department between 1945 and 1949, the number of squatters and their dependants decreased from 202,944 to 46,953.[31] These figures almost certainly bear no relationship to reality. Department of Labour files on individual firms show that the number of squatters remained stable while new employees tended to be wage labourers. Moreover the less well-off European settlers continued to rely almost entirely on squatters and made no effort to employ Africans as wage labourers. According to the 1949 Labour Department annual report:

> Many areas of the Kenya Highlands continue to rely on resident labour as the nucleus of their labour force. It has been in the past, and is now, a relatively secure and reliable form of labour for the farmer, and key positions are usually filled by such men.[32]

To complete the picture the report should also have added that dependants of squatters made up a large percentage of the new casual labourers. The restrictions placed on the growth of squatting stemmed from the changing character of settler agriculture. The government's decision to increase production and to encourage farming along more intensive lines during the war was implemented on an even greater scale in the post-war period. Large estates were subdivided and agricultural land was developed more productively. A number of parastatal bodies supervised the new farming practices and provided credit and market facilities.[33] Settler agriculture was further boosted by rising prices of agricultural commodities during the period.

The extension of land under cultivation made possible by the mechanization of settler agriculture could not be reconciled with the unregulated squatter system that prevailed. During the decade following the outbreak of the war the area under wheat in Nakuru and Laikipia districts increased from 26,642 to 97,480 acres (10, 790 to 39, 479 ha).[34] Agricultural change required greater control and supervision over Africans resident on farms and many settlers and officials expected that squatters would be eliminated altogether. But the settler community was not ready for this change. Instead squatters were forced to give up the last vestige of their independence without becoming full wage labourers. The new system of resident labour was designed to transform squatters primarily into labourers and not independent producers.

The emergence of the system of resident labour implied the general impoverishment of squatters. Wages could be left quite low as the few acres available to resident labourers could provide most of their subsistence requirements.

The economic consolidation of European agriculture implied the death of the squatter. European claims could now be asserted without the fear of squatter competition. But the consolidation of European agriculture had come too late.

The limits of settler power

Formally the European settlers had all the power they needed to dominate Africans living on their farms. The colonial administration did little to restrain European settlers or regulate life in the White Highlands. The first attempt by the administration to introduce a degree of social control, embodied in the Squatters' Bill of 1916, was withdrawn as a result of the furious reaction of European settlers.[35] Throughout the next two decades colonial officials in Nairobi were loath to provoke the wrath of the settler community.

Africans had no political rights whatsoever in the Highlands. They were there at the invitation of the settlers and technically they could be evicted from a farm on one to three months' notice, depending on the length of the contractual arrangement. During the first two decades of this century, local government in the settled areas consisted of district committees. These were chaired by the district commissioner and consisted of representatives of European settlers. Legally the settlers acted in an advisory capacity but in practice the district commissioner was unlikely to oppose settler opinions on most issues.[36]

The subordination of the African squatter in the Highlands to the interests of the settler was apparent in a set of rules that were partly legal and partly informal. All Africans had to carry a *kipande* (pass). The *kipande* was not merely an identification card; in the Highlands it served as a mechanism of labour control. Employers in need of labour often refused to endorse the *kipande* of labourers who wished to leave their service, forcing them to remain on the farm. The movement of Africans was carefully controlled through the *kipande* and a system of tribal passes ostensibly designed to prevent the theft of stock. Under the Township Ordinance of 1902, Africans could not stay in a township for more than 24 hours unless employed there. There were also restrictions on the movement of squatter produce and livestock.

The power of the settler was most evident within the confines of the farm. Physical punishment was not infrequent and even labour officers accepted it as normal practice. Even magistrates displayed a callous indifference towards the life and health of Africans. In one 1915 case of a settler beating one of his labourers to death, the penalty was a fine of 570 rupees or three months in jail for 'voluntarily causing hurt'. The only aspect of this case that disturbed the magistrate 'was that the accused did nothing for the body and never reported the matter'.[37] Another method of enforcing discipline was through the exaction of fines. Squatters were financially penalized for a wide range of 'offences' from lateness to the loss of livestock. The settlers were also in a position to force their squatters to sell their produce to them below the market price.

Despite their considerable and arbitrary power over African squatters, the European farmers were far from confident. They were aware of their relative weakness and the potential strength of their squatters. On the demographic level the White Highlands was not quite white. In 1918, one official – no doubt with a proclivity for exaggeration – stated: 'I am credibly informed that parts of Naivasha Province now look like a Native Reserve'.[38] A clear picture of the demographic patterns of settlement can be gauged from the case of Nakuru District, one of the most prosperous European settled districts in Kenya. In 1927 it had a total population of 31,396; only 1,190 of these were European.[39] The squatters in the district had 60,456 acres (24, 485 ha) under cultivation in 1928 and on paper owned 42,032 goats, 30,981 sheep and 4,312 cattle.[40] Such a sizeable squatter presence – 30 squatters per European – constituted a potential threat to the European claims to the Highlands.

It was not just demography but also economics that exposed the weakness of settler power. Very little of the land under European occupation was put under cultivation or used for grazing. In 1929, just over 10 per cent of European-owned land was under some sort of development.[41] Since the term 'development' was generously defined, even this figure gives an exaggerated picture. During the 1930s European farming declined under the impact of the Depression. The area under European cultivation decreased and many farms were abandoned. Land speculation was rife and the indebtedness of many farmers posed a grave threat to the future of European settlement in Kenya. The Commissioner for Lands and Settlement reported in 1937:

> During the recent visit of the Advisory Land Board to the Uasin Gishu and Trans Nzoia Districts, the Board was impressed by the large areas of underdeveloped and unoccupied farms. In some instances the farms appeared to have been partially developed and abandoned; in others no sign of past development could be discovered.[42]

Under these circumstances the settler monopoly over political power in the Highlands was insufficient to deal with squatting. There was an awareness of the fragility of European settlement in government circles that explains why the widespread breaking of squatting laws was ignored. Even the more prosperous settlers who had the means to rid their land of squatters did not push matters too far. As Paul Mosley notes in his study of settler economics in Kenya and Southern Rhodesia, the tension between productive farmers and absentee or Kaffir farmers was resolved through local squatter rules.[43]

Given the isolated position of European settlers, the Kenya government did its best to support the weaker farmers even if it meant tolerating the squatter system. Mosley's observation is apt: 'The governments of Kenya and Southern Rhodesia were at all times exposed to pressure to protect the weak farmers as well as the strong, in the interests of maximising the size of the European rural population'.[44] In Kenya even this protection could not postpone the inevitable. However, at the time many European settlers could imagine that the African squatter was a temporary barrier whose removal would guarantee the future of the White Highlands once and for all.

The final assertion of settler power

The years 1940-46 mark the high point of settler influence. As a result of the demand created by the Second World War settler agriculture finally took off. Economic success was paralleled by the extension of political influence. The demands of the war put great strains on the colonial state machinery and European settlers were called on to fill the breach. Alongside colonial officials, leaders of the settler community became involved in the running of the country. The European settlers were finally in a position to deal with the question of squatting.

Throughout the 1940s the settler-controlled district councils passed a succession of rules designed to eliminate the squatter as an independent producer. In many cases evictions occurred and throughout the decade tens of thousands of Kikuyu were forced off the farms. Having the upper hand, the settlers used the threat of evictions to force Africans on their farms to work harder and for less. According to our estimate, the squatters' standard of living must have at least halved during the years 1944-46 in Nakuru District.

Such attacks on the squatter way of life provoked widespread resistance in 1946-47 but the settlers kept up the pressure. In 1949-50 more squatters were expelled and those who remained on the farms experienced a steady deterioration in living standards.

Even the colonial officials were surprised by the ruthlessness of the settler assault on the squatter way of life. A 1947 government report noted that:

> in their anxiety to control squatters, Councils are still making orders reducing acreage and stock: orders follow each other at close intervals, giving neither the resident labour nor the farmer any feeling of security. This lack of security is tending in certain areas to promote unrest among the natives concerned.[45]

The indifference of European settlers to the steady impoverishment of Kikuyu squatters and to the implications of growing unrest created problems for government officials who were concerned with the maintenance of stability and law and order. In 1949 the Labour Commissioner complained that as a result of settler action against squatters the credibility of his department had been undermined. He claimed that 'years of hard work on the part of my predecessors and officers in the Department in gaining the confidence of the Africans have been lost as a result of what the African regards as oppressive measures'.[46]

There can be no doubt that the escalation of settler demands on Africans living on their farms drove people towards desperation and finally towards rebellion. The officials of the Labour Department openly argued that cuts imposed on squatter cultivation had made it impossible for Africans to subsist. The official in charge of the Labour Department in the Rift Valley directly linked the rise of resistance to the reduction on squatter cultivation and criticized the European district councils for not at least ensuring that squatters were compensated for their loss with higher real wages.[47]

Squatter policy

Economic weakness and conflict of interests among European settlers made it difficult to evolve a coherent anti-squatter policy. The obstacles to the establishment of a settler consensus were a cause of continuous frustration to the leadership of the European colonists. In February 1945, a leading settler spokesman, W.F.O. Trench, told a conference of European agriculturalists that the 'District Council had tried to get a unified policy but had not been successful'. He warned his audience that the squatter problem 'is a real menace to the integrity and security of the White Highlands and if we don't do something about it now we are absolutely sunk'.[48]

Settler divisions regarding squatting were based on a conflict of interest between highly capitalized and less prosperous farmers, and between dairy and stock farmers and those involved in cereal and plantation-related activities.[49] Dairy and stock farmers claimed that squatter livestock threatened to infect their cattle and called for major restrictions. In any case their need for squatters was considerably less than that of those involved in labour-intensive activities such as maize and wheat farming. Pyrethrum, tea and coffee growers also needed large supplies of resident labour.

David Throup has drawn attention to the leading role of Naivasha District Council in leading the anti-squatter drive.[50] He argues that in Naivasha the dairy and stock farmers formed a homogeneous block and new rules were brought in with little opposition. He notes that in 'this European cattle farming area the fear of diseased squatter stock proved far more powerful than the danger of disrupting the harvest by antagonising squatters'.[51] The leading position of Naivasha in the anti-squatter campaign is well documented. However, although the nature of their farming played an important role in influencing Naivasha settlers it was not the only reason they decided to take on the squatters.

The strategies adopted by district councils cannot be explained simply with reference to their different economic activities. For example, initially Trans Nzoia District Council adopted far-reaching measures against squatters. The Labour Commissioner, Meredyth Hyde-Clark, characterized Trans Nzoia's new rules as 'oppressive' and 'likely to lead to widespread discontent'.[52] Yet far from being pastoralists, Trans Nzoia settlers were primarily involved in cereal production. On the other hand, settlers in Uasin Gishu District, which was a wheat growing but also a mixed farming area, were relatively easy on squatters.

Conflicts between stock raising and cereal growing farmers were very real. Thus we find farmers from Laikipia, which came under the Aberdare District Council, complaining against the new rules restricting squatter rights. One farmer remarked that the Aberdare District Council was composed 'largely of wealthy stock farmers' who 'are completely ignoring the interests of the pyrethrum growing minority in the District'.[53] Although the conflict between stock farmers and cereal growers is an important influence in settler politics, it does not explain the differential reactions. Thus, for example, stock farmers in Uasin Gishu and Trans Nzoia were quite prepared to live with squatters and their livestock. In many instances stock farmers in this region were prepared to declare that their squatters' cattle was in fact theirs as a way of getting around legal restrictions.[54]

When all is said and done, it appears that the main forces behind the anti-squatter drive were the more prosperous sections of the settler community; European settlers with considerable capital were in a position to take a long-term view of the situation. In their case the long-term political implications of a sizeable African squatter population overrode the immediate problem of labour shortages. It was their fears about the political future of Kenya Colony that provided the main impetus behind the anti-squatter drive.

Two of the main influences behind the evolution of policy on squatters were Charles Mortimer and F.W. Cavendish-Bentinck. Both these settlers were intimately involved with the running of the colonial government, had access to the ears of the administration and were determined to defend the European monopoly on landownership in the Highlands. In 1935, a memorandum written by Cavendish-Bentinck emphasized the necessity for measures 'which must be taken to preserve the complete and absolute integrity of those areas . . . [the White Highlands] . . . and to secure for all time that ''privileged position'' which persons of European descent enjoy therein by virtue of the provisions of the Command Paper of 1932'.[55]

Mortimer firmly supported Cavendish-Bentinck's objectives. But as Commissioner for Local Government, Land and Settlement, Mortimer was acutely aware of the weak economic position of European settlers and their fragile hold over land in the Highlands. He felt that unless European settlement was established on a more stable foundation, African claims to the Highlands would be difficult to reject. In the 1930s he was particularly worried about the large number of unoccupied holdings, which undermined the case for European paramountcy in the Highlands.

Mortimer attempted to confront the problem by advocating closer European settlement. He attacked the speculators who drove land prices up while their huge estates remained underdeveloped and thereby prevented new European immigrants from taking up farming.[56] Cavendish-

Bentinck agreed with Mortimer and urged more financial help for new settlers and curbs on the rise of land prices. Like Mortimer his aim was to establish large-scale European settlement and thereby moral authority as the guardians of the Highlands. He wrote to Mortimer in August 1942:

> No one has yet succeeded in working out a sound scheme of co-operative farming applicable to Kenya where we do not want to have labour competing with semi-skilled African labour, but I am convinced that we have got to work out such a scheme if we are to get into the White Highlands a population sufficiently strong numerically to give us political security.[57]

It was this desire for political security that strengthened the anti-squatter lobby in the settler community. At a 'squatter conference' held in Nakuru on 26 June 1944 with government officials and settler representatives in attendance a hard line on the squatter question was adopted.[58] A declaration of war against the squatter was followed by the implementation of harsh restrictions on Africans living on the farms. Within months squatter unrest broke out in Naivasha and Thomson's Falls. By the middle of 1945 unrest had spread to all the districts of the White Highlands.

The severe sanctions imposed on African tenants was bound to provoke resistance. Government officials, especially from the Labour Department, were aware that it was merely a question of time before squatters took up the fight. In his handing-over-report, the Labour Commissioner, Wyn Harris, warned his successor that 'the only serious unrest which at present is likely is among squatters . . . squatter troubles in the not distant future are probable'.[59] Fearing an outbreak of mass action on the farms, officials from the Labour Department urged caution and implored settler leaders to slow down the implementation of the new rules.

Government officials were particularly concerned that the unrest among Kikuyu squatters in Naivasha, Thomson's Falls and Nakuru should be contained in those areas and not be allowed to spread to other parts of the White Highlands. In addition they were worried about reaction to the anti-squatter measures in Britain and sought to give them the minimum of publicity. Aware of these dangers, Cavendish-Bentinck adopted a parallel course of action. He took strong exception to suggestions that officials from London might be involved in the working out of future squatter policy. Harris agreed and noted that any outside enquiry 'would again raise all the old problems leading with land tenure'.[60] He told a meeting of officials and leading settler personalities that the discussion on squatter policy should take place behind the scenes, arguing that a public reopening of 'the problem would led to correspondence in the paper which might not all be of good value for the good name of the Colony'.[61]

Settler leaders like Cavendish-Bentinck also began to fear the political consequences of the anti-squatter campaign. But it was the field officers of the colonial government who were most sensitive to the potential for long-term instability. This concern turned into near panic when in October 1946 unrest broke out among Bukusu squatters in Trans Nzoia and Nandi squatters in Uasin Gishu,[62] a situation that led the government to pressure Trans Nzoia and Uasin Gishu Councils to slow down the implementation of anti-squatter rules. And in March 1947 the Commissioner for Local Government refused to confirm the new rules that Uasin Gishu wished to implement.[63]

The justification for government action was that the 'problem of the squatter' applied particularly to Kikuyu tenants in the lower areas of the Rift Valley Province – Naivasha and Nakuru. It was argued that there were good economic reasons for the anti-squatter rules in Naivasha and Nakuru but that elsewhere the motivation for removing squatters was primarily political. Meredyth Hyde-Clark, the new Labour Commissioner, wrote:

> The political motive is much more important in the Uasin Gishu and Trans Nzoia areas and is the raison d'être for the present proposed orders: employers definitely fear that the African population and the number of stock are increasing in such a way that the problem of removal and control is likely to be very difficult if not impossible in a few years time. If there is proper control, this attitude is untenable and there is little doubt that enforcement of the proposed amended orders will have an adverse effect on the labour supply and a general undermining of African influence on settlers and the administration alike.[64]

In fact Hyde-Clarke's arguments were a post-hoc rationalization of events. Political considerations behind the anti-squatter drive were just as important in Naivasha and Nakuru as in Trans Nzoia or Uasin Gishu.

Although a significant section of the settler community in Trans Nzoia and Uasin Gishu were against the new squatter rules because they feared a shortage of labour, the majority on the district councils responded with a hard line. C.L. Bolton, on behalf of Trans Nzoia District Council, wrote back to the Commissioner for Local Government in protest, suggesting that 'to go on dithering with this problem will also play into the hands of disloyal agitators who can see a chance of making political capital out of it'.[65] A memorandum passed by Uasin Gishu Council in April 1947 provided a clear statement of the settler outlook:

> Council believes that the African by and large, is still a savage and a child and that he understands and responds to firmness, that he fully understands the reason for Council's proposed order, and far from

losing confidence if the order is implemented and enforced, will gain respect and liking for the European.[66]

In fact the response of the district councils had more the character of an outburst than reasoned thought. With the threat of mass unrest and major disruptions of the supply of labour looming on the horizon the colonial administrators in Nairobi won the day. A more gradual approach towards the withdrawal of squatter rights was adopted in Uasin Gishu and Trans Nzoia.[67]

The modification of squatter policy in March 1947 was complemented by a coherent strategy of divide and rule. As colonial officials perceived it, the main threat to law and order came from the Kikuyu squatter. To meet this threat officials sought to isolate the Kikuyu from other squatters and advocated a differential treatment of squatters. District Commissioners and other officials characterized Kikuyu squatters as trouble-makers, those from North Kavirondo as victims of circumstances and Nandi squatters as loyal allies worthy of special privileges.

An interesting discussion on the different squatter 'races' in 1949 explains the differential approach. A memorandum by a labour officer on Nandi squatter stock provoked local officials to advance political arguments as to why Nandi squatters should be treated with care. Emphasis was placed on the dominant role of Nandi and other pastoral ethnic groups in the police. Carson, the District Commissioner Tambach, remarked that pastoral 'tribes form the bulk of the Police in this country' and any anti-squatter rules would 'naturally' affect them. He noted that in one location alone in his district there were 67 ex-Kenya Police, most of whom had relations on European farms.

Drawing on British colonial experience in India, Carson argued:

> It would be a grave mistake to antagonise a fine body of men on whom the security of the country in effect must depend. (I feel that the state of the Kikuyu and Kavirondo tribes today leaves little doubt on this matter). The position is one akin to the Punjabis and Pathans versus the Hindus, Parsees etc. It was the former who defended the latter and in this country it was the Samburu, Nandi etc. of the Kenya African Rifles (KAR) who helped to keep the home country safe for certain other tribes to make their fortunes in.[68]

Carson's argument for special dispensation for Nandi squatters was gradually accepted by European settlers. G. Swinton-Home, Chairman of the Soy-Hoey's Bridge Farmers Association in Uasin Gishu argued that the removal of Nandi squatter stock could unleash unrest. His warning to the DC of Uasin Gishu also contained wholesome praise of the Nandi:

> If the Resident Labour Ordinance, Uasin Gishu District is rigidly put into effect, it would . . . create a Political Situation, (in these days of

unrest and the infiltration of Communism into Africa) of extreme gravity amongst a tribe who are at present not politically inspired . . . it should be appreciated that this letter is written with the intention of assisting Africans, who by long and faithful service, deserve such help as their long time employers can offer.[69]

The upshot of this discussion was that anti-squatter rules against the Nandi were implemented only formally and officials turned a blind eye to infringements of district council rules.

The differential application of squatter rules illustrated the relative limits on settler power. European settlers had their hands full with the Kikuyu and were forced to make concessions to squatters from other ethnic groups. As a result the subsequent squatter movement that emerged came primarily if not entirely from the Kikuyu.

Notes

1. *Leader of British East Africa (LBEA)* 27 May 1911.
2. Public Record Office (PRO), CO 10533/398/16126, no. 415, Governor Grigg to Secretary of State, 12 February 1930.
3. Kenya National Archives (KNA), Lab 9/304, Resident Labourers. General Correspondence no. 74 P. Wyn Harris to Secretariat, 6 April 1945.
4. Redley (1976).
5. PRO, CO 533/310 23446 no. 695 J.H. Thomas to Governor Coryndon 3 July 1924.
6. PRO, CO 533/116 6361 Memorandum: Governor Belfield to Lewis Harcourt, 27 January 1913.
7. Rennie (1978), p. 96.
8. For a parallel development in South Africa see Bundy (1972).
9. Kaffir farming in Kenya was practised by the most undercapitalized sections of European settlers. This arrangement implied the exchange of access to land in return for a rent in produce, livestock and sometimes cash. Kaffir farming was most prevalent among Boer farmers in the Uasin Gishu District. These arrangements were rare in those districts (Nakuru, Naivasha, Nyeri and Thomson's Falls) where Kikuyu squatters lived in great numbers.
10. Naivasha District Annual Report (1916–17), p. 2.
11. Native Affairs Annual Report 1928, p. 100.
12. A typical expression of this fear was articulated by a Mr. Stimar at a meeting of the Kenya Colonists Association in September 1910: 'It was necessary for a farmer to get natives on his land for purposes of labour. There must be some quid pro-quo for labour. But the farmer objected to introducing on his farms a *Swahili* or other foreign native, who could undersell him in the market with say potatoes. It was ridiculous to sell potatoes at 75 cents per load when they were worth a penny per pound.' See *LBEA*, 29 September 1910, p. 3. Presumably a '*Swahili* or other foreign native' was any African independent producer who could undersell the European farmer.
13. *East African Standard (EAS)*, 13 February 1932.
14. United Kingdom, 1934 Cmd. 4556, Vol 1 *Report of the Kenya Land Commission*, p. 497.
15. From Agricultural Censuses 1930–38.

16. KNA, Lab 5/35/4/1426, 'A Note on the Squatter Problem', V.M. Fisher, Principal Inspector of Labour, 1936.
17. *EAS*, 22 July 1938.
18. KNA, Lab 9/1064, Marketing of Native Produce.
19. Odingo (1968), p. 268.
20. Cone and Lipscomb (1972), p. 66.
21. Rift Valley Province Annual Report, 1938, pp. 258–64.
22. Report of the Board of the Land and Agriculture Bank of Kenya, 1937, p. 26.
23. Nakuru District Annual Report, 1940.
24. *EAS*, 17 April 1942.
25. KNA, Lab 9/1043 no. 177, PC. *RVP* – Government House, 24 January 1941.
26. *EAS*, 10 October 1941; and 13 February 1942.
27. KNA, Lab 9/1 no. 46, 23 October 1945.
28. Harris (1947).
29. *ibid*, p. 4.
30. The Labour Officer stationed in Nakuru made the distinction between a squatter and a contract labourer on the following basis: a squatter cultivates in excess of half an acre and possesses stock; casual labour has no stock, cultivates under half an acre and has no legal claims to his produce. KNA, Lab 9/317, Nakuru District Council no. 15 Labour Officer to Labour Commissioner, 24 June 1946.
31. African Labour Census, 1947 and Kenya African Labour Enumeration, 1949.
32. Labour Department Annual Report, 1944, p. 33.
33. Cone & Lipscomb (1972) p. 97.
34. *EAS*, 11 November 1949.
35. For the debate on the 'Squatters Bill' of 1916 see the coverage in *LBEA* for that year.
36. Settlers, of course, could also put forward their interest through their representatives on the Legislative Council.
37. KNA, Jud. 1/752, file no. 8, Town Magistrate of Eldoret – Registrar of High Court, 13 September 1915, Uasin Gishu, Appointment of New Magistrate.
38. Ukamba Province Annual Report, 1917–18.
39. Nakuru District Annual Report, 1927.
40. In fact the area under squatter cultivation and the numbers of livestock under their ownership far exceeded the official figures available in Agricultural Census, 1928.
41. Agriculture Census for Kenya Colony, 1930.
42. Kenya Land Office (KLO), L.O. 31530, Development of Farms, General, Commissioner for Land and Settlement to PC, RVP, 14 April 1937.
43. Mosley (1983), pp. 20, 26.
44. *ibid.*, p. 234.
45. Harris (1947), p. 5.
46. KNA, Lab 9/304, Resident Labourers, General Correspondence Labour Commissioner to Secretariat, 16 June 1949.
47. KNA, Lab 9/318, The Resident Labourers, (Conditions of Employment) (Nakuru County Council) Order 1953, no. 56, Senior Labour Officer, RVP to Labour Commissioner, 12 October 1954.
48. *EAS*, 23 February 1945.
49. See Throup (1983) for an informative discussion of settler divisions on the problem of squatting.
50. *ibid.*
51. *ibid.*, p. 150.
52. KNA, Lab 9/601, Labour Legislation R.L.O. General Correspondence 1942–59 Hyde-Clarke to Chief Secretary, 12 August 1946.
53. KNA, Lab 9/600, Local Option Orders, Aberdare District Council, no. 65B, Letter from F.H. Crovit, 27 November 1945.

54. KNA, Lab/1057, RLO Legislation. Policy and Amendments. This file contains many examples of such transactions.
55. KNA, Att. Gen. 3/155: Reservation of Highland – Order in Council, Memorandum from the Elected Member RE: European Highlands, 25 April 1935.
56. KLO, L.O. 31530, vol 2, Development of Farms General, no. 45, Mortimer to PC, RVP 19 April 1937.
57. *ibid.*, no. 131, F. Cavendish-Bentinck to Mortimer, 31 August 1942.
58. For the proceedings of this conference see *EAS*, 31 June 1944.
59. KNA, Lab 9/2151, Handing Over Reports, P. Wyn Harris to E.M. Hyde-Clarke, 18 April 1946.
60. KNA, Lab 5/35, Squatters or Casual Labour, General 1939–46, no. 233, Record of meeting, 11 February 1946.
61. *ibid.*
62. See PC, RVP, DC/TN/2/4: Monthly Reports, October 1946 and KNA, Lab 9/326, RLO Trans Nzoia District Council no. 50, Vernon to Hyde-Clarke, 11 November 1946.
63. PC, RVP, DC/UG/2/4: Monthly Reports, March 1947.
64. KNA, MAA 8/124, Resident Labourers: Central Co-ordinating Committee for Resident Labour no. 1, 'Resident Native Labour in Kenya', Memorandum by M. Hyde-Clarke, 3 March 1947.
65. *ibid.*, no. 8, TNDC resolution passed on Resident Labour Legislation, 14 May 1947.
66. *ibid.*, no. 4, Memorandum approved by meeting of Uasin Gishu Council, held on 21 April 1947.
67. See Throup (1983), pp. 166–70, for a discussion of the climb-down in Trans Nzoia.
68. NLO, C/14; Resident Labour Matters Uasin Gishu, no. 2, Carson, DC Tambach to Labour Officer, Eldoret, 15 February 1944.
69. *ibid.*, no. 3, G.A. Swinton-Home to DC Eldoret, 28 January 1949.

Two

A Community Living on
Borrowed Time

The only Native political question of any importance is the control of native squatters on private and crown lands.[1]

Nakuru District Commissioner 1915

So long as the cultivation and stock of resident labourers were more or less unrestricted, these questions did not arise. Now they constitute a real problem which demands early attention. The Kikuyu resident labourer sees only one answer, i.e. land in the settled areas.[2]

Laikipia District Commissioner 1946

I want to inform you British that you are not to spoil the boundaries of Olenguruone *shambas*. If you just think since you came to Kenya you have never seen an African with a gun. I am the one to inform you that the Wakikuyu have more power than you have with your guns.

Just wait until the year 1949 you will have to be sorry for the rules which you are giving us now and when it will be my turn to order you the same way. I am Njoroge Waweru, my plot number is 167 and that is where I am staying.[3]

The Kikuyu squatter community was created, transformed and finally destroyed in just over four decades. The scale of the disruption to people's lives telescoped into such a short historic period had far-reaching consequences. Between 1903 and 1925 the Kikuyu squatter's way of life resembled that of a tenant in a semi-feudal setting. This life was rudely, and as the squatters feared, irrevocably disrupted in the late 1920s under the impact of the European settlers' offensive. For the next 15 years or so the Kikuyu squatters managed to defend their rights as independent producers, but after 1947 their proletarianization became irreversible.

The Kikuyu squatters' struggle to protect their rights as independent producers went through several phases. The first expression of general resistance in 1929 gave way to more localized actions against specific encroachments on squatters' rights. In the early 1940s a more widespread and organized movement took shape, culminating in the mass movement of defiance of 1946–47. In 1948 the squatter movement was transformed into a militant wing of Kenyan nationalism. At this stage the radicalization of the squatter movement took it beyond the confines of mainstream nationalism and into the front line of the struggle against European settler domination. The Mau Mau explosion that followed was the last stand of the Kikuyu squatter before his final destruction as an independent peasant producer.

Who were the squatters?

Squatters were composed of many different ethnic groups, but the most numerous were Kikuyu. The Kikuyu who emigrated to the Rift Valley between 1905 and 1920 came for three main reasons: to find land, to avoid military service with the Carrier Corps and to escape from the despotic rule of the newly appointed colonial chiefs and their agents. The most important factor influencing squatter migration was the shortage of land. Those most directly affected by it were those Kikuyu whose farms had been expropriated by Europeans between 1903 and 1907. But the restriction of land available to the Kikuyu people also created pressures on the *ahoi*, the traditional tenants, by the *githaka* holders, their landlords. Many *ahoi* were forced off their land and had no choice but to migrate to the White Highlands. They were joined by others who still had land in the Kikuyu Reserves, but whose holdings were insufficient for maintaining livestock and for the subsistence need of their families. An overwhelming proportion of ex-squatters interviewed on the motives for their families' migration gave land shortage in one of its forms as the cause for moving.[4]

In January 1919, the District Commissioner of Naivasha carried out a survey of squatting in his area. On 39 farms he found 1,406 squatters and their families. Table 2.1 gives a breakdown of the origins of these squatters.

Table 2.1: *Origin by district of squatters in Naivasha District, 1919*

		Percentage
Kiambu	343	24.3
Fort Hall	451	32
Dagoretti	538	38.2
Nyeri	74	5.25

It is noteworthy that 62.5 per cent of the labour enumerated in Table 2.1 came from Dagoretti and Kiambu, the two areas where most of the land alienation took place. These were the most densely populated areas of Kikuyuland. The majority of the squatters from these two districts seem to have come from the relatively small area between Dagoretti and Uplands, an area of great population concentration and European settlement. The high proportion of squatters from Fort Hall indicates that there were pressures other than the direct expropriation of land by Europeans in operation. Such pressures were shortage of land and restrictions on the traditional rights of the *ahoi* by *githaka* holders.

The desire to avoid military service with the Carrier Corps during the First World War was also a compelling motive for young men to leave the Reserve. The European settlers protected their labour force from conscription. For many Kikuyu squatters life on the European farm was a preferred alternative to conscription. Unpleasant memories of the Carrier Corps still linger on in ex-squatter memories. Boro Gicheru notes: 'I came to the Rift Valley in 1915 with my father. We had heard bad stories about the Carrier Corps. We left because my father refused to fight . . . Many Kikuyu left for that reason'.[6]

Many Kikuyu became squatters to escape the growing encroachments on their rights by *githaka* holders and the newly appointed chiefs and headmen. The only way to escape from this heavy-handed rule was to move out of the jurisdiction of the 'native authorities'. As Ngaramiti Kamau put it: 'I left Kiambu for the Rift Valley in 1919. We came to the Rift Valley because of the chiefs. If we did something that the chiefs did not like they would come to the house and free things from the people . . . If a chief hated you, you would have to leave.'[7]

The exercise of arbitrary power by local appointees of the colonial administration was particularly evident in Fort Hall. Tensions were high during the First World War when local poeple reacted against the onerous demands of the colonial government for recruits and forced labour directed through the chiefs. Many Kikuyu from Fort Hall left for the European farms to escape these impositions. The District Commissioner of Fort Hall complained in December 1917 that many Africans had refused to work on the roads and had decided to emigrate from the area.[8] The hostility against chiefs and headmen was so strong that by 1921 the colonial administration had to move in to depose them.[9]

There were other reasons for migrating to the Rift Valley. For a small minority (8 per cent of those interviewed) there was an element of economic pioneering in becoming a squatter. Certainly the abundance of uncultivated land in the European-owned areas must have contrasted favourably with the high density of farmed land in Central Province.

Squatters were recruited directly by European settlers or through the chiefs. The terms offered were quite generous, as they were designed to attract as much labour as possible. According to Kigathia, the son of Chief Kinanjui (who was an important recruiter of labour for the settlers), people were 'subjected to a sort of brainwashing. They were told that they would not be allowed to keep much stock in the Reserves. But if they went to the Rift Valley they could have as much land as they wanted'.[10]

The new squatters believed that life on the European farms would be similar to that of the Reserves. They saw the European landlord as a white version of the *githaka* holder. Although it was realized that in return for land rights they would have to contribute some labour, most Kikuyu assumed that such obligations were similar to their traditional tenancy arrangements. This view of the status of the squatter appears to have been confirmed by the initial experience of Africans in the White Highlands. During the early years of 1903–18 the European settlers were too weak economically to regulate the life of their squatters.

At this stage squatters were able to cultivate as much land as they wanted. The only area reserved for the landlord was the land he demarcated for his own use. As the land under European development rarely exceeded 10 per cent of the holding, there was plenty of land available for the squatter to choose. Kikuyu squatters were generally dispersed in small groups of two to three households depending on where good soil was located. This meant that they did not live in labour lines like casual labourers. Europeans often complained that it was difficult to supervise the Kikuyu squatters dispersed on their land, but there was little they could do about it.

Squatters obtained most of their income from the sale of their produce, mainly maize and potatoes. From early on trade in squatter produce is evident in the White Highlands. Unregulated markets sprang up during the second decade of this century in such centres as Elburgon, Naivasha and Gilgil. Squatters also traded with various pastoral people. One 1914 report notes the exchange of produce for livestock between squatters and Maasai taking place nearly every day in Naivasha.[11] Squatters strongly encouraged this trade, as they placed high value on the ownership of stock. Often, the squatters sold their produce to the European farmer or to an Indian trader and used the proceeds to purchase animals from the Maasai. One man who took part in this trade recalls:

> When I came to the Rift Valley I had no stock. I remember after the Great War when I bought my first sheep. After I sold the maize that I grew to an Indian I bought 3 sheep from a Maasai. The Maasai used to come and trade regularly to Molo and Elburgon. All the people bought stock whenever they could. From the food that I sold during a year I could buy three or four goats and a couple of sheep.[12]

Squatters did not have complete freedom to dispose of their produce. Often they were forced to sell it below market prices to the European farmer. There were other restrictions on squatter trade. A system of permits and licences made it difficult for squatters to send produce back to the reserves. Consequently the squatter was often forced to sell to the Asian traders who became established at all the centres in the Rift Valley.

In this early phase of squatting, Kikuyu tenants were able to benefit from their landlords' thirst for labour. Landlords with a reputation for cruelty and harshness often found themselves without tenants and squatters were able to move from farm to farm and bargain for better conditions. Mbucha Kamau recalled:

> When I got to the Rift Valley, I went on a farm near Gilgil. During the first years life was good for the European did not bother you and there was good land. Later the European wanted us to work for him all the time and he fined those people who did not show up for work. Many people including me left them and I came to Captain Harris' farm in Njoro.[13]

Such movements between farms testify to the limited power of the European to assert control over the African tenants residing in the White Highlands.

Fortunately for the European settler, the flow of Kikuyu migrants to the farms continued unabated between 1919 and 1923. Land shortages were becoming a growing problem in parts of Kikuyu land and the availability of land on the European farms was an attractive proposition. This uninterrupted flow of Kikuyu migrants had the effect of stabilizing the labour situation and strengthened the position of the European landlord. By 1923, the Native Affairs Departmental Annual Report could note: 'the number of natives residing on farms continue during the year to increase somewhat out of proportion to the actual labour requirements'.[14]

The considerable growth of the pool of Kikuyu migrants ready to work on the farms altered the balance in favour of European settlers. The period 1925–29 saw the first consistent settler offensive against squatters. Unilaterally European settlers began to change the terms of tenancy agreements, demanding more days of work and reducing the amount of livestock squatters were allowed to own. In most cases Kikuyu squatters were now obliged to provide 180 days in labour-rent. Local administration and the police also strengthened their supervision of Africans residing in the Highlands. In 1927 the Resident Native Labourers Ordinance began to be enforced and 1,050 squatters were convicted for offences under this law.[15]

The settler offensive against squatters provoked a shift in the pattern of migration. Migration to the farms more or less ceased in 1927 and there was a flow of Kikuyu back to the Reserves. According to one contemporary estimate, during the years immediately following 1927, 'more persons have returned to the reserves than have left'.[16] In fact this reversal of the migration pattern was of short duration and dramatic as it was, it came to an end by 1930. There simply was not enough land in Kikuyu land to accommodate the returning squatters. By 1930 most ex-squatters

were back in the White Highlands – with the full realization that there
would never again be any room for them in the Reserves. Table 2.2
shows what the return of Kikuyu expatriates would have meant for
landholdings in the Reserves.

Table 2.2: *The relation of labour migration to the Kikuyu Reserves, 1931*[17]

Kikuyu districts	Area (acres)	Resident Kikuyu population	Acreage per head of Kikuyu population	Kikuyu outside the district	Acreage per head if non-resident Kikuyu return
Kiambu	254,720	104,021	2.45	37,256	1.70
Fort Hall	373,120	171,852	2.17	40,073	1.76
Nyeri	194,560	121,210	1.60	18,303(?)	1.34
Total	822,640	297,091	2.07	95,637	1.67

In his annual report for 1928 the District Commissioner of Dagoretti
put the matter succinctly. More squatters would return home if they
could. But 'I have no hesitation in saying that their portion of the Kikuyu
Reserves cannot under existing conditions accommodate the natives
indigenous to this area, who reside at present outside the Reserve
boundaries'.[18] The Kikuyu landowners and chiefs were also worried
about the prospects of thousands of ex-squatters returning home.
M. Vidal, the District Commissioner of Kiambu, reported in June 1929
that the chiefs were alarmed at the influx of squatters owing to the shortage
of food in the Reserves and the shortage of grazing.[19]

For the ex-squatters the return home provided a bitter lesson. At least
in economic terms they could no longer expect to find a 'home' in their
districts of origin. They had become irrevocably uprooted from their land
of origin. For most of them there was no alternative to exchanging their
labour for land on the European farms. And as the shortage of land and
lack of opportunities began to affect an ever-increasing section of Kikuyu
society, more and more Africans were forced to seek their livelihood
outside the reserves. It is at this point in 1929 that the cumulative effects
of land expropriation created the conditions for the separate development
of the squatter community.

The emergence of squatter society

Although 1929 represents a turning point in the history of the Kikuyu
squatters, the European settlers were not able to press home the advantage just yet. For at least the next 15 years most European settlers had to
make do with a system of labour tenancy. Lack of capital, the
Depression, the large labour requirements of European pyrethrum

growers and the new demand for labour during the Second World War limited the drive to transform the squatter from a tenant into a wage labourer. Although the general tendency was to encroach upon the rights of squatters, these 15 years were inconclusive in terms of resolving the balance of power between European landlord and Kikuyu tenant. A temporary breathing space provided for the consolidation of the squatter community.

The Great Depression and its devastating impact on European agriculture was a major boon to Kikuyu squatters. The settlers' problems were their opportunity. Squatters were able to strengthen their economic position and reassert themselves as independent producers. Many squatters who became unemployed chose to squat illegally on Crown Land and unoccupied farms, thereby challenging the property rights of Europeans in the White Highlands. In 1933, the Chief Native Commissioner reported:

> Native squatters on unoccupied farms have been a source of trouble. Every endeavour has been made to deal with them in conjunction with the Police, but shortage of personnel has rendered this difficult, especially as the natives residing illegally usually concentrate on the large estates and in forest country.[20]

The shortage of labour due to the increased production of pyrethrum in the late 1930s further strengthened the position of squatters. Sometimes squatters demanded that their old privileges be restored. In Rumuruti, squatters who had previously resided without sheep and goats refused to sign on unless they were allowed to keep them.[21] The fears of settlers were clearly expressed at a meeting of farmers in Gilgil in 1938:

> Several farmers spoke of indisicipline and unrest amongst the local labour force . . . It would seem that there is a strong inclination towards the worst form of trade unionism starting amongst the local squatter labour, even amongst the old men, who have been on the farms for 15 to 20 years. Attempts by local farmers to assist in the reafforestation of the district, by the issue of free seeds, young trees, have been met by flat refusals and threats to leave the farm in a body. The considerable increase in the acreage under pyrethrum has not assisted towards a contented labour force.[22]

The forceful steps taken by squatters to defend their interests in the 1930s was based on the elaborate socio-economic structures that were established by them in the Highlands. The stagnation of settler agriculture during the Depression gave squatters new scope to expand their production and trade. Many squatters became traders in the produce of their brethren. The District Commissioner of Naivasha noted in 1933 that Kikuyu traders were gradually supplanting Somalis.[23] By the mid-1930s an elaborate system of squatter markets operated in most centres in the Highlands. The most important market, Elburgon (in Nakuru District), dealt in maize, fruit, eggs, sugarcane, fowls, vegetables and potatoes. Elburgon also became the centre of the profitable squatter export trade in maize and potatoes.[24]

The growth of the squatter economy and of a class of squatter traders was paralleled by the development of Kikuyu squatter social and cultural institutions. By the mid-1930s Kikuyu Independent schools and churches were well established in the Highlands – in 1938 there were at least 16 in the districts of Naivasha, Nakuru, Laikipia and Uasin Gishu under the aegis of the Kikuyu Independent Schools Association and the Karinga Schools Association. The squatter demand for education was based upon the realization that they were being left behind by their brothers in the Reserves. The District Commissioner of Nakuru wrote in 1937 of the great desire of natives in the District for schools.[25]

The leadership of the Independent school and church movement was basically composed of the new group of squatter traders and a smaller group of educated Kikuyu, many of whom were teachers or farm clerks. This group also tended to be influential in the Kikuyu Central Association (KCA), the nationalist political movement which spread to the Rift Valley in the late 1920s. Under the direction of this group the KCA expanded its activities in the Rift Valley. Meetings were often held in secret in churches and schools and the KCA grew alongside the Independent churches and schools. In 1937 the District Commissioner of Laikipia complained:

> The main bug-bear in the district is the large number of schools on farms. It is difficult to understand the views of farm owners for, having granted permission for the schools, they complain bitterly that they are nothing more than erections for political agitators and the district organization for farm labour.[26]

The support for the Independent churches and schools was widespread and by 1938 large numbers of squatters (two to three thousand) assembled in townships for 'Sports Days' and other meetings.[27]

A community under siege

Despite the development of trade and new social institutions the squatter community had fragile foundations. Theirs was a precarious existence which depended on the strengths and weaknesses of the European settler. Survival and prosperity required adaptability and organization. After the events of 1929 squatters realized that only the evasion of settler power could secure their future. As a result the squatter communities acquired many of the attributes of a frontier mentality – they were aggressive, resourceful and independent.

Under settler pressure squatters learned to seize opportunities. As individuals they were highly mobile. After 1929, many of them left the farms to find their livelihoods elsewhere. Many of the younger generation tried their hand at trading and moved about the country in search of opportunities. Njoroge Kagunda recalls:

> Nobody liked working for the settlers . . . So in 1931 I went to Kisii . . . I liked the place . . . There were about 65 Kikuyu families there when I arrived . . . The Kisii were friendly to us and we had a good life. We were the ones who started business there and we introduced new crops to the Kisii. Many Kikuyu sold to the Kisii. Some Kikuyu went to Nairobi to buy old clothes and sold it to the Kisii.[28]

The absence of any fixed land rights provided the Kikuyu squatters with an incentive to move around in search of new opportunities. In the 1930s one sees the rise of a distinct group of squatter traders. Young squatters who sought to escape from the restrictions imposed on them on the farms moved around seeking to make a living as traders. Mwangi Njuguna's family lived on a farm in Elburgon. In the 1930s he started buying vegetables from squatters in the area, transporting them as far as Uganda.[29] Samuel Muiruri worked as a forest squatter in Maji Mazuri. He became one of the many Kikuyu contractors working with sawmillers. In 1940 he expanded his activities and started trading in timber.[30]

Trading activities were not restricted to a small group of professional traders. Great numbers of squatters were involved in part-time trading. Markets mushroomed all over Nakuru District in the 1930s. Settler-imposed barriers to African commerce were circumvented by a network of black market relations. Restrictions placed on the movement of Africans in the White Highlands and on the marketing of squatter produce forced the traders to pursue a life that was semi-legal.

The numerous petty regulations imposed on Africans living in the White Highlands meant that inevitably law-breaking would be an everyday affair for the squatter population. Illegal activities ranged from outright illegal squatting to visiting friends on a neighbouring farm without the permission of the European landowner. One could paraphrase Marc Bloch to say that law-breaking was as natural on the European farms as strikes are to large-scale capitalism.[31] The significance of law-breaking among squatters becomes clear when one considers that between 1939 and 1946 resident labourers refused *en masse* to sign the new labour contracts, and were thus living illegally in the White Highlands.

Under these circumstances squatters became remarkably adaptive. As settlers put more pressure on the squatters in the 1940s many of the more resourceful among them began to look for alternative forms of economic activity. From 1945 onwards, when regulations governing the lives of squatters became more onerous, many of the younger generation turned to trading and related activities. Others became resident on the farms as skilled workers such as tractor drivers, carpenters and other key personnel.

This social differentiation within the squatter communities was paralleled by regional differentiation. Especially after the tightening up of regulations after 1945 there was a growing divergence in living standards among Kikuyu tenants in the Rift Valley. The position of squatters varied from district to district, depending on the District Council Orders designed to control resident labour. In 1945, in Nakuru District, the main focus of this study, a squatter had to work 240 days each year, and in return could cultivate two acres of land (.81 ha), with an additional acre for each wife after the first. In neighbouring Naivasha the labour-rent was 270 days and only one acre was allowed for cultivation, or a maximum of two acres if the squatter had more than one wife. In Laikipia District, 270 days of labour were required, and one acre per adult up to a maximum of three acres was allowed.[32] Regulations regarding squatter stock varied from ward to ward within a district. In Molo ward of Nakuru Distrct no squatter stock was allowed.

The lack of uniformity in the squatters' conditions was further reinforced by climatic and soil differences. Squatters in the drier parts of Nakuru and Naivasha could produce less surplus produce than their counterparts in the more fertile wards. Again the degree to which the European landholder enforced the district councils' rules also had important consequences for the lives of squatters. The Forest Department, private forest contractors and Boer farmers had a reputation for allowing African resident labourers to cultivate in excess of the limits imposed by district council rules. Consequently pockets of African independent producers were to be found prospering here and there alongside their less fortunate brethren.

Nakuru District, with a population of around 45,000 squatters, illustrates the uneven position of resident labourers. The Elburgon–Njoro region was by far the most desirable area from the squatters' point of view since it had the highest yield of maize and was also capable of producing relatively high yields of potatoes. One Labour Inspector estimated in 1945 that the average annual income from cultivation per squatter family in Nakuru district was 374 shillings while in the Elburgon–Njoro area it was 1,187 shillings. The adjoining Molo–Turi area was also quite prosperous, with the highest yield of squatter-grown potatoes in the district.[33] In other parts of the district, such as Rongai, Subukia and Bahati, squatters were considerably worse off.

These regional differences had important social consequencs. The more prosperous and self-sufficient squatter communities were able to develop a network of independent institutions – religious, educational and political. Although these institutions had a presence throughout the White Highlands, they were more developed and stable in the more prosperous regions. Squatters in areas like the Elburgon–Njoro region were better able to defend themselves than their less prosperous counterparts.

The geography of resistance

Squatter participation in the Mau Mau movement was widespread throughout the White Highlands. However, the scale of activity was uneven. It is possible to identify three centres of political activity in the 1940–52 period: Elburgon-Njoro area in Nakuru District, the Lakeside area in Naivasha and the region around Ol Kalou/Wanjohi Valley in the then Laikipia District. The one feature that these areas had in common was that they supported some of the most active and developed Kikuyu squatter communities in the White Highlands.

The development of prosperous squatter communities in Ol Kalou, Wanjohi Valley and the Lakeside area were directly the result of a limited European presence. The squatter communities could develop relatively unhindered, free from supervision and control.

Many of the large estates in the Naivasha lakeside area were secured by absentee landlords. European agricultural activity was restricted to a small part of the estates and African squatters faced few restrictions on the size of their landholdings. Squatter agriculture was therefore extensive and well organized. Under the aegis of a Kikuyu Independent Church, the local squatters formed a vegetable-growing and marketing company, an enterprise that came to the attention of the administration in 1945 when the Lakeside squatters refused to sign the new labour agreements. A local official reported:

> another matter which should be investigated by the Administration is the formation of a semi-religious organization which has its headquarters or church . . . on the Lakeshore. These men though apparently harmless have a certain subversive effect on the labour in the neighbourhood. This is most marked in connection with vegetable growing activities since it is believed the organization has something to do with the marketing of vegetable produce belonging to natives in the Naivasha area.[34]

The solid resistance against the new labour agreements led to a firm government response – a number of squatters were evicted and the vegetable company was closed down.[35]

Despite greater police surveillance, illegal squatter cultivation on an extensive scale continued throughout the 1940s and a regular pattern of trade in vegetables emerged between the Lakeside and Nairobi. This network became a useful line of communication between the squatters and activists in Nairobi. Illegal economic activity and political organization developed side by side. In October 1950 an official reported 'an extremely unsatisfactory state of affairs in respect of illegal cultivation and illegal residence' and to add to the difficulties 'a considerable amount of political activity of the very worst type was encountered'.[36] The high incidence of Mau Mau activity recorded in the area clearly underlined these fears.

In the Ol Kalou and Wanjohi areas squatters were able to maintain their position as independent producers despite the enforcement of district council rules in the 1940s. The Afrikaner settlers who owned many of the farms in the area tended to be undercapitalized and resistant to agricultural change. Many of them looked upon squatters as tenants who could provide them with rent either in the form of produce or in cash. The local squatter community had a long tradition of independent activity and compared to other areas it was relatively prosperous and well organized. The Kikuyu community had a strong identification with the area and looked upon it as theirs. The description of this area in the Nakuru District Annual Report of 1951 is revealing:

> Unfortunately in the Ol-Kalou and Wanjohi Valley areas, he found among farmers, many of them Afrikaaners, reluctance to accept any form of control and he described it as an area not under full control from which trouble can be expected. In Mr. Penn's opinion Mau Mau thrived in the area, though very much underground and manifested itself mainly by a surly and uncooperative attitude, backed by the fact that *most of the Kikuyu genuinely believe that the White Highlands were rightfully theirs.*[37]

In 1950–51 a number of strikes and physical assaults on European settlers occurred in response to district council efforts to alter the position of their squatters. A determination to protect the rights established in previous decades gave a strong impetus to the growth of Mau Mau.

The region became an important centre for the organization of resistance. The close links that the squatters had with the Kikuyu district of Nyeri proved to be an important line of comunication, especially during the phase of armed resistance. The squatter community's tradition of self-sufficiency and isolation provided a strong foundation for the squatter movement. The squatter community felt strong and quite able to protect its interests against what was seen as European encroachment on its rights.

The key role of the Elburgon–Njoro region in the movement has already been alluded to. As early as 1919, Njoro had become a centre for trade in squatter maize. During the 1920s Elburgon established itself as the centre of the squatter potato trade. The high yield of potatoes and maize obtained by the squatters in the area attracted many migrants from the Reserves. 'Everybody heard how good it was in Elburgon. That's why my family came here. From the crops you sold you could buy sheep and goats'.[38] By 1939, Elburgon had the largest squatter market in the Rift Valley. Every Friday between 2,000 and 3,000 Africans attended the market to buy and sell. European settlers and administrative officials looked upon this 'boom' with concern. The District Commissioner of Nakuru wrote in 1938: 'Among the natives, the Kikuyu are getting such excellent prices for their maize that their whole energies are bent on the production of this one crop leading to difficulties with squatters whose land hunger is voracious . . . and a positive menace in the Elburgon area.'[39]

This expansion of the maize and potato trade stimulated the formation of a class of squatter traders centred on Elburgon who marketed produce as far as Nairobi and Uganda. In 1939 Elburgon was said to be the 'favourite' choice of Africans applying for township plots in the settled areas,[40] and, according to a 1945 administrative survey, was the most popular centre for traders both from outside and inside the district.[41]

The activities of squatters in the Elburgon area were exceptionally diverse since its forests provided them with plenty of economic opportunities outside agriculture and trading. Many worked on squatter-type contracts for the sawmills and the Forest Department and a number used the skills they had acquired to launch their own enterprises. Some became self-employed contractors and charcoal-burners in the 1930s. The economic development of the squatter community was paralleled at the social and political level, with Elburgon becoming the centre of the Independent church and schools movement. A boycott of Indian shops in 1948 was initiated in this area.

This highly developed squatter community had the political capacity to defend its position. When the Government began to enforce the district council rules in 1945, the Elburgon squatter community quickly mobilized a campaign of resistance. In fact the Elburgon–Njoro area provided the leadership for the squatter movement as a whole. Samuel Kibunja, the leader of this movement, worked for the Forest Department in the Elburgon–Njoro area. After the declaration of a State of Emergency Elburgon experienced considerable Mau Mau activity and physical violence. Not surprisingly it was one of the first areas in the district to experience mass repatriation.

The issues that shaped squatter resistance

Between 1929 and 1948 Kikuyu tenants residing on European farms underwent a thorough process of radicalization. There were many issues that provoked this reaction. Squatters faced a fundamental threat to their way of life which was also perceived as a breach of European promises. They were threatened with landlessness and at the same time experienced a steady erosion of living standards. Cut off from their homes in the

Kikuyu districts squatters gradually confronted a world that was becoming increasingly hostile. In addition they had to live under humiliating conditions with no rights – not even political ones. As the settlers became ever more strident in their attitudes the squatters rose up against the provocations.

Land and land rights

By the end of the Second World War a clearly expressed popular consciousness existed in the squatter community. This consciousness developed on the basis of the cumulative experience of life on the farms, expressed a strong grievance about the loss of rights to land and emphasized the legitimacy of squatter claims to land in the White Highlands. There was a widespread view that the squatters had a moral contract with the European settlers: in return for their labour they were entitled to land for grazing and cultivation. According to popular accounts until 1929 the contract was kept and the squatters prospered. However this Golden Age came to an end when the settlers reneged on their promise. This theme reoccurs in songs, petitions and statements throughout the 1940s. Chief Koinange recalled this breach of faith in 1948:

> I received a letter from Mr. Northcote saying that I may ask people to help cultivate on European farms in order to increase friendship. I did that. When such agreements were discussed we were all happy together, no one could classify the other as white, black or red . . .
> After the great war 1914–1918 Lord Delamere went to South Africa to find out how he could trouble the Kikuyu, while he had land that could be occupied by the whole of Kiambu's population. When he returned he arranged a meeting at Ruiru Club of Europeans; he advised them to deceive the Kikuyu. The Europeans requested that Kikuyu men should be collected and get free tickets to go to the Highlands to work on the farms and their good fame spread over the country and Europe . . . After these people's departure, the Europeans came back and occupied this land and forests, they broke the agreement that we had.[42]

The breakdown of the earlier forms of landlord-tenant relations provided the main impetus for protest. A general consensus among squatters emerged which stressed the theme of dispossession and betrayal. Many of the squatters rightly saw their own impoverishment as directly linked to the prosperity of European settlers. A profound sense of injustice prevailed. In a 1947 petition to the Secretary of State to the Colonies one of them wrote:

> Thousands of acres of land which rightly belonged to Your Petitioners was allocated to the European settlers at whose mercy they were thrown in the capacity of resident labourers. In the beginning the terms of service were not so bad in as much as the Squatters were

allowed as much land as they required, they could have had as large a herd of cattle as they pleased, they could possess as many goats and sheep as they liked or could afford and they could grow food to their fullest requirements but when the white man, it seems, felt he was well established *he started biting the very hands that fed him.*[43]

A sense of injustice was combined with a grave sense of insecurity. European settlers made up the rules as they went along and after 1945 the conditions of tenure became extremely unstable. Labour Department officials were sensitive to the implications of such a quick succession of regulations and warned that 'lack of security is tending in certain areas to promote unrest'.[44] Lack of security and the fear of landlessness led many of the more enterprising squatters to turn to trading in one of the townships in the Highlands. During the 1940s there was a veritable flood of applications from squatters for township plots. In 1951 the District Commissioner of Nakuru linked this development to the fear of eviction among Kikuyu residents.[46]

The fear of eviction was based on the expulsion of thousands of squatters who refused to sign labour contracts in 1946. In fact until the period just before the State of Emergency evictions for economic reasons were rare. But it was sufficient for there to be a few cases for fear about the future to spread. The experience of 1946 demonstrated the ease with which evictions could be implemented. As European settlers began to talk more openly of evicting squatters from their land, the Kikuyu on the farms became acutely aware of their precarious position. Officials who wanted to prevent unrest had no answer to the anxiety that many squatters had about security for their old age. By 1951 there was a growing perception that old squatters would be evicted at the conclusion of their contracts.

No return home

By 1929 it had already become clear to squatters that they were not welcome back in the Kikuyu districts. At the time Chiefs Koinange, Waruhiu, and Josiah, leading figures of the Kikuyu establishment, petitioned local officials to prevent the return of squatters.[47] By the post-war period pressure on land had intensified, creating problems even for those who had recently left Kikuyuland.

The District Commissioner of Kiambu was particularly sensitive to what he saw as an explosive situation if the squatters were to return home. In May 1946, when squatters evicted for their refusal to sign labour agreements returned to Kiambu, he warned that hundreds of people were 'wandering about the district with no land and little hope of getting any'. He urged the government to find land for the ex-squatters and warned 'no one will dispute that if European land is saved and native land ruined the final result will be ruin for all'.[48]

The tenuous links that squatters had with their original homes in the Reserves made the threat of eviction all the more significant. News of hostility towards ex-squatters, especially from the Kikuyu landlord class, began to filter back into the White Highlands in the second half of the 1940s. Similar difficulties were experienced by non-Kikuyu squatters. When squatters returned from Trans Nzoia to their previous homes in North Nyanza the local African district council passed a resolution that 'these squatters should not be allowed to return, as they had lost all their land and there was no room for them in Kitosh area'.[49] The African reserves could provide no future for the squatters and the situation highlighted just how precarious their existence had become.

The threat of impoverishment

Insecurity of tenure was compounded by the threat of impoverishment. The steady encroachment on squatters' rights implied also a deterioration in living standards. The strict enforcement of anti-squatter regulations in 1946 led to a drastic decline in living standards. Many squatters who were able to earn over 2,500 shillings a year in 1940 from their produce and livestock were now forced to make do on an income of 400 shillings. An increase of monthly remuneration from 7 shillings to 10 shillings did little to ameliorate this.[50]

The Labour Department was taken aback by the intensity of the attacks on squatter living standards. In a number of instances labour officials intervened in 1946 to ensure that squatters received at least a monthly wage of 12 shillings. Otherwise with the reduction of rights to land, argued the Labour Commissioner, 'it will be impossible for the families to exist'.[51]

In 1949–50 the way of life of squatters took a qualitative turn for the worse. Stimulated by high market prices and government assistance, European agriculture continued its expansion. In Nakuru this expansion was directly at the expense of the squatter community. In 1950 the District Commissioner reported that the 'tendency of farmers to engage squatters either without sheep or with a number below the maximum is on the increase'.[52] The severe reduction in squatter-held land and stock was not compensated for by an increase in wages. In Nakuru, the average rate for squatters in 1950 was 11 shillings a month.[53] This amount barely covered the poll tax or the price of a bar of soap and a pair of khaki shorts.[54] Even in 1946, the Labour Commissioner estimated that squatters needed 12 shillings per month just to exist. Four years later, with a significant rise in prices, the fall in real wages of squatters was clearly drastic. One labour officer warned: 'wages of farm labourers continue to be low; as far as can be ascertained they are at present 20% above the average 1938 rates. With the enormous decrease in the purchasing power of money these low wages can be no inducement to the African to work'.[55]

Kikuyu tenants were forced to work longer for a smaller real wage and with diminishing access to land and grazing. One District Officer, A.A. Hayes, who was well acquainted with the situation in Rongai and Molo, noted in January 1951: 'To the squatter, life generally is a fight; he needs the money which he gets from the production of crops, on his allocated acreage in order to subsist'.[56] Hayes was not the only official aware of the situation. A Conference of Labour Officers and Inspectors concluded in May 1951 'that the time has arrived for the Labour Department to enter the arena, in an endeavour to step up wage rates'.[57]

The drastic reduction of squatter incomes bred resentment and a sense of desperation, especially as impoverishment manifestly coincided with the increasing affluence of the European landlord class. Warning of growing lawlessness and an imminent breakdown, Hayes argued that the Kikuyu squatter 'has very little to lose'.[58] With that assessment most Kikuyu squatters would have agreed.

Stolen maize

Squatters greatly resented the restrictions placed on their freedom to sell their produce. Often their landlords claimed the right to purchase it and enforced a sale below market price. One of the main complaints of squatters was the low price that the Maize Marketing Board offered for their produce. They had no choice but to sell their surplus maize to the Board through the European landlord. In 1950, for example the African squatter received 14–15 shillings for a bag of maize from the European settler. Europeans, however, received 32 shillings a bag as a result of government subsidies, and the profit made by a European farmer on his squatter's maize could often cover his wage bill.

Resentment at what was seen as theft grew because of both the racial discrimination and the poverty of life that Africans faced in the White Highlands. It was also the issue that caused the government the most embarrassment. This indefensible exploitation of the squatter was the focus of considerable agitation within the Labour Department. A group of its officials wrote to the Governor in May 1951:

> It is submitted that the present differences in price between Native grown maize both in the Native areas and the settled areas, and the price paid for European maize is unfair. The same price should be paid to each dependent on the quality of the maize. This difference in price is undoubtedly one of the greatest stumbling blocks to racial harmony in the Colony today.[59]

For most squatters sale of their maize constituted a significant portion of their income – often as much as 70 per cent. The discrimination in the price of maize affected every Kikuyu squatter and was a grievance that expressed the oppressive features of life in the White Highlands in a most tangible form. It symbolized the oppressive regime and established a direct link between their impoverishment and the prosperity of European settlers.

The European District Officer in charge of anti-Mau Mau propaganda in Molo Nakuru district made the connection with the Kikuyu revolt in June 1951:

> I have mentioned previously that the one point for which I cannot find any answer is in the price differential which relates to squatter maize . . .
>
> It must be realised that every squatter in the Settled areas knows that, on the maize which he has grown, his master immediately makes a profit on sale. He knows too that, although some of his maize is fed to casual labour on the farm, most of it is sold . . . indeed he probably helps pack it for despatch.[60]

Discrimination and no political rights

Discrimination and lack of civil rights enforced the subordination of the African community. Squatter economic activity was carefully monitored and considerable obstacles were placed in the path of African traders and craftsmen. The role of the African was to labour for European settlers; any other activities were strongly dicouraged by the colonial administration. A hierarchy prevailed with white landlords on top, Asian traders and craftsmen in the middle and Africans at the bottom. Kikuyu squatters, and particularly squatter-traders, were bitter about the restriction on their activities that was enforced by the Asian monopoly over wholesale and much retail commerce. One squatter list of grievances declared: 'our traders sell soap and tea leaves brought from Indian shops for they are not allowed to order them from far away places'.[61]

Local governments provided virtually no services for squatters. As far as the administration was concerned the squatter community did not merit any medical, social or welfare services. This view was vociferously shared by European settlers: squatters were temporary labourers who did not need the provision of public services. The District Commissioner of Nakuru commented in 1948:

> Welfare amenities are generally totally lacking on farms with a few exceptions, and the opinion has been expressed by those who should know better that the African is privileged to be allowed to dwell in the White Highlands and should not expect more than his pay and food.[62]

As a result of growing political unrest among squatters a number of token gestures were made by the colonial administration and an African Welfare Centre was set up in Dundori. As the Labour Commissioner himself admitted, this was a cosmetic exercise designed to placate public opinion in Britain. He wrote: 'we cannot escape the repercussions of home politics . . . I should certainly be sorry to learn of any decision which would prejudice the continuance of Dundori as it is concrete evidence which can be brought to the notice of uninformed public opinion at home'.[63]

Three years later, in 1951, newly arrived civil servants in Nakuru District were appalled by the lack of social services. Proposals were drawn up for reforms, the most radical being that of Hayes who suggested that some of the profits from squatter maize '*must* be returned to the farm labour in social services'.[64]

In the framework of the European-dominated social structure of the White Highlands the grievances of resident labourers were reinforced by the unequal power relationship between black and white. It was clear to the Africans that their presence was tolerated merely in order to serve Europeans. It is worth quoting the Nakuru District Commissioner's description of race relations in 1948:

> In fact the principal races are virtually segregated into distinct compartments, [the settled areas are a] jealously guarded preserve for Europeans, penetrated by those of other races . . . who are necessary for his continued existence . . .
> The disparity between the European and African in the settled areas is both obvious and deplorable and is at present almost impossible of reconciliation as it is unfortunately a fact that within this district no single African approaches European standards of life.[65]

The subordination of African interests to those of the European landlord was enforced through the systematic denial of civil rights. Africans throughout Kenya Colony were excluded from real political power by the colonial administration. But in the Highlands even the institutions of local government that existed in the African Reserves were absent. The African squatter had no legally recognized channels for the articulation of his interests. In contrast to the situation in the reserves, in the White Highlands there were no legally sanctioned chiefs, headmen or local native councils or native courts. In the 1930s native tribunals were established, but these catered mainly for Africans in the townships; Africans on the farms resolved differences through an informal 'court' of respected elders.

The absence of political rights gave European settlers direct power over Africans living on their farms. The European-run district councils' local rules regulating squatter life in line with the changing needs of the landlords were bad enough, but on the farms coercion and arbitrary force prevailed without the semblance of legality. On the farms the settler was King. African residents were often penalized through a system of fines and often suffered the indignity of physical punishment.[66] The settler's power extended to controlling squatters' movements and other aspects of their daily life. The cumulative deterioration of the squatters' way of life coincided with the growing prosperity of European agriculture. To many Africans it seemed that this prosperity was a result of theft – their own dispossession.

One of the more balanced accounts of the squatter way of life was given by the Nakuru District Commissioner at the outbreak of the Mau Mau rebellion in 1952:

> Lack of security and lack of amenities, were, as ever, two potent factors in determining the African attitude. The resident labourer, possibly born in the Highlands, has nothing to look forward to in his old age save his precarious existence drawn out as a dependent of his family, living on sufferance on the farm in which he spent most of his life, or else eviction to exist on the charity of his class in his reserve. Nor have his wages risen in proportion to the rising costs of his few essentials or in ratio to his employers' profits. His recreations are limited and some employers, fortunately a minority, would even deprive him of his weekly visits to a market or centre to exchange commodities and gossip with his friends.[67]

After the first major wave of squatter protest colonial officials became aware of the implications of excluding Africans from any institutional arrangement. The absence of any participatory institutions meant that the administration was out of touch with African sentiment and in no position to channel frustration or contain unrest. Indeed, there was not even a group of recognized African mediators who could help the government defuse protest. As the situation became more volatile the colonial administration became aware of the need to establish the limited system of local authorities that existed in the Reserves.

Discussions were initiated in administrative circles in early 1946 on the question of establishing a framework of African institutions in the settled areas. The Chief Native Commissioner wrote of the urgent need 'to find some means of establishing much closer contact between Africans living in non-native areas and Government'.[68] The objective of this discussion was the creation of a respectable moderate African leadership through the new institutions, but it had few prospects of realization. The European settlers were in no mood to share power and any form of African local authority would of necessity only be allowed a symbolic significance. Accordingly an African Advisory Council was established in 1947 in the Nakuru District 'to give Africans an opportunity of lawfully expressing their thoughts and views in public'.[69] This council, composed of government appointees, had no executive or legislative function, it could only 'advise' the District Commissioner. Moreover, the council composed of Africans from the townships had little relevance for squatters as its activities were directed towards the difficulties Africans faced in Nakuru Town.

59

Token gestures like the establishment of the African Advisory Council made little difference in the prevailing political climate. After the enforcement of the anti-squatter rules in 1946 the application of settler power became more ruthless and pervasive. It had become evident to Africans that what was at stake was their very survival as tenants with land rights. This settler campaign was particularly offensive to the younger generation of squatters, many of whom had been born on the farms. The callous racism of the European settlers provoked strong passions among younger, economically entrepreneurial and educated Kikuyu. This bitterness was succinctly summarised by a Mau Mau activist from Elburgon: 'The settlers and the squatters did not mix. Africans were considered as dogs. That is why we became annoyed and moved into the forest. You know, for me Mau Mau means to hate'.[70] The explosive nature of racial tension in the Highlands was clearly recognized by government officials. At a meeting of Provincial Commissioners in November 1948, the Deputy Chief Secretary warned that 'European settlement in this country must be doomed unless race relations could be put on a satisfactory footing'. The Rift Valley Provincial Commissioner added that the 'intransigent attitude of so many settlers was dictated by fear'.[71] However, the administration had no solutions to offer. It simply hoped that the problem would sort itself out.

A community on the frontier

The African squatters were perhaps the most misunderstood of Kenya's social groups. The colonial administration dismissed them as the most backward of the African population.[72] This ethnocentric assessment was based on such criteria as education and acculturation to Western ideas and practices. Since there was little in the way of the so-called 'benefits of colonialism' – social services and education facilities were conspicuous by their absence – the reputation of squatters for being traditionalist and conservative was prevalent in government and settler circles. Indeed for certain authors it is this conservatism that explains the high level of squatter involvement in Mau Mau.[73]

The absence of social services and education certainly limited the options open to squatters. But lack of facilities did not mean they passively accepted the fate assigned to them. Squatters were anything but traditionalists. After 1929, when the option of returning to their areas of origin was no longer available, they moved throughout Kenya to establish new communities. Kikuyu squatters became highly mobile, remarkably adaptable and in spirit truly pioneering. Ex-squatters established trading communities in Maasailand, Kisiiland and West Suk.

Indeed one of the main preoccupations of the colonial administration was how to control the movement and life of Kikuyu squatters. For the administration the problem of control was most acute in the forest areas. According to 1945 figures there were 43,000 Kikuyu squatters and members of their families employed by the Forest Department and private timber contractors and firms. This figure is certain to be an underestimate since the government lacked the means to inspect all forest stations. Forest squatters, like those on farms, were given rights to cultivate land and to graze livestock in return for labour. In the large forest areas it was practically impossible to keep an eye on the dispersed landholdings of Kikuyu squatters.

Squatter communities in the forest lived virtually outside the law. Just as the anti-squatter campaign got under way the government finally remembered that thousands of squatters were also living in the forests, in part because of pressure from European farmers worried that squatters facing new rules on the farms would escape to the forests. To reduce the attraction of life in the forests, settlers argued that district council orders should cover forest squatters living on Crown Land.[74] On closer inspection it became clear to officials that forest squatters lived outside European supervision.

An inspection of the squatter community in Elburgon Forest in March 1945 revealed a near complete lack of supervision of squatters' conditions and activities. Moreover, inspectors were taken aback by the relative prosperity of the squatter community. Some squatters worked on their own account as fuel contractors; a butcher and a shopowner combined 'squatting' with their commercial activities; and even the headmen and forest guards were involved in illegal cultivation and trade.[75] The inspector admitted that he had no information on the number of squatters in the area but speculated that 'with regard to the acreage under cultivation there must be a considerable number of them'.[76] Supervision was extended and regular inspections were instituted to control the community in Elburgon Forest. Control was never effective, however, and the Kikuyu there continued to live a life of semi illegality. In June 1952, seven years after the first serious inspections, the local labour officer argued for a combined operation of the police and the army to get on top of the situation. 'About 200 persons are required as it takes in a big area,' he wrote.[77]

Far from being exceptional, Elburgon was typical of most Kikuyu forest squatter communities. In Thomson's Falls, forest stations in Ol Arabel Valley and Ol Bolosat Forest Reserves presented similar problems. In October 1947 the local labour officer demanded that forest squatters be concentrated in villages to facilitate inspections, describing the state of affairs as 'extremely serious'. His main concern was that lax control 'in the Forest areas is having a demoralising effect on resident labourers on farms'.[78]

By this time there was a growing awareness in government circles that squatter communities in the forests meant trouble. In 1946 forest squatters refused to give information for the census and throughout the 1940s their settlements were seen as centres of unrest. In Uasin Gishu and Trans Nzoia, where political activity was always considerably less than in Nakuru, Naivasha or Thomson's Falls, it was the isolated Kikuyu forest squatter communities that were at the centre of 'subversion'. Ainabkoi, Kipkabus, Timboroa, Kaptagat in Uasin Gishu and Mount Elgon Forest Station in Trans Nzoia were also seen as centres of unrest.

For the administration the only solution to the breakdown of control was the prevention of further Kikuyu migration into the forests. In 1948 the Labour Commissioner resisted demands by private sawmill companies for more labour, arguing that: 'The attitude of the Labour Department is that, particularly in view of the very high proportion of Kikuyu . . . 30,000 out of 32,000 . . . it would be fatal to agree to any increase in the number of resident labourers in the forest area'.[79]

The forests served as a haven for all squatters. Resident labourers on the farms travelled to the forest to evade government officials and police. Inside the forest economic transactions could take place without the knowledge of European settlers and police. An account of an inspection of Bahati Forest in Nakuru District in January 1948 shows a community fiercely independent and resentful of all control:

> Any African that I saw working I did not bother. Only Africans that roamed about the forest, whom it appeared, had nothing to do, but carry big sticks and swords did I request to show whom they were working for. I can state on oath that 90 per cent of this type had no means of identity, or did not wish to show it.
>
> Say for instance I came across 5 or 10 natives and ask for their means of identity one would pretend to show his Kipande or reach inside his shirt, the rest would bolt into the forest and never be seen again . . .
>
> Natives not working for anybody have threatened to beat my Kangas [police] . . . in one instance a native pulled a sword on my Kangas slashed at them and ran away . . .[80]

The inspector also observed that in the early morning crowds of Africans left the forest for Nakuru. Lorries and buses stopped regularly, picking up and depositing passengers, indicating that large numbers were living in the forest illegally.[81]

If forest squatters had indeed been conservative or backward they would not have been seen as a threat. What infuriated Europeans was that forest squatters refused to accept their rules and had developed a frontier culture. A community confident of its way of life and aggressive in pursuit of its interests did not show the respect towards Europeans that was expected. A group of missionary teachers who inspected Kikuyu schools in the forests in 1951 were taken aback by the hostility they encountered. One of the group, Major Dewilt of the Africa Inland Mission, observed that 'both at Bahati and Maji Mazuri he found the forest squatters the most anti-Christian, anti-European and anti-Government collection of people he had found anywhere in the country. In the forests they ran things as they wished and resented any interference from outsiders'.[82]

The problem of control was not restricted to the forest areas. On many farms, Kikuyu squatters were able to establish communities that were more or less free from European supervision. These communities developed their own economy and tended to thrive. They also emerged as key centres of resistance. During the 1946 wave of unrest, government officials found a direct correlation between resistance and lack of supervision. A report on the refusal of squatters to attest – sign contracts – in the Kinangop area of Naivasha concluded:

> We have found that squatters show more willingness to attest in the North Kinangop than in the South, this is largely due to the fact that North Kinangop is more open country and the farmers in this area have made more endeavour to keep the native stock and cultivation under control. It is noticeable that where the squatter stock has not been strictly controlled in the past there is now 100 per cent refusals to attest.[83]

The freedom from European supervision on some farms was considerable. In the Ol 'Joro Orok area, Ol Arabel Valley and in Rumuruti where the Kaffir farming system was prevalent, squatters had their own markets, butchers shops and other amenities on the farms. In Ol Arabel Valley, Afrikaner farmers paid little attention to squatter black market activities as long as they received rent in kind. In November 1947, labour inspectors discovered illegal squatter settlements near the forest areas in Ol Arabel.[84] The lack of control over squatters is indicated in a report on three farms owned by B.H. Curry, C.D. Colville and A. Dykes in the Rumuruti area. The inspector reported:

> All three farms are vast stocks of land: Colville's place resembles a native reserve rather than a ranch. Rough guess is that they have between one to two thousand acres under maize and I estimated the crop standing at 6 bags to the acre a crop of perhaps 9,000 bags or more. Then this is sold, as one Kikuyu told me, at 35 shillings a bag in the reserve . . . I would say they are getting more out of the farm than is Colville himself.[85]

The local labour officer observed with perhaps a hint of exaggeration that 'each squatter owned a small village with herds of women and children tilling the land. Each little village with eight or nine well filled maized cribs, flocks of sheep and goats gave the impression that the squatter had reached the stage where he could comfortably afford to pay income tax'.[86]

Since the report of squatter cultivation in Rumuruti coincided with the first inspection of the area in 1948, it may be held that such extensive flouting of control was rare. It is interesting to note, however, that inspections carried out three years later showed the area to be still out of control. A report on Dykes' farm shows that squatters could have as much land as they wanted. Two mills on the farm indicated the considerable squatter maize that was cultivated. Nor was Dykes an eccentric backward settler. The labour inspector wrote, not without irony: 'It might be mentioned here that Mr. Dykes is one of the most influential men in the district and was at one time, Chairman of the District Council. There is no doubt, therefore, of his knowledge of the District Council Rules'.[87]

Squatters on Soysambu Estate, which emerged as the centre of the 1946 resistance, enjoyed little interference from their landlord. They lived in isolated villages miles away from any European. A report on Soysambu drawn up in October 1946 gives a flavour of squatter life on the frontier:

> estate shows more lack of control, and contained more serious resultant conditions than any Estate previously inspected, which is partly due to the native huts and cultivation being in very fertile pockets of silt soil in broken country situated 10–12 miles from the manager's house and to inspect the area entails a ride or walk of 10 miles from the nearest point that it is possible to approach in a car, and as a consequence chiefly due to a long period of immunity from inspection or control.[88]

This squatter community of over 1,000 people lived a life of virtual autonomy. The Labour Commissioner remarked that no European had visited the community for over a year and that he 'formed the conclusion that it was in fact regarded as an extension of the Kiambu District and completely uncontrolled'.[89] Nearby, on the northern border of Soysambu, inspectors discovered a triangular patch of land, 13 miles long and five miles at the base, which was used as a grazing ground by Kikuyu from nearby farms. According to the local labour inspector no control whatsoever had been exercised on this area.[90]

Inspections of squatter communities and attempts to enforce district council orders often precipitated a flight of Kikuyu residents. Kikuyu squatters in many cases exercised the option of establishing new illegal communities outside European control. Thus in June 1945 we find a European farmer, H.T. Cunningham, complaining that three of his squatters had removed themselves from his Trans Nzoia farm on the boundary of Elgon Location and established themselves on the edge of the nearby Forest Reserve. Upon further enquiry it was discovered that the ex-squatters were residing inside Elgon Reserve and were paying a cash tribute to the local chief.[91] More permanent outlaw communities were in existence near the boundary of Naivasha and the Maasai Reserves along the southern wall of the Great Rift Valley. The escarpment, which rises in a series of steps to a height of nearly 19,000 feet, is heavily forested and makes an excellent hideout. Settlements containing a mixture of Maasai and Kikuyu at Ololobwach, Nasapukia, Olesampula and Kamamias were inaccessible to the administration and police. According to intelligence reports Mau Mau activists had a strong presence in the area. These settlements were truly no-go areas. In 1951 and 1952 attempts were made to inspect the settlements, but government officials failed to make contact with the Kikuyu residents. Finally, on 21 November 1952, a large-scale military raid involving the King's African Rifles, the Lancashire Fusiliers, the Kenya Regiment and the Kenya Police was made on the area. Before the arrival of the troops all the men escaped and the forces of the state had to make do with capturing women and children.[92]

The social affirmation of independence from European control

The Kikuyu in the Highlands were driven by a combination of enterprise and a desire to evade the harsh restrictions imposed by the European landlord class. In a sense it was not possible to live in the White Highlands without breaking the law. In adapting to this environment the Kikuyu squatters became inventive and resourceful. Quick to seize opportunities, they were open to new possibilities. Of all the African communities in Kenya, Kikuyu squatters were the group most exposed to Western skills and technology.

From the late 1920s onwards, one sees African squatters performing multifarious tasks demanding new skills. Even a brief examination of farm files reveals that squatters worked in a number of specialized trades: lorry drivers, tractor drivers, stonemasons, carpenters and clerks were the most common on the farms.[93] In the forests, squatters performed most of the tasks necessary for the running of sawmilling operations.

The powerful desire for education by Kikuyu squatters provides the most forceful invalidation of the 'squatters were traditionalists' thesis. During the 1930s a number of government reports verify this point. The District Commmissioner of Nakuru observed in 1937: 'One thing that has emerged strongly during 1937 is the great desire of natives in the District for schools, as hitherto the Education Department has had practically no policy or provision for native education in the settled areas'.[94]

The eagerness for education provided the impulse for the establishment of a popular Independent schools and church movement on the farms. One of the leaders of the Independent schools and churches movement recalled that: 'In Elburgon our churches and schools started in 1931. In the beginning we held services outside and then we started building with wood. We collected 2 shillings from most squatters in the area to pay for teachers and books'.[95]

Many European farmers were suspicious of the new African schools and churches, but there was little they could do about them if they hoped to maintain a stable labour force. The Labour Officer of Nakuru wrote to his superior in 1938:

> As you are aware the question of the provision of education facilities for native employees in settled areas is now a most important factor in attracting labour, especially in industries, such as pyrethrum, in which a large number of juveniles are employed.[96]

It was precisely the burning desire of squatters to improve their way of life that created unease among the Europeans. Since the squatter community could only advance its interests through relying on itself, it was forced to establish its own counter-institutions. For government officials and European settlers squatter institutions were a threat because they were necessarily outside their control. Squatter economic activities operated on a black market and represented a challenge to the concept of a White Highlands where the African laboured for the European landlord. But the institutions that tended to provoke the greatest European reaction were those in the sphere of education and religion. For the colonialists these were inherently subversive institutions since they were entirely under the control of Africans. In the context of the White Highlands any African initiative which did not depend on the permission of the Europeans was by implication illegal or semi-legal.

In the squatter communities there was a strong correspondence between freedom from control, economic initiative, prevalence of religious and educational institutions and later political action. For the European, squatter counter-institutions were very much of an enigma. Europeans were particularly apprehensive about religious movements among squatters since they felt that such forces were unpredictable and beyond rational considerations. Thus in July 1945 a labour inspector in the Naivasha Lake area connected the refusal of vegetable-growing squatters to sign contracts with the presence of a mysterious religious organization. It appeared that these 'semi religious organizations' whose church was on Captain Rawson's farm on the Lake Shore organized the marketing of squatter produce in Nairobi and exercised a 'subversive' influence on nearby squatters. The labour inspector strongly recommended 'that this organisation be closed down in the settled area as we are convinced they have a bad influence on the labour of the area in which they carry on their business'.[97]

As it turned out when the inspector visited the church he found no evidence of subversion. He reported that on 'inspecting their church the only literature which was found was of a religious nature, of almost every known religion'.[98] Suspicion of religious groups ran deep among government officials and in August it was suggested that the refusal of squatters to attest in parts of Naivasha was perhaps linked to the proximity of an American Mission in the area.[99]

Although far from subversive, Kikuyu religious movements did express the resentment of squatters with European rule and were often a reaction against society as it was.[100] More precisely, a lack of confidence in European rule provoked a similar response in relation to white missionaries and their institutions. In Kikuyu society one of the first significant mass reactions to European domination took the form of a campaign against missionary interference in female circumcision. Missionary endeavours to eliminate female circumcision were seen as a fundamental attack on Kikuyu culture. In 1928–29 they led to a major crisis threatening an outbreak of resistance.[101] One long-term legacy of the female circumcision crisis was the formation of breakaway Kikuyu churches and schools. European missionaries lost adherents to the African Orthodox Church which organized its own Kikuyu Karing'a Schools and to the African Independent Pentecostal Church which launched the Kikuyu Independent Schools Association (KISA).[102]

In the Kikuyu Reserves KISA in particular achieved considerable success, but Independent churches and schools had considerably less adherents than those of European missionaries. In contrast in the Rift Valley, Independent churches and schools tended to exercise dominant influence in the Kikuyu communities. The various squatter frontier settlements, especially in the forests, became the stronghold of the Karing'a churches and schools.

The growth of Independent churches reflected the need of the squatter community for its own institutions. European society confronted the squatters as a hostile force ready to destroy their communities. For European settlers such institutions represented a challenge to the exercise of control over the farms. Considerable efforts were made to restrict the influence of Kikuyu schools and churches. Thus in June 1932, we find the District Commissioner, Nakuru launching an investigation of Richard Kimathi wa Njuguna, a school teacher in Elburgon.[103] It appeared that Kimathi had established an independent school without official sanction.

The case against Kimathi was brought by an African teacher, Justus, who ran a competing Scottish Mission school. Justus, put up by the District Commissioner, claimed that Kimathi was an 'agent of the Kikuyu Central Association marking his meetings under the cover of schooling'.[104] For the District Commissioner this statement was sufficient evidence to force Kimathi out of the area.

By the late 1930s local administrators throughout the White Highlands were expressing concern at the growth of independent schools. The Director of Education in Nairobi indicated in April 1938 that a European supervisor was to be posted in Nakuru to keep an eye on the Kikuyu schools.[105] Discussions in April and May proved inconclusive, as no supervisors were posted nor funds allocated for government-financed schools. The District Commissioner reported: 'It was recognised at these meetings that the various poorly organised Independent and Karinga movements are continuing to increase their hold on the local natives, which is objectionable both because of their influence on labour and the poor standard of the curriculum'.[106] This consultation with education officials did not lead to any action or policy innovation. In practice district commissioners continued to harrass independent, particularly Karing'a schools.

Despite the hostile attitude of officials, the Independent schools continued to thrive. Thus in February 1939 we find a Mrs. S.T. Thorne of Poultry Farm, Njoro complaining: 'My farm school registered no. 2619 has practically closed down owing to the existence of two "Independence" schools in the vicinity which I understand are not under any control'.[107] The same month the Provincial Commissioner warned of Independent schools springing up in the forests and demanded action from the Director of Education.[108] The scale of this growth of the Independent movement was confirmed later in 1939 in a survey carried out by the District Commissioner in Uasin Gishu.[109]

Settlers and missionaries saw Independent schools quite rightly as representing an alternative pole of allegiance. In the White Highlands among the Kikuyu the battle for allegiance was being won by the independent schools and churches. Their growth was clearly at the expense of European-inspired competitors. An illustration of the relation between Independent and missionary education is shown by the example of Kinari school in Bahati Forest, Nakuru. In the late 1940s James Kamuro had been a KISA teacher at the school. To further his training Kamuro was sent to the Africa Inland Mission (AIM) training school at Kijabe, where according to a European missionary he was 'converted to Christianity'. He returned in late 1950 as an agent of the AIM and set about teaching in line with his missionary training. The reaction of the squatter community was predictably hostile. Kamuro faced ostracism from squatters who demanded his expulsion from the area. A group of AIM missionaries sent out to support Kamuro were taken aback by the ferocious hostility which greeted them and could do nothing to save the situation.[110]

Many observers could not grasp the hostility of squatters to European Christianity. For many missionaries this hostility appeared to be an expression of some primeval morality. In fact hostility towards someone like Kamuro or European missionaries had a more down-to-earth basis. The squatters could not afford to tolerate individuals within their communities whose loyalty was in question. In their eyes Kamuro was an outsider, an agent of European influence and therefore a threat to the survival of their community. For Europeans, Independent schools represented subversion. For squatters they represented community control and ultimately survival.

If Europeans were concerned about the Independent movement they were positively irrational about the spread of the so-called 'dreamers" churches, millenarian organizations that developed among squatters from the 1930s onwards. A rejection of the European and a desire for dignity and freedom predisposed squatters towards a millenarian solution. The *murathi* (*arathi*, plural) or prophet of traditional Kikuyu religion emerged preaching salvation now in a semi-Christian and anti-European form. The earliest millenarian church in the Highlands was the *Watu wa Mungu* (God's people), which emerged in Kikuyuland in 1930 and had spread to the European-owned farms by 1931. The message of salvation for the African and punishment for the European usurpers found a resonance within sections of the squatter communities. For colonial officialdom the *Watu wa Mungu* represented a dangerous and potentially explosive force. Adherents were perceived as a threat to law and order and faced police harassment and expulsion from the European settled areas.

In May 1934 five adherents of *Watu wa Mungu* residing in the vicinity of Elburgon were rounded up. According to D.M. Stephens, Assistant Superintendent of Police at Nakuru, all five had 'a peculiar and wild facial expression and appear to be slightly deranged'. Stephens was not sure whether this was 'a result of their faith or whether they were previously unbalanced and so adopted the faith'.[111] Millenarian religion was seen by Europeans as beyond rational control, but the policy of repression failed to eradicate *Watu wa Mungu* from the farms. Although it had marginal influence within the Kikuyu squatter community it continued to gain adherents. It attracted support in Naivasha and many squatters living on Mount Margaret Estate and Mungu Estate were converted in 1937. Although they were forced to leave by their employers, other adherents were detected on farms in the Kinangop plateau.[112] Seven years later the area still continued to provide a residence for the sect.

From 1944 onwards police reports indicate a growing millenarian pressure on the farms. In addition to the *Watu wa Mungu*, other *arathi* representing new sects were circulating among squatter communities.[113] Although there was no evidence that these sects organized against the existing authority, officials continued to view them as subversive. When the 1946 squatter resistance broke out, local officials tended to blame it on religious sects. The Acting Provincial Commissioner was forced to concede that 'no specific instances of members [of *Watu wa Mungu*] causing dissatisfaction amongst labourers on farms has been brought to my notice'. Nevertheless, he wrote, 'a policy of "moving on" can and is being maintained'.[114]

The anti-squatter drive in the 1940s provided fertile terrain for the growth of millenarian religions like *Watu wa Mungu* and other so called 'dreamers' religions' like *Dini Ya Roho*. New sets sprung up on the farms. The sect *Dini ya Jesu Kristo*, which in 1947 acquired national prominence because of an armed confrontation with police in Kiambu, had its origins in the Londiani area of Nakuru District. The influential *Dini ya Msambwa*, which eventually came to enjoy mass support among the Bukusu, had as its main base of support the Bukusu squatters in Trans Nzoia.[115] This mushrooming of millenarian sects provided a clear testimony of heightened tensions and instability in the Highlands.

Although the growth of millenarian sects was often seen as an affirmation of traditional African cultural and spiritual norms, it is much more useful to see this phenomenon as an expression of the breakdown in existing values. In the Rift Valley it was the threat to squatter communities or the closing down of the frontier that precipitated anxiety and insecurity, making African tenants predisposed to new possibilities. In this sense millenarianism represented but an extreme symptom of the general rethink going on in the squatter communities. Although such sects existed throughout Kikuyuland, they were much more in evidence in the White Highlands. Official reports tend to confirm this trend. In May 1946, C. Tomkinson, the Provincial Commissioner of Central Province, wrote to his district commissioners in Kikuyuland on this subject. He noted the apparent growth of millenarian sects on the European farms and wanted more information on their influence in the Kikuyu districts. The sects were, he argued, exercising a 'bad influence on the younger Kikuyu on farms' and were 'being used for propaganda purposes such as the refusal by resident labourers to renew their agreements'. He concluded that 'it appears that their activities are increasing in the Highlands, but to the best of my knowledge they have not increased their following much in the Native Land Units'.[116] The replies of the district commissioners confirmed this assessment; only in Fort Hall was there a noticeable increase in millenarian activity.

Police reports confirm that millenarianism was a response to the closure of the squatter frontier. The theme of escape from bondage or a search for freedom from European control is reiterated time and again in detective reports and interviews with adherents of the sects.[117] It is a sentiment shared widely by squatters and one which when politicized endowed the squatter response to European domination with coherence and force.

Notes

1. *Nakuru District Annual Report 1914–15.*
2. Kenya National Archives (KNA) Lab 9/600, Local Option Orders, Aberdare District Council, DC Laikipia to PC RVP, 4 January 1946.
3. KNA, DC/NKU/6/2, Olenguruone 1974 50 no. 42, 'Translation of a letter found at the door of the hut of Ngoroge Waweru', 3 August 1948.
4. A select questionnaire of Kikuyu ex-squatters – 30 originating from Kiambu, 30 from Nyeri and 14 from Fort Hall – reveals the following information: 68 emigrated to the Rift Valley because of landlessness; six emigrated to the Rift Valley to seek their fortune. 53 went to areas where they had friends or relatives; 21 went to areas where they had no contacts.
5. Minute Report 1919 (File cover is missing) held at the archives of the Provincial Commissioner, Nyeri (PC Nyeri).
6. Interview with Boro Gicheru, Njoro.
7. Interview with Ngaramiti Kamau, Shifonde Forest Station.
8. KNA, PC/CP 6/3/1, Native Affairs – Emigration from Reserves, DC, FH to PC, Nyeri, 21 December 1917.
9. A European missionary based in Fort Hall wrote: 'The D.C.s are at their wits end how to tide over the transition. At present they are feverishly deposing old men who have lost control of their people, and are putting mission boys in their place'. Public Record Office (PRO), CO 533/287 no. 16051, H.D. Hooper to Friends, 24 January 1922.
10. Interview with Kigathia.
11. PC, Nyeri, Minute Report 1919 (File cover is missing).
12. Interview with Nyihia Misirori.
13. Interview with Mbucha Kamau.
14. Department of Native Affairs Annual Report, 1923.
15. Judicial Department: Annual Report, 1927.
16. See the memorandum by S.G. Fazan, 'The Economic Survey of the Kikuyu Reserves', United Kingdom, 1934 Cmd. 4556, *Kenya Land Commission: Evidence*, Volume 1, p. 916.
17. These figures probably underestimate the number of Kikuyu outside the reserves. The Kikuyu squatter population alone must have been around 90,000. This estimate is arrived at from Agricultural Censuses and from reports which note the prevalence of illegal squatters not on contracts. The source of the table is s. 6. in *ibid.*
18. KNA, Annual Report of Dagoretti Sub-District, 1928.
19. PC, Nyeri, Lab 31/2, Kikuyu Squatters Returning to Reserve, DC, KPU to Acting CNC, 4 June 1929.
20. Native Affairs Department Annual Report, 1933.
21. *East African Standard (EAS)*, 31 March 1939.
22. *(EAS)*, 9 October 1938.
23. Naivasha District Annual Report, 1933.
24. KNA, PC/NKU 2/1064, Marketing of Native Produce, no. 53, 'Report on Elburgon', 3 December 1937.
25. Nakuru District Annual Report, 1933.
26. Laikipia-Samburu District Annual Report, 1937.
27. Nakuru-Naivasha-Ravine District Annual Report, 1938.
28. Interview with Njoroge Kagunda.
29. Interview with Mwangi Njuguna.
30. Interview with Samuel Muiruri.
31. M. Bloch (1966), p. 170. Bloch notes that 'agrarian revolt is as natural to the seigneurial regime as strikes, let us say, are to large-scale capitalism'.

32. Kenya Government, 1947, *The Problem of the Squatter: Economic Survey of Resident Labour in Kenya*, part 6.
33. KNA, Lab 9/317, Nakuru District Council, Labour Department Report, November 1945.
34. KNA, Lab 5/1, Intelligence Reports 1945–48, 'Resident Labour, Inspector's Report' July 1945.
35. *ibid.*
36. KNA, DC, NKU 2/385, Labour Department, Monthly Reports, S. Davidson, Assistant Labour Officer, Naivashu to Labour Officer, Nakuru, 9 January 1951.
37. Nakuru District Annual Report, 1951, p. 37.
38. Interview: Ngihiu Muiruri, 16 February 1972.
39. Nakuru-Naivasha-Ravine District Annual Report, 1938, p. 3.
40. *ibid.*, 1939.
41. KNA, Lab 5/1 Intelligence Reports 1945–48 'Intelligence Report for July 1945' Labour Officer, Nakuru.
42. KNA, MAA 8/106, Internal Security Mumenyereri, see English translation of excerpts from *Mumenyereri*, 12 July 1948.
43. KNA, Lab 3/41, *Squatter Complaints* no. 214, see Squatters Petition to Creech-Jones, 10 July 1947.
44. Harris (1947).
45. Nakuru District Annual Report, 1951.
46. DC, NKU, Notes of DC for Annual Report, 1951 (no file number).
47. PC, Nyeri, Lab 31/2, Kikuyu Squatters Returning to Reserves, Assistant DC Kiambu to DC Nakuru, 14 June 1929.
48. PC, Nyeri, *ibid.*, DC Kiambu to PC, CP, 10 May 1946.
49. PC, RVP, Lab 27/5 vol. 5, Squatters and Squatter Stock Extract from North Nyanza African District Council Minutes, June 1950.
50. I have not been able to arrive at a satisfactory estimate of the real reduction in squatter income. The regulations were unevenly enforced and most of the figures of officials are rough estimates. Farm files indicate that even the minimum monthly wages were often underpaid. In Nakuru District it appears that the formerly prosperous squatter community experienced a major cut in living standards which brought them just above subsistence. This is evident from interviews and the alarm expressed by officials of the Labour Department. The most useful estimates of squatter living standards are available in a report on the subject by A.A. Hayes, District Officer, Molo, see DC, NKU, LG 5/2/5/9, Social Welfare Centres, Safari Report, 7 January 1951 and a memorandum by the Labour Officer in charge of Nakuru District on wage rates in 1950, PC, RVP, For 3/5/20/1 vol. 1, Forests. Welfare, Report on Welfare Amenities, 1 May 1950.
51. KNA, Lab 9/316, Naivasha County Council, no. 69 Labour Commissioner to All Inspectors, 8 March 1946.
52. Nakuru District Annual Report, 1950.
53. PC, RVP, Lab 27/5, vol. 5, Squatters and Squatter Stock, R.L.O. Inspector's Conference, Minutes, 21 May 1950.
54. *ibid.*
55. DC, NKU, LG 5/2/5/9, Social Welfare Centres, Safari Report, 7 January 1951.
56. *ibid.*
57. PC, RVP, Lab 27/5, as cited in note 53.
58. DC,NKU, LG 5/2/5/9, as cited in note 55.
59. PC, RVP, Lab 27/5, as cited in note 53.
60. DC, NKU, LC 5/2/5/9, as cited in note 55.
61. KNA, MAA 8/106, Internal Security, Mumenyereri, see English translation of excerpts from *Mumenyereri*, 19 April 1948.
62. Nakuru District Annual Report, 1948.

63. KNA, Lab 9/2202, The Dundori African Welfare Centre, Labour Commissioner to Chairman, Social Welfare Committee, Nakuru District Council, 10 August 1948.
64. DC, NKU, LG 5/2/5/9, as cited in note 55.
65. Nakuru District Annual Report, 1948.
66. Farm files available at the Labour Office at Nakuru indicate that punishment was frequent and often condemned by labour inspectors.
67. Nakuru District Annual Report, 1952.
68. KNA, MAA 9/875, African Advisory Councils in Settled Areas, Chief Native Commissioner, Minute, 23 May 1945.
69. Nakuru-Naivasha-Ravine Annual Report, 1947.
70. Interview: Francis Mucherere.
71. KNA, MAA 2/5/49, Minutes of Meeting of Provincial Commissioners, 2 November 1948.
72. KNA, MAA 9/875, African Advisory Councils in Settled Areas, Chief Native Commissioner, Minute, 23 May 1945.
73. Buijtenhuijs (1973) p. 249.
74. KNA, Lab 9/10, Labour, Squatters, Forest Areas no. 1, Secretariat to Conservator of Forests, 11 October 1944.
75. Lab O. NKU, Inspection Report, Elburgon Forest, March 1945.
76. *ibid*.
77. KNA, DC, NKU 2/397, Monthly Reports. Labour Office, June 1952.
78. KNA, Lab 9/10, Labour, Squatters, Forest Areas no. 107, Labour Officer Thomson's Falls to Labour Commissioner, October 1947.
79. *ibid*, no. 134 Labour Commissioner to Member for Agriculture, 10 August 1948.
80. KNA, Lab 2/388, Labour Inspector's Report no. 47, Report for Month of January 1948, Subject – Bahati Forest, Forest Officer.
81. *ibid*.
82. DC NKU, Ed 12/2/3 vol. 1 Native and Somali Schools, Report of meeting to discuss religious teaching in Bahati, 26 May 1951.
83. KNA, Lab 5/1, Intelligence Reports 1945–48, no. 47A, Resident Labour Inspectors' report for May 1946.
84. DC Nyandarua Lab 27/3 vol. 3 R.L.O. Attestation of Squatters, Labour Officer, Thomson's Falls to P.J. Van Dyk, 13 November 1947.
85. *ibid*., no. 68, R.L.I. monthly intelligence report for December 1948.
86. *ibid*., no. 69, Labour Department Annual Report, 1948.
87. Lab Office Nyandarua, Personal File of Dykes A. Farm, May 1951.
88. KNA, Lab 5/1, Intelligence Reports 1945–48 Addendum, Labour Officer to Labour Commissioner, 8 October 1946, Resident Labour Inspector's report to Soysambu Estate (Eburru) Area.
89. KNA, Lab 9/601, Labour Legislation R.L.O. General Correspondence 1942–59 no. 78A, Labour Commissioner to Chief Secretary, October, 1946.
90. KNA, Lab 5/1, Intelligence Reports 1945–48 'Addendum . . .' (see note 88).
91. KNA, DC, KMGA 1/29 Kikuyu in North Nyanza 1945–55 no. 14, DC, Kakemega to PC, Nyanza, 4 January 1946.
92. DC, NKU. See file entitled Settlement on Border of Naivasha Farms. The most detailed description of these communities is contained in a memo written by an unnamed officer stationed in Ngong to the CNC, 11 June 1952.
93. See the files on individual farms at Labour Office, Nakuru and Molo.
94. Nakuru-Naivasha-Eldama Ravine Districts Annual Reports, 1937.
95. Interview: Onesmus Gachocho.
96. KNA, DC, NKU 2/148, Education Native no. 79, Labour Officer, Nakuru to Principal Labour Officer, Nairobi, 12 May 1938.
97. KNA, Lab 5/1, Intelligence Reports 1945–48 no. 7H, Resident Labour Inspector's Report, July 1945.

98. *ibid.*
99. *ibid.*, 11A Squatters Inspector's Report, August 1945.
100. For a discussion of some of the explanations for the rise of protest religions in Kenya see Wipper (1977), Chapter 1.
101. See Rosberg & Nottingham (1966), Chapter 4, for a discussion of this crisis.
102. See Rosberg & Nottingham (1966), p. 125. For a useful overview of Independent schools and churches see Kanogo (1987), pp. 79–92.
103. KNA, DC, NKU 2/148, Education Native no. 9, DC, NKU to Forester, Elburgon 23 June 1932.
104. *ibid.*, no. 17, H.J. Afford, Forester to DC, Nakuru, 30 June 1937.
105. *ibid.*, no. 77, Acting Director of Education to DC, Nakuru, 16 April 1938.
106. *ibid.*, no. 81 DC, NKU to PC, RVP, 13 May 1938.
107. *ibid.*, no. 105 Mrs. S.T. Thorne to DC, NKU, 22 February 1939.
108. *ibid.*, no. 107 PC, RVP to Director of Education, 23 February 1939.
109. *ibid.*, no. 116 DC UG to PC, RVP, 24 December 1939.
110. DC, NKU, Ed 12/2/3, vol. 1 Native and Somali Schools, Report on Bahati Forest, 2 June 1951.
111. KNA, DC, FH 2/1/4, False Prophets (*Watu wa Mungu*), D.M. Stephens, Assistant Superintendent of Police, Nakuru to the Superintendent, CID Nairobi, 12 May 1934.
112. KNA, PC, CP 8.7.3, Political Unrest 1934–57 no. 36A, H.A. Nisbet, Labour Officer Nakuru to Principal Labour Officer, Nairobi, 23 December 1937.
113. DC, NKU, Conf. 12, Report on Native Religions, 12 November 1942.
114. KNA, PC, CP 8/7/3, Political Unrest 1934–57 no. 63B, Acting PC, Minutes to DC, NKU, 13 May 1946.
115. See Wipper (1977), Chapter 13.
116. KNA: PC, CP 8/7/3, Political Unrest 1934–57 no. 64 PC, CP, Tomkinson to all District Commissioners, Central Province, 20 May 1946.
117. See DC, NKU, Conf. 12, Report on Native Religions, 12 November 1944, and DC, NKU, Misc. 34/1, Mission and Chaplaincies.

Three

The Politicization of
the Squatter Communities

By the mid-1940s the Kikuyu squatter community was in a state of ferment. The wave of squatter resistance against settler society that dates from this period was to last into the 1950s. Agrarian movements rarely endure over such a protracted period of time. And it was precisely because the squatter revolt acquired characteristics not usually associated with peasant movements that it achieved such vitality and duration. Kikuyu squatters became politicized through their interaction with external social forces and it is the dialectic of this relationship that helps explain the duration and coherence of the revolt.

The Bukusu squatters in the Trans Nzoia areas of Kiminini, Lugari and Kamakoiya serve as a useful contrast to the Kikuyu. Here was a community whose experience was similar to that of the Kikuyu squatters but whose resistance was episodic and relatively unpoliticized. What explains this differential response?

The Bukusu squatters, faced with the fate of protracted impoverishment, began openly to resist the settler offensive in September 1946 when the so-called Kitosh Crisis broke out. Alarmed settlers and local officials reported that according to their informants Bukusu squatters were planning a land invasion of unoccupied European farms in the south-west corner of Trans Nzoia. A series of strikes on European farms in the area forced the administration to take the reports seriously.[1] Police action preempted the planned land invasion and for the moment the administration felt it had the situation under control.

In fact the years following the Kitosh Crisis were ones of instability and unrest. Strikes and go-slows were frequent occurrences on the farms and in 1949 a campaign of arson reminded the European settlers that the situation was far from normal.[2] However, Bukusu resistance, unlike that of the Kikuyu squatters, did not assume a political form. Instead, religious cults like the *Dini ya Masambwa* gained a strong following among the squatters in Trans Nzoia. The rejection of settler society was expressed through support for a religious movement profoundly hostile to European domination. It is worth noting that this response was no passing phenomenon. As late as December 1960, a meeting of European officials in Trans Nzoia observed that: '*Dini ya Masambwa* and its related movements were securing a strong following in the settled area among the increasing numbers of unemployed and other uneducated Africans. In Trans Nzoia its adherents showed . . . truculent and subversive attitudes'.[3]

At least in the mid-1940s the experience and response of the Bukusu squatters had striking parallels with those of the Kikuyu. Yet Bukusu squatter resistance remained localized and without a political focus. The experience of the Bukusu squatters suggests that the emergence of the Mau Mau movement needed more than the impetus provided by agrarian grievances. The additional ingredient was the intervention of urban-based militants and the drawing into the radical wing of the nationalist movement of squatter activists. It is our argument that through this relationship both the Kikuyu squatter movement and the nationalist movement underwent major changes. The squatter movement became politicized and in turn became a significant constitutency pressuring the nationalist forces to take a radical direction.

Early political influences

The early nationalist organizations that emerged in Nairobi and the Kikuyu Reserves, such as the Young Kikuyu Association and the Kikuyu Central Association (KCA), were initiated in the 1920s by the missionary-educated younger generations.[4] Motivated by the aspiration for better economic opportunities and more civil rights the new Kikuyu petit-bourgeoisie saw in the KCA a vehicle for the pursuit of its claims. It was a small, even elitist movement without a coherent social programme. Nevertheless, although organizationally weak, the KCA was in a unique position to articulate Kikuyu grievances. Its leaders were literate and possessed a working knowledge of the framework of the colonial system. The weight of the KCA depended not on its numbers but on its ability to represent the views of the Kikuyu masses. Before the war the KCA seldom initiated protest. Rather through its leadership it gave shape to the periodic outbursts in the Kikuyu Reserves. In the White Highlands the KCA was numerically relatively weak, but the widely held grievances of the squatter community there provided issues that KCA leaders could take up and promote. For the KCA, the squatter community was a natural constituency in its battles against the Kikuyu establishment. Moreover, the absence of native authorities in the White Highlands meant that even a handful of KCA activists could monopolize the go-between role in a highly compartmentalized society. The KCA acted as a conduit of information between the reserves and the farms. Consequently, disturbances in Kikuyu reserves such as the controversy over female circumcision became part of discussion on the farms.

Opportunities for the growth of KCA influence in the White Highlands first arose during the settler offensive against squatters in the late 1920s. The reductions imposed on squatter livestock in 1929 provided the impetus for the first mass movement of protest on the European farms.

The new regulations fostered a mood of insecurity and anger among the Kikuyu squatters. In early 1929, strange rumours were circulating throughout the White Highlands. One such rumour suggested that if squatters signed the new labour contract they would be bound to labour for European settlers for 30 years. Another widely believed rumour claimed that, just before he died in 1929, Paramount Chief Kinyanyui had ordered all Kikuyu squatters to return to the Reserves. These rumours were symptomatic of the acute sense of uncertainty that prevailed on the farms. Uncertainty combined with a profound sense that injustice had been done generated a mood of defiance. Kikuyu squatters throughout Naivasha, Laikipia and Nakuru districts refused to sign their labour agreements and returned to the Reserves. In some areas strikes broke out on the farms.

The extensive support for the movement of protest gave many settlers the impression that they were faced with a well-organized plan designed to overthrow their institutions. One of them wrote:

> We are living in troublesome times, and a Kikuyu rising is imminent. Settlers are beginning to hold meetings and a Vigilance Committee has been formed . . . We are supposed to have the visiting Bolshy Organizers on our and surrounding farms. For the last 5 months all the Young Kikuyu have been uppish and cheeky and have refused to turn out to work.[6]

In fact 'visiting Bolshy Organizers' were a figment of the European settler imagination. It was the general sense of grievance rather than the shadowy agitator that was responsible for the unrest. The KCA played the role of promoting the squatters' cause and articulating their grievance, but at this period it was an essentially informal organization based on a network of personal relations. It could represent the cause of the squatters but it could not initiate or organize action.

After the defeat of the 1929 protest the KCA receded into the background in the White Highlands. It grew in numbers as many young educated Kikuyu, who were excluded from the establishment in the Reserves, began to migrate to the White Highlands, in search of a future. But while numerically stronger, the KCA had little opportunity to exercise leadership. During the 1930s, especially during the period of prosperity generated by the pyrethrum boom, squatters could look after themselves and needed little in the way of representation. Because of labour shortages, the balance of power shifted in their favour and they were able to minimize the effects of European control. A report of the Provincial Commissioner to the Rift Valley testifies that in this period the rules regulating squatter economic activity could not be enforced.[7]

The illegal occupation of European-owned land became prevalent. The absence on active service of many settlers during the Second World War made the control of squatters particularly difficult. In 1944 the Chairman of the Solai Farmers Association complained that squatters:

> were taking and cultivating land where they liked and the position in Solai was said to be chaotic. Some big farms of 10,000 to 20,000 acres in extent were alive with squatters and farmers had no idea of their numbers.
>
> Many of them would not even work for the owner of the land on which they squatted and in some cases had, it was alleged, actually refused to come out to work when asked to do so.[8]

It was not until 1944 that the forces of law and order were in a position to bring the situation under control. Control now also meant the application of the new anti-squatter rules with their far-reaching consequences. The mass movement of disobedience provoked by these provided the conditions in which KCA and any form of nationalist movement could thrive. For their part the squatters were receptive to new organization and new leadership.

The crystallization of the squatter movement

The closer control of squatters brought about by the enforcement of new district council rules provoked widespread fear and anxiety. Throughout 1945 there was widespread unrest on the farms. Rumours, an important barometer of social tension, were circulating at a feverish pace.[9] On some farms it was rumoured that if a squatter signed the new labour contract, he would not be able to accept a dowry for his daughter.[10] Most of the rumours emphasized the theme of enslavement; signing the new contracts was depicted as a first step in that direction. On many farms and in the forests, squatters spontaneously refused to sign the new contracts. The greatest resistance came from squatters who had become accustomed to living under relatively unregulated conditions. On one forest estate, where squatters lived relatively unsupervised, all 140 forest squatters refused to sign the new agreements. Many of the forest resident labourers took it upon themselves to go to neighbouring farms to build up support. One official commented:

> I have received information that these Forest squatters have advised labour on farms to refuse to accept new agreements, with the result

that these natives are waiting to see what action we are taking as regards Forest labour . . . and should we show weakness, more trouble will ensue when new orders come into force.[11]

Other squatters went on strike. On one estate in the Thomson's Falls area the informal Kikuyu farm council directed that women or children should not pick pyrethrum as a protest against the reduction of the plots of land available for their cultivation.[12] This spontaneous outburst of resistance, which affected Kikuyu settlers throughout the Highlands, coincided with the establishment of the first legal African political organizations in the settled areas. The Kenya African Study Union (KASU), the predecessor of the Kenya African Union (KAU) was able to establish branches in many of the major townships in the settled areas. KASU, a moderate constitutionalist organization was founded in 1944 in Nairobi and developed a membership mainly composed of Kikuyu businessmen and civil servants, whose grievances it primarily articulated. A number of prominent Kikuyu from the Highland townships were present at its founding conference,[13] and to strengthen its authority a number of KASU officials attempted to become spokesmen for the squatters. Thus, for example, M.C. Benson, the secretary of the Ol Joro Orok branch of KASU, petitioned the Chief Native Commissioner about the drastic consequences of the new district council rules for the squatters.[14]

KASU and KAU never established a base among squatters on the farms and their activities were restricted to the townships. Most squatters were deeply suspicious of KASU/KAU, a sentiment which was later to turn into bitter hostility.[15] In contrast the KCA, which was banned and operated as an illegal organization, had strong grassroots support. This organization, initially based on an informal network of personal relations, acquired a relative degree of coherence in the 1940s. Initially this group consisted of educated Kikuyu, skilled artisans, traders and other prominent local figures and recruitment was carried out on a selective basis. The organization resembled many of the secret societies to be found in peasant communities. Although some of its activities were open (e.g. petitioning), oathing bound the membership to secrecy about KCA activities. The need for secrecy became even more essential after 1940, when the KCA was declared illegal by the government. The growth of squatter resistance provided the KCA with an opportunity to extend its influence since it promised united action and political expertise. Unlike KAU, the KCA had strong roots in the squatter community.

Many second generation squatters sought to escape the bleak future that life on the farms offered them, and these provided an additional link with the KCA. Some of them became traders, while others obtained skills and became artisans on the farms and in the townships of the settled areas. Many of these young men joined the KCA and they formed a direct bridge between the association and the Kikuyu on the farms. One such man was Kimani Muchohio, a KCA official in Njoro: 'It was not life working for the settler. So I went to Kijabe School where I was till 1938. After I finished I became a carpenter on a farm. I joined the KCA in 1940'.[16] Muchohio's biography was representative of local KCA activists.

The KCA was organized in Nakuru and Naivasha districts into loose branches: branch 'N6' extended geographically from Molo to Njoro, the Miti Miingi branch covered the Elmenteita, Gilgil area. These branches were divided into smaller area committees. Area committees of the N6 branch operated in Molo, Njoro and Elburgon. The basic unit of the KCA organizational structure was the KCA farm committee. Not every farm had a KCA committee. Recruiters of the group preferred to hold initiation meetings on the larger farms in order to avoid detection by the settler. As the organization grew larger, more and more farms formed their own committees. A provincial committee was formally responsible for communication. It seems that this committee met only two or three times up until 1950. Communications with the Kikuyu Reserves and other branches in the Rift Valley were established via Kikuyu traders moving from place to place.[17] The KCA organization was informal. But the very existence of a system of communication, no matter how diffuse, provided an important weapon for the squatter movement. In late 1945 the local leaders of the KCA decided to organize a more coherent resistance against the district council rules. The spontaneous protest against the new labour agreements among squatters was given a new direction and leadership. Three divisions of the KCA – N6, Thomson's Falls and Soysambu – provided the initial focus for this struggle.[18] The transformation of the KCA from a select elitist pressure group to a more broad-based force was itself one of the most important innovations of the squatter movement.

The Olenguruone factor

The active intervention of the KCA in the squatter movement was stimulated by the important events taking place in Olenguruone. Olenguruone has become a symbol of Kenyan anti-colonial resistance. This struggle also provides a unifying link between the squatter movement and the subsequent revolt in the Kikuyu Reserves. The origins of this dispute go back to the squatter protest movement of 1929 when many of the squatters reacted against the new burdens imposed on them by returning to the Kikuyu Reserves. When they discovered that there was no room for them there, most returned to the Highlands. Others migrated to Maasailand where they were later joined by squatters who sought a better way of life free of settler restrictions. One of these immigrants to Maasailand recalled:

We stayed on the farm until 1933. We left because the settler said to us that we couldn't keep any more goats. We went to Merilili in Maasailand. When we got to Maasailand, we approached a Maasai who gave us land and in return we gave the Maasai a portion of the food we grew.[19]

This community and others in Maasailand looked as if they would have a prosperous future. But many European settlers saw this development as a threat to their control of squatters. One farm manager complained to the Officer in charge of the Maasai Reserve:

During the past few months a large number of Kikuyu, who were previously working . . . as squatters have left and gone to live with their families in the Maasai Reserve . . . There appears to be some idea in the minds of the Kikuyu, that they are allowed to make this movement, and that once settled in Maasai Reserve that most likely they can avoid Hut Tax.[20]

The administration had its own reasons for being unhappy with the establishment of a Kikuyu community in Maasailand. In particular, the penetration of Kikuyu into Maasailand undermined the policy of maintaining rigid tribal boundaries. Through administrative pressure and harassment (including the burning down of Kikuyu huts) the Kikuyu ex-squatters were moved to Olenguruone settlement in 1941.[21]

Almost from the beginning the Kikuyu settlers at Olenguruone came into conflict with the administration since they considered it had been given in exchange for land they had lost to the white settlers and that they were therefore entitled to exclusive ownership of it.[22] In contrast the colonial administration was determined to control and regulate closely the Kikuyu living there. When the settlement rules were translated into Kikuyu the ex-squatters were shocked to find that they were referred to as *ahoi*, i.e. as tenants. They at once rejected the rules and indicated that they would refuse to sign the settlement agreements. In June 1943 a meeting was held at Olenguruone between the Kikuyu settlers and the Chief Native Commissioner at which the spokesmen for the Kikuyu settlers, Samuel Koina and Mbote Karamba:

. . . protested and contended that they should be in the same relation to their holding in Olenguruone as they had been to their original *Ithaka* (i.e. as landowners) which they had lost in Kiambu district, a principle which had been admitted in the grants made at Lari and Kerita.[23]

The Chief Native Commissioner reiterated the government's position and told the ex-squatters 'that as trespassers in Maasai they had received most generous treatment'.[24]

The meeting ended with both sides refusing to yield. According to a government account: 'After Mr. Hosking's Baraza in June 1943, the settlers did not, as they were clearly told, sign the agreement or leave the settlement. The influence of the malcontents spread, showing itself in the form of deliberate hindrance of the agricultural experimental work which was steadily going on'.[25] The Kikuyu settlers were determined to fight. As far as they were concerned, the government had pushed them about and broken its promise. One of the Olenguruone KCA leaders noted:

> When the rules were introduced we became very angry for when we came to Olenguruone we had come to be paid for our *shambas* which were turned into forest reserves in Kiambu. This they did. We were given 8 acres. But later they introduced the rules. We realised that we had been made like forest squatters.[26]

Their common experience on the farms and in Maasailand gave the Olenguruone Kikuyu a strong sense of community consciousness which formed the basis for united action.[27]

A group of tough and independent-minded Kikuyu provided a strong leadership for this community. To cement resistance, most Kikuyu settlers were given the KCA oath. In 1943–44, the unanimous hostility towards new agricultural rules indicated the effectiveness of this oathing campaign. The government's attempts to implement crop rotation and prohibit grass-burning and the growing of maize were simply ignored. However the government was not prepared to accept defeat. It issued an ultimatum threatening eviction unless the agricultural rules were implemented.

The Olenguruone settlers responded by initiating a widespread movement of protest that coincided with the outburst of squatter resistance on the neighbouring farms and was to have far-reaching consequences. The Olenguruone settlers initiated a new oath of unity, one which subsequently formed the basis for the Mau Mau oath. It represented a commitment to defy the government and had been taken by the whole population of Olenguruone by 1946.[28]

> In 1946 we took an oath which was different from the ordinary KCA oath. We were the first ones to take the oath because we had been sent from Maasailand and Turi, and when the settlers saw that we cleared the grass, they wanted to take it and we became very angry.[29]

In the spring of 1946, the Olenguruone Kikuyu showed their 'anger' by ignoring a government rule ordering them to plant grass on three of their eight acres,[30] and throughout 1946–47 they refused to co-operate with government officials. Their struggle to use what they regarded as their own land in whatever way they chose lasted until 1950, when the last of the Kikuyu settlers were evicted from Olenguruone and transported to the inhospitable Yatta area. By this time their fight against the government had become a symbol of anti-colonial resistance. In his Handing

Over Report of the settlement in May 1945, P.J. Browning described the situation with great perspicacity:

> I have been horrified at the lack of foresight in planning the settlement . . . There is a complete lack of confidence in the orders and promises of the '*Sereikali*' . . . [Government] . . . and I feel bound to say that there is some justification for the attitude . . .
>
> The treatment given to the court proceedings, will have far reaching repercussions in not only the Kikuyu Reserve, but throughout the whole of Kenya. The present unity of these men . . . is a force not to be trifled with. They now believe strongly in their rights to this land, they have faith in their cause.[31]

The struggle at Olenguruone had significant long-term implications. Through this experience the squatter movement became politicized and acquired an organizational form. Although its organization was primarily based on an informal network of militants it still represented a major advance over the previous forms of localized reactive resistance. At the same time, the politicization of the squatter movement had a critical impact on the KCA. Under the pressure of events the KCA was forced to open its doors and extended its core of activists. To some extent the squatters made the KCA their own and their brand of emerging agrarian radicalism strongly influenced the movement's outlook. The importance of this development soon became clear on the European farms.

The resistance on the farms

The struggle at Olenguruone had a great impact on squatters in Nakuru District. A direct road connected Olenguruone to Molo and Elburgon and Kikuyu settlers regularly visited Elburgon to sell their produce. The Elburgon KCA activists were in constant contact with Olenguruone.[32] Early in 1946 a number of activists from Olenguruone left for the farms to obtain support for their struggle from squatters. They administered the new oath of unity to a number of KCA activists in the Elburgon area and on the huge Soysambu estate. The choice of Soysambu indicated a degree of political sophistication, as protest was timed to coincide with the visit to this farm by Arthur Creech Jones, the Under-Secretary of State for the Colonies.

The oathing campaign found ready support among KCA leaders on the farms, who had their own reason for spreading the oath to other farms. The fusion of the squatter movement with that of the Olenguruone settlers provided a powerful stimulus to the spread of resistance. The District Commissioner of Nakuru and Naivasha reported in 1946:

> Taking full advantage of the power of oath swearing, many hundreds of squatters were induced not to re-attest in the hope that either

farming would be paralysed or District Councils' Resident Labour legislation jettisoned . . . it has become necessary to imprison 97 men from one farm . . . [Soysambu] . . . for a deliberate flouting of the laws of the land and this on the day before the arrival in the District of the Under Secretary of State for the Colonies; the organizers thought their demonstration well timed.[33]

The squatter oathing campaign of 1946 sheds new light on Mau Mau historiography. Contrary to conventional wisdom, the use of the oath of unity began in 1946 and large-scale oathing began in the Highlands and not in the Reserves. This point, stressed in one of my earlier articles, has been challenged by a number of scholars.

John Spencer uses interviews with his informants as evidence that the oath of unity came from Githunguri in Kiambu.[34] This assertion flies in the face of other substantial evidence. According to participants the connection with Kiambu was established *after* squatter activists were evicted from the Rift Valley. This is corroborated by intelligence reports from the Labour Department and the Special Branch. The squatters did not need help from outside; on their own they had spread the oath into every corner of the Rift Valley. Thus by the summer of 1946 the oath had even spread among squatters on European farms in Nyeri, an area that had no political links with Kiambu. In June the Nyeri District Commissioner wrote of the strength of feeling on a nearby farm. When the labour inspector visited the farm not one squatter was prepared to sign the contract: 'it appeared that they had all taken the githitu oath that they would not do so, unless they were allowed 5 heads of cattle'.[35]

Squatter resistance spread throughout Nakuru, Naivasha and Laikipia. By June 1946 it had spread to the Uasin Gishu District. The Labour Officer of Uasin Gishu District noted:

This is the first occasion that the Labour Office had come across reluctance amongst squatters to re-attest in this district and is obviously the result of the false rumours spread by agitators that have been circulating the Naivasha-Nakuru districts in recent months and is now permeating the Uasin Gishu district.[36]

The centre of the struggle took place in and around Soysambu Estate in Naivasha. In April 1946, resident labour inspectors began enforcing new rules in Naivasha that reduced the number of sheep squatters could keep from 40 to 15, and the acreage of cultivation from, in practice, almost an unlimited area to one or three acres (0.4 to 1.2 ha), according to the number of wives a squatter had.[37]

The 145 squatters on Soysambu refused to sign these new agreements, but no immediate action was taken against them as some of the labour officers sympathized with their plight. The Labour Commissioner instructed his officers that the wages of squatters in the Naivasha area should be not less than 12 shillings a month otherwise it would 'be impossible for the families to exist on this reduction'. He stated: 'This will not make much difference to the political difficulties of attesting contracts, but it will at least assure that squatters who wish to attest can in fact exist'.[38]

The determination of the Soysambu squatters to make a stand was closely linked to their long tradition as an autonomous and prosperous community. The landlord had a reputation for ruling his huge estate in the manner of a benevolent feudal baron, and squatters were spread over the estate with freedom to cultivate as much land as they wanted.[39] Many of the squatter villages were miles away from European supervision and a Kikuyu community had developed in a more or less independent fashion. This relatively undisturbed community provided the KCA with an ideal base for its operations in the Highlands. By 1946, the majority of the Kikuyu on the estate had taken the KCA oath.

The government tried to defuse a potentially explosive situation. In particular the Administration wanted to avoid the possibility of a general strike in the White Highlands. Meredyth Hyde-Clarke, the Labour Commissioner, warned the Governor that he had 'traced a definite connection between the attitude displayed at Soysambu and a similar attitude of the Olenguruone settlers'.[40]

On 6 June a meeting was held between the Soysambu squatters and the Labour Commissioner. Two major Kikuyu figures, Senior Chief Koinange and Chief Waruhiu, were brought in to assist the Labour Commissioner. The chiefs warned the squatters that there was no room for them in the reserves, and that therefore they must remain on the farms under the new rules. A temporary agreement was reached with the squatters; in return for a promise that no steps would be taken to reduce the area of cultivation, a number of squatters agreed to stay on until December. The Labour Commissioner, however, failed to achieve his goal: to persuade the squatters to sign the agreement. He reported: 'In view of the very tense attitude at Soysambu and the extreme suspicion displayed towards the European community, whether official or settler, I was unable to obtain the reattestation of the contracts of these squatters'.[41]

The inability of the government to obtain any measure of cooperation from the Soysambu squatters inevitably paved the way for a showdown. During the month after the 6 June meeting attempts were made to placate the squatters and to isolate those whom the administration saw as the 'ring-leaders'. These tactics failed, as by July the squatters' attitude towards the administration had clearly hardened. On 20 July the Soysambu squatters told the Nakuru Labour Officer that they would not give any information for the purposes of the government census.[42]

On 23 July the Registrar of Natives and other officials visited Soysambu in order to persuade the squatters to cooperate with the census and the district council rules. They received a hostile reception. The Registrar of Natives reported:

> It soon became apparent . . . that they had no intention of their listening to the advice or complying with any orders, their spokesman stated that they had refused the census information last November and would continue to refuse. They further stated that they were not prepared to divulge particulars of their families and stock required by the Senior Labour Officer to facilitate their removal from the Estate following their refusal to attest under the new conditions.[43]

The squatter leaders demanded that they should all be transported to Nakuru town for a trial to be heard against them, there and then. Convinced of the strength of their cause, they felt that a mass trial would serve to publicize their case. The visit of the Under-Secretary of State for the Colonies to Nakuru District would also give their demonstration more prominence. The Registrar was taken aback by this request but he agreed to transport 20 of the leading squatters. The Kikuyu refused to be split up and decided to walk to Nakuru as a group.[44]

Next morning 97 of them arrived in Nakuru. In court they reaffirmed their intention of not cooperating with government regulations. Before proceeding with the case, the magistrate called in the secretary of the KAU in Nakuru, Joseph Kinyua, who was asked to try to persuade the squatters to reconsider their attitude. 'After Mr. Kinyua had spoken to them for some time, they again became noisy and aggressive. They stated that they did not know who Mr. Kinyua was, neither did they know whom he represented. They were not prepared to listen to any of his reasoning'.[45]

The stand taken by the 97 Soysambu squatters earned them a month's hard labour and a 100 shilling fine. But the trial and the publicity attached to it inspired others to take a stand. An intelligence report observed in July: 'Indications suggest that Soysambu has initiated a landslide of refusals to attest'.[46] Next month it was reported that 'the attitude of the Kikuyu to accepting contracts, has if anything hardened'.[47] Throughout the rest of the year squatter resistance to the district council rules spread from farm to farm. The government held meetings with squatters in Laikipia, Naivasha and Nakuru districts in order to counter the influence of so-called 'outsider agitators'. At many of these gatherings the administration was able to use local KAU officials to put its point of view. Thus at a KAU meeting held at Subukia Police Post in Nakuru District, Charles Kamau, a KAU official from Njoro, told the assembled squatters that '. . . many were lazy and . . . as long as they remained so they would never get on. He asked them to think over things they heard and not to do anything suddenly or be led astray by any old story that was spread around'.[48]

The effect of these meetings seems to have been negligible and the intervention of officials of KAU served to reinforce the squatters' suspicions of that organization. The KCA also held public assemblies during the year. At these meetings grievances were aired and future plans discussed. Sometimes prominent Africans were invited to attend these assemblies. One such meeting took place at Bamboo Farm on 20 September 1946. Eliud Mathu, the first African member of the Legislative Council, was invited in order to acquaint him with the situation. At this gathering 700 squatters representing 33 farms and Olenguruone settlement unanimously refused to accept the new labour contracts for the following reasons:

1. the reduction of squatter stock to 15 heads of sheep
2. the reduction of cultivation to 1 acre per family
3. wages are too low
4. squatters' children have no facilities for education and inadequate medical services.
5. food crops strictly controlled – can't sell them or move them when we like.
6. Orders of District Councils impoverishing squatters completely.[49]

Mathu reported to the Labour Commissioner: 'Their objective is to leave the settled areas as soon as possible to return to the Native areas or to go to a place where Government can procure land for them'.[50]

The necessity for coordination of activity led to the emergence of a system of communication on the farms. Links between KCA farm committees were established and coordination occurred through regional committees. The most effective local organization was the Naivasha Committee, operating in the area around Soysambu. In November the Naivasha Committee organized a meeting to discuss future plans. The meeting, attended by more than 300 squatters representing 42 farms, decided to initiate a publicity campaign – letters and petitions were to be sent to the Governor, African political figures and newspapers.[51]

The threat of open political resistance provoked repression. From July onwards, eviction of defiant squatters was stepped up; over 5,000 Kikuyu were evicted from Nakuru District alone. By the end of the year there was a veritable flood of squatters forced back to Kiambu, their home district. Since this area was already overcrowded the District Commissioner of Kiambu feared the worst. He wrote to his superior, the Provincial Commissioner of Central Province: 'I am becoming very concerned about the question of squatters particularly from Nakuru and Naivasha areas, returning to this district. I am threatened with a large inundation; and where they are to go I have no idea'.[52]

The eviction of large numbers of squatters and the dismissals of individual militants had a stabilizing effect. After February 1947, defiance of the new rules became sporadic and unorganized. Faced with the threat of eviction and the lack of prospects in the Reserves, most squatters decided to stay put. However the squatters did not lapse into passivity – resistance was postponed while the activists continued to operate underground.

The politicization of the movement

The defeat of the movement on the farms coincided with the extension of squatter activity in the Reserves. Through the evicted squatters an important alliance was consolidated between the militants on the farms, in the Reserves and Nairobi. The evicted squatters stayed together and with the help of the KCA formed the Kikuyu Highlands Squatters Landlords Association (KHSLA). All eight of the prominent spokesmen of the KHSLA were KCA activists.[53] Gitau Kamau was chairman of the important KCA committee on Soysambu estate, while Samuel Kibunja, from Elburgon, who became the main spokesman of the KHSLA, was a close associate of George Ndegwa, the former secretary of the KCA.

The focus of the KHSLA's activity was in Kiambu District, in the Kikuyu reserve. It acted as the voice for the 3,000 ex-squatters, who were camping near Limuru as a group to demonstrate their plight and to demand land for themselves. The KHSLA, through George Ndegwa, hired a lawyer to draw up a formal petition for them. On 18 November a delegation of 3,000 ex-squatters visited the District Commissioner of Kiambu and demanded that food be issued to them and land be given to them to settle on.[54] They were told that there was no land for them in Kiambu and that they should return to the Highlands and re-attest at once.

Two days later four lorry-loads of ex-squatters went to Nairobi to present the Governor with a list of their grievances. The District Commissioner of Nairobi addressed them and advised that they return to their homes. The squatters did not heed him and remained camped at the Law Courts the next day. The District Commissioner addressed them again and stated that he would take a delegation from them to see the District Commissioner of Kiambu, on the condition that they disperse immediately. The squatters left Nairobi that evening. At the meeting with the District Commissioner of Kiambu, the delegation was told that the attitude of the government remained unchanged but that a final meeting with senior government officials could be arranged.[55] The squatters were warned that any more disturbances or demonstrations would not be tolerated. The 'final' meeting was arranged for 30 December 1946. The ex-squatters camping near Limuru were split as to what course of action they should pursue. A minority of militants wanted another demonstration to take place in Nairobi immediately.[56] Others, however, were prepared to give up and return to the Highlands. But it seems that the majority wanted to await the results of the meeting with the government.

The 30 December meeting included eight squatter representatives and an impressive government delegation led by the Chief Native Commissioner, W.S. Marchant.[57] Marchant reiterated the government's position; it had no intention of reconsidering the case. If the squatters wanted work, there was plenty available if they cared to return to the Rift Valley and abide by the new council rules.[58] Kinyanjui wa Gicheru gave the squatters' position:

> They went to work on farms in the Highlands on certain conditions which had been gradually whittled down. He wanted stock and land on a similar basis to the Europeans. How were their own Kiambu and Limuru lands to be returned to them if they were not allowed to stay in the Highlands? They had found these lands good and fertile but were not told that they would have to enter into contract – otherwise they would not have gone.[59]

The government was not prepared to make any concessions to the squatters. They were told they had no claims to land and were warned against demonstrating in Nairobi in the future.

The ex-squatters did not heed the government's warning. On 1 February 1947, 250 of them, including women with their babies, invaded Government House and demanded to talk with the Governor. The Governor held a short meeting with the ex-squatters and suggested they return to the farms. Upon concluding his talk, he told the squatters to leave Government House, but they remained sitting on the ground. When it became clear that they had no intention of leaving, the police moved in and arrested a number of the leading demonstrators; the rest were forced into lorries, which took them back to Limuru.[60]

The absence of any concrete gains led to increasing demoralization among the ex-squatters in Limuru. Their food supplies were running low and their petitions to the government demanding food were being ignored. In February, their number was increased by newly evicted squatters.[61] Meetings were held throughout Kiambu in a last-ditch attempt to obtain local support; plans for seizing a piece of forest land and further demonstrations in Nairobi were discussed. A police officer reported that they were 'becoming more and more secretive in these meetings and now post sentries to keep anyone who is not one of them away from the place'.[62]

Frustration and demoralization among the squatters in Kiambu began to take their toll. Plans for future protest action in Kiambu or Nairobi were abandoned and in late February a decision was made to return to the Highlands.[63] A number of ex-squatters were left behind in Limuru to coordinate the activities of the KHSLA. In April a meeting organized between the ex-squatters and a group of Olenguruone settlers agreed to coordinate each others campaigns.[64]

The KHSLA remained active in Limuru until the end of 1948. During this time it published a series of petitions to the Governor and the Secretary of State for the Colonies, and addressed one to the United Nations.[65] Contacts were also established with KCA activists in the Reserves and Nairobi that exposed the ex-squatters to nationalist and radical influences. Radical anti-colonial ideas corresponded to the experience of the ex-squatters and tended to politicize their outlook.

The ex-squatters experienced intense hostility from the Kiambu Kikuyu establishment. Their activities were continually obstructed by the Kikuyu chiefs and headmen, who saw them as a threat to law and order.[66] The hostility towards Rift Valley Kikuyu in Kiambu became more prevalent after December 1947. A religious sect, the *Dini ya Jesu Kristo* clashed with a police patrol at Gatundu in Kiambu. Led by their prophet, Reuben Kihiko, the members of this sect killed two African constables and a European inspector. Since this sect was composed of ex-squatters who had recently returned from the Rift Valley all ex-squatters came under popular suspicion.[67]

The 1945–47 period prefigured subsequent developments. The network of activists that emerged provided an important core leadership for the Mau Mau movement. It provided an organizational focus that ensured that the squatter protest would no longer be local. At the same time the tension that developed between squatters and the Kiambu establishment anticipated the violent hostility that was to explode into a critical civil war during the Mau Mau years.

Uneasy alliance

The years 1945–47 saw the transformation of the squatter movement into a significant force of protest. The breadth of its activities was certainly unusual for an agrarian-based protest movement. Resistance on the farms and at Olenguruone spread to Kiambu District in the Kikuyu Reserves, culminating in protest action in Nairobi. This action, orchestrated through the KCA and KHSLA, was made possible by the emergence of a network of politicized squatter activists. In the course of this agitation it became clear that the old relationship between the KCA and squatter protest had changed. Under grassroots pressure the KCA had acquired a more thoroughgoing activist dimension. More significantly the squatter protest threw up a new generation of leaders who were able to pursue action on behalf of their constituency. They did not leave the task of representation to the old KCA leaders but took it upon themselves to articulate the grievances of squatters.

The main effect of the emergence of squatter militants was not so much to radicalize the KCA as to intensify its combativeness. Squatter activists were not necessarily more radical than the older generation of KCA leaders. What distinguished them was rather their determination to go further than the older generation in the pursuit of their goals. A tension between the two wings became evident during the course of squatter agitation in late 1946 and early 1947. While sections of the squatter movement wanted to step up action, others counselled a moderate stance so as not to offend the Kiambu Kikuyu establishment.

The tension that surfaced at this time was temporarily resolved, since at this stage attitudes were far from hardened. Even the most moderate section of the nationalist movement could not afford to attack publicly the tactics of squatters. For their part, the squatter militants were too weak to advance on their own and needed the assistance and resources of the more established Kikuyu leaders. An uneasy truce had emerged, one that neither side had any interest in breaking at this time.

The growth of a militant wing of squatter activists is one of the main legacies of the 1945–47 period. It was very much the product of the 'nationalization' of the squatter movement and was connected to a similar pattern of development in the Kikuyu Reserves and Nairobi. Squatter activists became strongly influenced by this contact with Nairobi and Kiambu. Through contacts with militants from these parts they became politicized and made more aware of the national dimension of their struggle. A shift in the political outlook of squatters through growing exposure to events in Nairobi and the Kikuyu Reserves is the product of this period. Thousands of squatters were forced back into Kiambu and a regular pattern of migration was established between the Reserves and the Highlands. Others moved to Nairobi and came into contact with more experienced activists. Through these movements squatter activists became dispersed and part of a wider network of protest.

The hostility faced by the squatters residing in Kiambu from the Kikuyu establishment contributed to radicalization, driving the squatter activists into an informal alliance with other Kikuyu militants. This was particularly the case in Nairobi where ex-squatters played an important role in radical nationalist circles. According to one intelligence report on Shauri Moyo, an African settlement in Nairobi, ex-squatters featured prominently in the collapse of law and order.[68] Squatter activists were closely linked with the militant 'Forty Group', which at the time constituted one of the most significant sections of the radical wing of the nationalist movement in Nairobi.[69]

The growth of a militant wing of the squatter movement was paralleled by similar developments in Nairobi and the Kikuyu Reserves. A revolt against the Kikuyu establishment was in the making. In Fort Hall, agitation against the terracing of land and compulsory labour for women led to the outbreak of violence in September 1947.[70] In Nairobi, unrest was extensive and the forces of law and order were faced with the threat of losing control in some of the African locations.[71] The specific causes of these outbreaks varied from area to area but in each case those leading the protests represented a new force in anti-colonial politics.

This was the political climate that shaped the political outlook of the squatter activists. Kikuyu society was going through a process of social and political differentiation. Literally excluded from the Reserves, the squatters gravitated towards those opposed to the status-quo. It was only a matter of time before those who opposed the existing colonial arrangement would constitute an independent militant force.

The new militants

The new militants who emerged in the course of the struggles of the 1940s, and who later came to constitute the core of the movement known as Mau Mau, represented a distinct social group in the White Highlands.

The Kikuyu squatter community was by no means homogeneous. Different economic opportunities in the various regions of the Highlands led to uneven development of the farms and, as argued earlier, local differences had important future political implications. The areas which had the greatest scale of squatter economic activities were also the most politically active.

On the farms social differentiation initially proceeded along the lines of division of labour. Most farmers had a number of trusted men who formed a distinct stratum on the farms. They were also on squatter contracts but in contradistinction to the rest of the Kikuyu their duties had a specialist or supervisory aspect. They were the headmen, the milk clerks, the drivers and the house servants, many of whom enjoyed privileges that clearly distinguished them from other squatters. Kamau Kigera was a headman on a farm in the Lake Naivasha area. His wealth was testified to by his 28 wives and 6,000 goats.[72] This pattern of differentiation was altered in the 1940s when the rationalization of European farming led to the modification of the existing division of labour. Henceforth, the trusted men were increasingly replaced by educated and skilled specialists.

The gradual transformation of the status of squatters as tenants stimulated many of them to look for new economic opportunities. A shift towards trade and commerce ensued which became an important force for speeding up social differentiation. A degree of trading activity had always characterized the squatter economy. Now this avenue was utilized to the full. In some cases squatter traders were able to accumulate considerable wealth; this was particularly the case on farms where European settlers encouraged some form of share cropping or cash tenancy. One squatter in the Naivasha Lake area had 1,400 acres (567 ha) under cultivation, ran a profitable enterprise and provided the Naivasha Prison with 52 pounds of vegetables every day.[73]

The scale of squatter enterprise was quite extensive. A senior labour official summed up the results of his investigation thus: 'I found on farms a very considerable number of small contractors, chiefly Africans, engaged in cutting, making bricks, clearing bush, charcoal burning, cutting fuel etc'.[74] Another inspector reported that many 'farmers complain that their labour is too much inclined to go in for petty trucking and harvesting, probably due . . . to the ready market which can be found for garden produce and poultry'.[75] In a previous article I noted that this group of traders, artisans and other skilled and educated Kikuyu played a leading role in the squatter movement and later in Mau Mau.[76] This has been challenged by Tabitha Kanogo who argues that on the contrary this group 'had a stake in settlerdom', that traders had 'business to protect' and that 'those with wealth also saw Mau Mau as a disruptive movement'.[77]

Kanogo's arguments are based on a confused analysis of the squatter social structure. In the White Highlands the most energetic and ambitious squatters became traders, artisans or skilled workers. However, very few of them managed to develop a stake in settler society. This group was different from the stratum of prominent, often educated African businessmen in the townships of the White Highlands or to the Kikuyu elite in the Reserves. Squatter traders lived precariously. Virtually every aspect of their activity could be construed as illegal and they suffered from close regulation by the European settlers and the police. The combination of strong ambition thwarted at every stage and economic insecurity drove this group towards political resistance. Rather than having a stake in the system, the way they saw it was that they had little to lose and everything to gain.

Kanogo questions whether these traders had any role to play and even disputes the importance of their mobility for organizing the squatter movement.[78] She puts forward the proposition that it was the 'unemployed' who played this role – not by offering evidence but through a process of abstract deduction. 'How', she asks, 'could they attend the meetings that took place between the White Highlands and Central Province leaders if they were employed?'[79] In fact it was precisely the channels of communication that served the squatter economy so well – the black-market network and the semi-underground connections – that proved to be indispensable in the organization of the movement. The life of illegality that characterized the day-by-day existence of the squatter traders proved invaluable for establishing a base line of communication for the movement.

Kanogo also questions the role of skilled workers, headmen (the *nyapara*) and milk clerks (*karanis*) in the leadership of Mau Mau. She argues that the *nyapara* and *karani* were in the pockets of the European settler, they 'owed their privileged position to him'.[80] Inevitably the

European settlers had their right-hand men and their spies. And quite clearly not every *nyapara* was a Mau Mau leader. Indeed, as we later show, one of the first objectives of the movement was to rid the farms of uncooperative *nyaparas*. However Kanogo is quite wrong to imply that the more privileged section of the squatter community was in the pockets of the European farmers. Many of the skilled men, including some *nyapara*, got their jobs precisely because they arose as leaders of the squatter community. Thus the elders' councils (*kiama*) that existed on the larger farms often had within their ranks the so-called trusted men of the European settler.

The stratum of traders, artisans and skilled workers was an integral part of the squatter community. In a sense they were its natural leaders. But they could not do as they pleased – they always had to abide by the existing consensus. Those few that ignored the general interests of the squatter community were ostracized and during the early 1950s were often eliminated by Mau Mau. It is always possible to dispute interpretations – but when it comes to facts Kanogo's arguments entirely disintegrate. Let us look at the evidence.

Police intelligence and labour inspectors' reports all point to the key role of the traders, artisans, skilled workers stratum in the leadership of the squatter movement and of Mau Mau. In the Nakuru Labour Office there are departmental files on every farm in the district. These indicate dates of arrests, convictions and evictions. The names of artisans and 'trusted men' figure disproportionately among those detained. This is backed up by other sources. A number of intelligence reports on the situation in Nakuru District in 1951 cite activists who should be considered for preventive arrests. Not *one* of the people on the list is an ordinary squatter. However the list contains two headmen, 12 artisans and skilled workers and nine people who could be considered as semi-traders and businessmen.[81] A detailed report written by Ian Henderson, Assistant Superintendent of Police in 1949, confirms the same trend in the settled areas of Uasin Gishu. According to his sources the 'chief agitator and leader' was John Murege, a *karani*. The other agitators included a forest scout, a headman at a sawmill, a trader who often travelled to Uganda, an owner of a farm shop and the principal of an independent school.[82] An unusually informative intelligence report written in February 1951 by S. Davidson, a labour officer stationed in Nakuru, confirms the general trend. Thus on one farm under his surveillance the head of Mau Mau is the *nyapara*, Paulo Mundio, and his right-hand man is Njugune Waweru, the schoolteacher.[83]

Information available from the files of W.B. Lambert, who was in charge of a screening team stationed at Subukia, provides useful evidence on this question. Thus we find the following individuals officiating at oathing ceremonies in August 1952 at Elburgon Forest: Kungu Nganga, a clerk; Kingori Wambugu, a cashier; Njoroge Kimani, an *askari*; and Maina Njoroge for whom we have no record of occupation.[84]

In March 1948 we find Ruiru Kagichu, a handyman on Olo Bonge farm in Eburru and a trusted employee for 12 years, at the centre of unrest. After leaving Olo Bonge, Ruiru gained employment at a nearby farm where again he was blamed for leading squatter unrest and was promptly dismissed.[85] Gitau Gathuri exemplifies the local militants who were the backbone of Mau Mau. In 1951, he was trading at Dundori Centre in Nakuru District, while residing on Cold Harbour Estate. An intelligence report of that period refers to him as the 'youth leader' of Mau Mau in Dundori and Ol Kalou.[86] Gitau Gathuri had emigrated to the White Highlands in 1918 and worked for a number of settlers, always on the look-out for new opportunities. Although he had no formal education he succeeded in obtaining a relatively prestigious post. Put in charge of transporting his employer's cream to the factory in Naivasha, his salary of 50 shillings a month was five times the rate paid to squatter labourers. During the 1930s he joined the KCA and became one of the local leaders of the organization. He observed:

> . . . during the war life was not so bad, the Europeans told people to give money for war but the people usually refused. In 1946 a lot of people joined the party, by this time things had gotten worse as the settlers wanted us to be like slaves to them . . . There were a number of people like me who used to go around oathing people. Being a trader made it easy for me to go around.[87]

The predominance of traders and artisans in the KCA and the Mau Mau leadership is striking even at a cursory glance. Edward Mugo, a KCA activist in Molo, was a charcoal burner. Ngaramiti Kamau, one of the founders of the KCA in Nakuru District, was a butcher. Harum Kafuguro, who played a leading role in the KCA in the Naivasha Lakeside area and later at Olenguruone, worked as a milk clerk. He stated:

> I joined the KCA in 1937 because the salary was too little and because of trouble from the settlers . . . During this time I also taught in an independent school. I left in 1940 because the settler refused to increase my salary. In 1940 I started buying and selling sheep in Laikipia. I bought them from the Turkana and sold them to the squatters.[88]

Eliud Kiberenge, whom we will shortly meet in connection with the Ngata affair, lived on that farm while trading in second-hand clothes. It is interesting to note that the six activists sent from Elburgon to Thomson's Falls to learn the administration of the *batuni* (the Mau Mau warriors) oath worked as either traders or contractors in the area.[89]

The spread of the oath in the late 1940s vividly illustrates the social base of the local leadership of Mau Mau. The farm committees of Mau Mau were generally led by the foreman, milk clerk or some of the other skilled employees. Kinanjui Mutegi, one of the most respected of the movement leaders in the Elburgon–Njoro area, worked as a *nyapara* on Salder's farm. According to him: 'We spread the oath the following way. First *nyaparas* and teachers were oathed, since they were the most respected men on the farms. Then they were made responsible for spreading the oath on the farms'.[90] Michael Waweru, a young activist in Elburgon gives the following account:

> We would go to a farm and approach a *nyapara*, the milker in charge of the dairy or the farm clerks. We would take him to a meeting and explain to him everything. If we wanted the milker and we know you were his friend, we sent you talk with him and get his confidence. We would then have you take him to a meeting, where we explained to him the movement and how we want to fight. He would then help us to organize a committee on his farm'.[91]

The emphasis of the oathing campaign on prominent Kikuyu might at first sight seem strange. One would have expected a degree of hostility between the skilled men on the farm and ordinary squatters. In particular, the headmen and foremen in their supervisory capacity were bound to provoke a measure of resentment from other squatters on the farm. But Mau Mau activists saw the skilled men as the most trusted section of the squatter community. They knew that many of these men had become influential even before they obtained their positions. The oath administrators calculated that if these people could be won to the objectives of Mau Mau then the rest of the squatters would fall in line.

Those Kikuyu in responsible positions had in some sense to be accountable to the squatter community. In an isolated community such as this no one could afford to provoke public opinion, and pressure from below acted as a deterrent against any Kikuyu identifying too closely with the interests of the employer. Hence the squatters were able to exercise a significant measure of control over every member of the community. When someone overstepped the mark the squatter community was quick to respond. Numerous strikes against unpopular headmen are recorded in Nakuru District in the 1940s.[92]

As the activities of Mau Mau accelerated, the need to eliminate unsympathetic headmen became more crucial. During 1950–51 a campaign of intimidation was launched against headmen who were loyal to their employers, taking the form of farm strikes and various forms of intimidation, including physical assault. F.D. Corfield noted that in 1950 Mau Mau tried to consolidate its position in the settled areas via various tactics: 'Among them were attempts to ruin a farm by packing it with Mau Mau labour – this was achieved by either intimidating the head man, or introducing a competent "wrecker" as headman.'[93]

Of course, there were a number of 'loyal' headmen and other trusted servants of Europeans who refused to become involved with Mau Mau. However, these men, regarded by the squatters as traitors (except for the non-Kikuyu among them), were few and far between. Most headmen were at the forefront of squatter resistance.. The following letter from a European settler to the Labour Commissioner describing the effects of the squatter campaign of 1946 is instructive on this point:

> We are very worried about the re-signing of our squatters as they have all refused to do so . . . All these men and their families have done very good work . . . I've talked to the head boy who we've had for 28 years and is involved and has always signed before. He says they've all been told that government is bringing a term of conscription by them signing for one or two years but in reality it means 30 years.[94]

The discovery that 'trusted men' were often the local leaders of Mau Mau was to cause a rude shock to settlers and Government. The District Commissioner of Laikipia noted in 1953: 'It is most depressing to see the natural leaders amongst the labour in the farms, artisans, craftsmen, headboys, old and trusted retainers being uncovered by the Screening Teams every time as the Mau Mau Committee on *every* farm screened'.[95]

The absence of a significant group of collaborators in the White Highlands is in sharp contrast to developments in the Kikuyu Reserves. The survival of the Kikuyu squatter community depended on a united stand against the settler onslaught. The headmen, artisans and traders formed a distinct stratum on the farms, but by themselves they were an insignificant force compared to the European establishment. Moreover their position and authority was dependent on their close relations with the squatter community. Consequently, the political interests of those two groups merged within a common movement.

This was not the case in the Kikuyu reserves. There, a group of missionary-educated Kikuyu elite members, landowners and businessmen, who were closely tied to colonial structures, constituted the basis for a class of collaborators. This difference between the Kikuyu reserves and the settled areas was noted by Colonel T.H. Henfrey, who was in charge of recruiting loyalist Kikuyu to the Home Guard in the Rift Valley Province. In the settled areas 'our problem is different from that of the Central Province', he explained. There 'you have a people who have a land right and who readily answer the clarion call to defend hearth and home'.[96]

In other words very few Kikuyu in the settled areas had a stake in the colonial system. Henfrey reckoned that at the most 10 per cent of the Kikuyu in the settled areas might support the government, and most of this support came from Nakuru town and the other townships. The majority of the active collaborators were wealthy traders or government servants. One such man was Parmenas Kiritu, a prominent shopkeeper in Naivasha, who became the local head of the 'Loyalist' Torchbearers associations.[97] In the Elburgon area the most prominent collaborator was Wairiri Kigera. He was a wealthy businessman, who had a reputation for being the richest African in the European settled area. His efforts on behalf of the colonial regime were well rewarded. A European Home Guard officer wrote on behalf of Kigera's application for a concession to become the local distributor of flour:

> The sole distributor in Elburgon is an Indian if there is to be another appointed we should like to see this in the hands of an African.
> Wairiri Kigera himself has assisted me actively in the Home Guards of Elburgon. We believe that as he owns shops and lorries both in Elburgon and Nakuru, he has too much to lose by consorting with terrorists.[98]

Active collaborators like Wairiri Kigera and Parmenas Kiritu were in a minority even within the small group of Kikuyu businessmen in the townships.

Kanogo's claims that: 'Contrary to Furedi's findings, there was a high inverse correlation between socio-economic status and response to Mau Mau among the squatters' misses the argument.[99] We have never claimed that the most wealthy Kikuyu, such as Wairiri Kigera, were natural supporters of Mau Mau. Nor do we suggest that there is a connection between wealth and prestige and participation in the revolt. What we suggest is that the mobile sections of the Kikuyu squatter community became politicized because their aspirations were thwarted at every turn by the settler-dominated institutions of the White Highlands. The most affluent Kikuyu, with a stake in colonial Kenya, collaborated with the authorities in the Highlands just as much as their counterparts in the Reserves. But due to the specific circumstances that prevailed in the Rift Valley, this group of collaborators was far more insignificant than in the Reserves.

The experience of oppression and economic discrimination was shared by all Kikuyu in the White Highlands. Even the most economically active Kikuyu faced the prospect of police harassment and eviction. Thus a movement of resistance arose which, although heterogeneous in its social composition, had a solid base of support. This was due to the coincidence of interest between different strata of Kikuyu that emerged in opposition to the power structure in the White Highlands. The hostile environment forced the Kikuyu into a permanent state of semi-secrecy and underground organization. This was necessary even for simple operations like the movement of livestock and the disposal of produce. It was inevitable that the much more dangerous endeavour of political resistance would develop along similar lines. Like peasant movements throughout the world the Kikuyu squatters turned to mass oathing and secret organization.

Notes

1. Kenya National Archives (KNA), Lab 5/1, Intelligence Reports 1945–48 81G, Labour Officer, Kitale, Intelligence Report for October 1946.
2. Wipper (1977), p. 234.
3. PC, RVP: DC/TN/3/1 *DYM*, no. 76, Minutes of Liaison meeting held in the DC's office, 19 December 1960.
4. For the formation of the KCA see Rosberg and Nottingham (1966), pp. 35–104.
5. The history of this rumour is well documented in Lab. 31/2, *Kikuyu Squatters Returning*, at the PC Nyeri's Office.
6. Public Record Office (PRO), CO 533/395/16126, undated and unsigned, circa January 1930.
7. KNA, Lab 9/1043 no file name, no. 177, PC, RVP to Government House, 24 January 1941.
8. *East African Standard* (*EAS*), 25 February 1944.
9. For a case study of the role of rumour as a significant social force see G. Lefebvre *The Great Fear of 1789, Rural Panic in Revolutionary France*, London (1973). George Rudé in the introduction writes: 'So rumour, panic and fear, for all their irrationality and for all the reflections they cast on the fraility of human behaviour, are presented as a new and significant dimension in the historical process . . . ' As Lefebvre himself puts it, 'What matters in seeking an explanation for the Great Fear is not so much the active truth as what the people thought the aristocracy could and would do, and it was not so much what had happened as what the townsmen and peasants believed to have happened that stirred them into feverish activity'. *ibid.*, p. xiii. For an African example see S. Marks *Reluctant Rebellion: The 1906–1908 Disturbances in Natal*, London (1970).
10. KNA, Lab 5/1, Intelligence Reports 1946–48, no. 118, Squatters Inspectorate Report, August 1945.
11. *ibid.*
12. *ibid.*
13. Interview with Onesmus Gachoka, 10 May 1972.
14. This letter dated 1 November 1945, is the earliest squatter political document I found during the course of my research. See KNA, Lab 9/600, Local Option Orders, Aberdare District Council, no. 40, M.C. Benson on behalf of squatters from Rumuruti and Naivasha Districts to CNC. The last sentence of the petition reads, 'Please ask Government to give us land to leave all our parents and children while working settler farms' expresses the central focus of Kikuyu squatter agitation.
15. See my discussion of KAU in Chapter 4 below.
16. Interview with Kimani Muchohio, 25 May 1972.
17. KCA organization developed informally through a process of experimentation. It was also continually evolving. The description of the structure of the KCA may give a picture of formality and routine which the organization clearly lacked. In any case the description of the structure of the KCA only applies to the period leading up to the mass oathing of 1947 and 1948.
18. Interview with Gitau Gathuri, 16 February 1972.

19. Interview with Onesmus Mwando Kibuku, 16 March 1972.
20. KNA, PC, RVP 6A/1/3/1, Olenguruone, Manager, Besiroko Limited to The Officer in Charge of Maasai Reservation, Ngong, 4 September 1936.
21. The Colonial Office made the acceptance of the RLO of 1937 contingent upon the addition of new land to the reserves, where evicted squatters might be settled. See PRO, C.O. 533/641, no. 38223 12 October 1936. Olenguruone was bought from the Maasai for this purpose. The settlement, consisting of 34,700 acres (1,4054 ha), was directly on the border of the Highlands just above Elburgon and 38 miles from Molo.
22. The precedent for this demand was the Kikuyu settlements established in Lari and Kerita in return for land lost to Europeans.
23. DC, NKU, Adm 15/20/15, Olenguruone Eviction, Note of a Baraza held at Olenguruone on 21 June 1943.
24. *ibid*.
25. DC, NKU, Adm. 15/20/15, Olenguruone Eviction, Draft Notes Olenguruone, A Resumé of Events. This 10 page document was written sometime in 1949.
26. Interview with Harun Kafugoro, 21 March 1972.
27. Even up to this day the Olenguruone Kikuyu settlers maintain a close contact with each other. They have an informal welfare organization through which members keep in touch.
28. Two or three government informers, who were well known to the Olenguruone leaders, did not take the oath. The Police relied on Gichere wa Mbiura for intelligence on the situation in Olenguruone. Gichere wa Mbiura was a close associate of the well-known government Kikuyu expert, Dr Louis Leakey, and acted as an informer back in the days when the settlers were living in Miriri. According to Mbiura, even the local government-employed headman and advisors were oathed. See Lab, Molo: PF 389, District Officer Olenguruone, Director of Intelligence and Security to Officer in Charge of Maasai District, Ngong, 6 January 1945.
29. Interview with Onesmus Mwando Kibuku, 16 March 1972.
30. DC, NKU, Adm. 15/20/15, Olenguruone Eviction, Draft Notes Olenguruone, A Resumé of Events.
31. KNA, DC, NKU/6/2, Olenguruone 1947–50, no. 8, H.O.R., P.J. Browning, 6 May 1945.
32. A police report warned: 'Sums of money are said to have been paid to young men and in Elburgon by people from the settlement. It is suspected that the money was a retaining fee and that these young men may move into the settlement to oppose the forces of Law and Order'. See KNA, DC, NKU/6/2, Olenguruone no. 47, Assistant Superintendent Police, Nakuru District, Intelligence Report, 27 October 1949.
33. Nakuru-Naivasha-Ravine Annual Report, 1946.
34. Spencer (1977), p. 160.
35. The District Commissioner confused the *githati* oath, a traditional Kikuyu oath, with the new oath of unity. See KNA, Lab 3/40, Resident Labour and Squatters no. 24, D.C. Nyeri to Labour Commissioner, 10 June 1946.
36. KNA, Lab 5/1, Intelligence Reports 1946–48, no. 138, Labour Officer, U.G. to Labour Commissioner, June 1946.
37. The drastic consequences of this order were not lost on the relevant officials. Both the Chief Native Commissioner and the Labour Commissioner protested against the enactment of this order.
38. KNA, Lab 9/316, Naivasha County Council no. 71, Labour Commissioner to D.C. Nakuru, 29 March 1946.
39. In 1946 over 1,000 acres of this estate were under cultivation.
40. KNA, Lab 9/601, R.L.O. General Correspondence no. 78C, Labour Commissioner to Registrar of Natives, June 1946.
41. *ibid.*, no. 54, Labour Commissioner to Commissioner for Local Government, 7 June 1946.

42. *ibid.*, no. 78C.
43. *ibid.*
44. *ibid.*
45. *ibid.*
46. KNA, Lab. 5/1, Intelligence Reports 1946–48 no. 57C, Intelligence Report, July 1946.
47. *ibid.*, Intelligence Report, August 1946.
48. *ibid.*
49. KNA, Lab 3/41, Squatters Complaints no. 39A, E Mathu to Labour Commissioner, 20 September 1946.
50. *ibid.*
51. *ibid.*, no. 77A, Police Report on KAU meeting at Naivasha, 17 November 1946.
52. PC, Nyeri, Lab. 31/3/vol 3, Squatters and Squatter Labour no. 50, DC Kiambu to PC, CP, 11 December 1946.
53. They were Samuel Kibunja, Mkono Kiare, Gitau Kamau, Kinanjui wa Gichoru, Mungai Kirihiko, Ng'era wa Ndere, Kagatho Gachuerie and Njororge Nganga.
54. KNA, Lab 3/41, Squatters Complaints no. 79, DC, Kiambu to CNC, 25 November 1946.
55. *ibid.*
56. *ibid.*, no. 97, Director of Intelligence and Security to Member for Law and Order, 12 December 1946.
57. The official minutes of this meeting are available at KNA, 3/41, Squatters Complaints no. 122.
58. *ibid.*
59. *ibid.*
60. KNA, Lab 3/41 Squatters Complaints no. 115. One of the lorries overturned near Limuru, killing one ex-squatter and injuring 14 others. Many squatters felt that far from being an accident, this was a deliberate act.
61. *ibid.*, Report of Assistant Inspector, Tigoni police station, February 1947.
62. *ibid.*
63. KNA, MAA 8/124, The Central Co-ordinating Committee for Resident Labour no. 2 Informer's report of meeting of resident labourers in Limura, 13 March 1947. Some of the squatters decided to sign the new resident labour contracts, others indicated their intention to work on a monthly ticket contract.
64. DC, NKU, Adm./15/20/15, Olenguruone Eviction no. 71.
65. KNA, Lab 3/41, Squatters Complaints, no. 258 contains copy of petition.
66. Interview with Boro Gicheru.
67. The *Dini ya Jesu Kristo* was one of the many small messianic sects that existed on the farms in the Highlands. After a dream in which God ordered Reuben Kihiko 'to deliver my people from bondage' he decided to build a church on a European farm in the Londiani area of Nakuru District. When he was told to obtain permission to get wood for his church from the European farmer: 'He replied that trees belong to God so does the earth'. He established two churches on two farms by early 1946. One man recalled: 'This was when it was proclaimed that squatters must sign contracts. He asked some people to contribute some money quickly and refuse to sign the contract for time was nigh'. In December 1946 Reuben was imprisoned for building a church on a farm without permission. When he was released from prison, he ordered his followers to throw away their European clothes and replace them with goat-skins to prepare for their journey home. In November 1947, he returned to Kiambu with a small band of evicted squatters. KNA, MA, A 8/106, Internal Security. Mumenyereri, no. 37 contains an article on this sect published in the Kikuyu newspaper, *Mumenyereri*.
68. PC, Nyeri, Adm. 18/1/1/10, Monthly Intelligence Report, Nairobi District, September 1947.
69. Furedi (1973).

70. Throup (1983), pp. 234–50.
71. PC, Nyeri, Adm. 18/1/1/10, Monthly Intelligence Reports, September–December 1947.
72. Interview with Thuo Kigera, 19 February 1972.
73. KNA, DC, NKU 2/385, Labour Department – Monthly Reports, Annual Report for year 1950 – Labour Department, Thomson's Falls.
74. KNA, DC, NKU 2/388, Labour Inspectors' Report 1946–48, no. 37, Senior Resident Labour Inspector's Report, November 1947.
75. KNA, Lab 5/1, Intelligence Reports 1945–48, no. 5i, Resident Labour Inspector's Report for June 1945.
76. See Furedi (1974a).
77. Kanogo (1977), pp. 247–48.
78. *ibid.*, p. 248.
79. *ibid.*
80. *ibid.*, p. 247.
81. PC, RVP: DC, NKU 5/1. Correspondence re Kikuyu, Screening, see reports for June 1951.
82. KNA, DC, UG 4/1, Monthly Labour Reports, Reports for November 1949.
83. KNA, DC, NKU 2/385, Labour Department – Monthly Reports, Intelligence Report for February 1951, 7 March 1951.
84. NLO, Misc. I. vol. 2, Misc. Correspondence re Kikuyu: Rehabilitation Centre, Bahati, Statements, 30 April 1955.
85. KNA, DC, NKU 5/2, Labour no. 9, P.E.D. Wilson, Labour Officer, RVP to Labour Commissioner, 23 March 1948.
86. KNA, DC, NKU 2/385, Labour Department – Monthly Reports, no. 8, Report for January 1951.
87. Interview with Gitau Gathuri, 30 March 1972.
88. Interview with Harun Kafu Goro, 21 March 1972.
89. Interview with Frances Mucherere, 6 March 1977.
90. Interview with Kinonjui Mutegi.
91. Interview with Michael Waweru.
92. NLO. See farm files for the period.
93. United Kingdom, 1960 Cmd. 1030, *Historical Survey of the Origins and Growth of Mau Mau.*
94. KNA, Lab 9/317, Nakuru District Council, no. 78, Letter from Ol Joro Orok to Hyde-Clark, 26 September 1946.
95. Laikipia District Annual Report, 1953, p. 2 (emphasis added).
96. *EAS*, 21 July 1953.
97. Rosberg and Nottingham (1966), p. 352.
98. This correspondence is located in the District Commissioner Nakuru's office. I am indebted to Moti Tamarkin for drawing my attention to it.
99. See Kanogo (1987) p. 131. The conflict of view between Kanogo and myself on the social composition of Mau Mau is profound. Since Kanogo's contribution is an impressive one based on serious research it is worth speculating how this conflict in evidence has come about. The documentary evidence for the period 1945–52 shows conclusively the central role of the skilled and of the mobile squatters and ex-squatters in the movement of resistance. It is possible that the pattern may have become modified after the expulsion of squatters in the early years of the Emergency. Possibly, after the expulsion, a significant proportion of those ex-squatters who went into the forest were those with the least means of economic support in the Reserves. It is possible that this group may have provided Kanogo with the evidence that the poorest section of the squatter community were the most active in Mau Mau.

Four

The Split: The Emergence of Mau Mau

In the White Highlands, the squatter campaign against the new district council rules had exhausted itself by February 1947. Pockets of squatter resistance persisted but generally most Kikuyu resident labourers were reluctant to pay the price of eviction for their defiance. The Nakuru Labour Officer reported in February: 'I formed the opinion that the back of the "Squatter Resistance" movement has been broken and there were indications of a more general willingness to attest – not by any means a wholesale willingness to attest . . .'[1] Squatters who tried to resist the district council rules were immediately evicted and the leaders sometimes imprisoned.[2] Many of the evicted squatters who returned signed on as monthly labourers. Employers were also sometimes reluctant to hire more squatter labour in case they might provoke future unrest.[3]

The defeat of the squatter campaign forced many activists to rethink their strategy. There was a growing recognition that new tactics were required and that future action required greater organization than was the case in the 1946 protest campaign. The younger generation of militants had become hostile not only to the colonial regime but also to the Kikuyu establishment. Even the nationalist leaders of the KAU were treated with suspicion. By late 1947 the nationalist movement, incorporating the KAU and the KCA, had undergone a major process of differentiation. On one side was the moderate older generation devoted to the strategy of constitutional reform. Against them was a younger generation of activists with strong constituencies in Nairobi, the Rift Valley and parts of Nyeri and Fort Hall. What divided these two wings of the nationalist movement was not so much political objectives as the *means* to be used to realize them.

By late 1947 the tension between the two wings could barely be contained within the existing movement. The determination of activists in Nairobi and the Rift Valley to extend oathing on a mass scale to escalate resistance finally brought matters to a head. The divergence between the two wings led to a *de facto* split. It is at this stage that the movement known as Mau Mau emerges as a distinct force. No longer constrained by moderate elements the radical wing was free to experiment and develop new tactics for its struggle.

The growth of militant nationalism

Despite the defeat of the squatter movement the situation did not return to the *status quo ante*. Settlers continued to feel uneasy about the general hostility Africans manifested towards Europeans throughout 1947. One Intelligence Report observed that 'various reports have been received of labour going "sour" on their employer for no apparent reason and it is difficult to believe that some political motive is not behind these sudden and unaccountable changes of attitude'.[4]

In September 1947 the arrest of Kikuyu settlers from Olenguruone provided a focus for squatter agitation.[5] Activists from Olenguruone toured Nakuru District seeking support for their cause. Prominent Kikuyu politicians, including Jomo Kenyatta, converged on Nakuru District to provide support and extend the influence of KAU. A mass rally organized by the KCA in Njoro township on 21 September expressed well the mood of the squatters. Since the KCA was an illegal organization the meeting was advertised as a KAU 'tea party'. Many of the 1,000-strong audience had already taken the KCA oath. Kenyatta, who was the main speaker, used the occasion to link local grievances to the broader goals of African nationalism. Many in the audience readily responded to the parable he told:

> A European, his houseboy and his dog went on *safari*. At one point during the journey they stopped to rest. Two of them ate something – the European and his dog. When Kenyatta asked if a dog is better than an African, the people became very angry.[6]

The assembly was also addressed by Samuel Koina, the leader of the Olenguruone Kikuyu. He emphasized that if the Kikuyu were removed from Olenguruone, then the government would have to find them land in the Kiambu Reserve.[7]

During the meeting a debate erupted concerning the *kipande*, the registration certificate that all African adult males had to carry with them at all times. Many of those in attendance decided to burn this *kipande* in protest against the system of pass laws.[8] Others, more moderate in their outlook, including Kenyatta, counselled against taking such drastic action.[9]

The Njoro meeting was a prelude to a new outburst of squatter protest during which the KCA initiated a large-scale oathing campaign. This campaign was a response to the growing consciousness that a greater measure of solidarity was essential for the future of the squatter community. The failure of the evicted squatters to obtain even the most minimal concessions, and the repression of the Olenguruone settlers, highlighted the weak position of Africans living in the Highlands. Many squatter activists drew the conclusion that protest had to be more radical and extensive if it were to be effective. The oathing campaign was designed to cement the Kikuyu community behind as yet undefined radical action. According to most squatter activists interviewed, this oathing campaign was the starting point of the so-called Mau Mau revolt. This view is also corroborated by intelligence sources.[10]

Intelligence sources believed that the oathing campaign was concentrated around Naivasha. Thus a memorandum of the Director of Intelligence and Security states that Mau Mau 'started its activities towards the end of 1947 and in 1948, several "oath" ceremonies are known to have taken place in the Naivasha district'.[11] This observation was based on the fact that the first oathing ceremony to be discovered was in the area. In fact squatters in the Elburgon, Molo and Njoro areas of Nakuru District had already been oathed during the latter part of 1947.

The oathing campaign coincided with the first serious political differentiation among the Rift Valley Kikuyu since the shift towards mass oathing and increased radicalism was not supported by all the KCA leaders. The older and more conservative section of the KCA felt that KAU should become the main vehicle of protest. During his visit to the Highlands Kenyatta advised leading KCA members that they should join KAU and curb the enthusiasm of the younger militants. A number of KCA activists followed this advice and by 1949 assumed control over the KAU branches in the area. This new local KAU leadership rejected the policy of direct action advocated by the younger militants. The former KCA activist and chairman of the newly formed KAU branch in Molo, Thuo Kigera observed: 'We the KAU officials believed that change should come about constitutionally and did not believe in violence'.[12]

Many leading KCA activists had achieved a measure of success in business or in trade and felt that they had too much to risk if they got involved with the new campaign.[13] Some of them felt that mass recruitment contradicted the original aims of the KCA. When they joined the KCA it was a selective secret association, recruiting only the 'leaders'.[14] They saw themselves as the representatives of the Kikuyu community and the idea of a mass movement was foreign to their inclinations.

The attitude of the conservatives in the KCA towards the growing radical underground movement contained a mixture of fear and hostility. Their main preoccupation was the fear that militant protest would get out of control. However pleas for restraint went unheeded on the farms. Repression and the continued deterioration of economic life meant that radical solutions found a strong resonance among squatters.

By the end of 1948 the militant wing of the KCA had become a distinct and influential force with a substantial body of support in the squatter community. The Chief Native Commissioner reported in 1948 that in the Rift Valley 'there is definitely evidence of a go slow policy among young labourers though the older generation remains unaffected'.[15] The younger generation of squatters had become impatient and sought to raise the stakes. Although a number of activists were urging more action, the movement's political objectives were diffuse and undefined. At this stage the emphasis was on attaining unity and on defending the existing way of life against settler encroachment. The Ngata affair in March 1948 and the boycott of Indian shops late in September illustrate the activities of the Mau Mau movement in Nakuru District.

On 13 March 1948, senior government officials received a despatch from Resident Labour Inspector Davidson which reported that an illegal squatter association had been discovered on Ngata farm. It noted:

> There was an illegal Squatter Association to which people were being asked to subscribe the sum of Shs 100/- to collect funds to promote strikes and other trouble. Three of the squatters refused to attend this Association and were beaten up by the other squatters.[16]

Upon further investigation it was discovered that this association extended 'further than Ngata farm and is known to have branches in that area'.[17] Although the government did not know it at the time, this was the first Mau Mau activity that it had stumbled on. More than three years later, in October 1951, this was realized by Inspector Davidson himself.[18] What the government also did not know was that by this time the 'illegal squatter association' was active throughout Nakuru District.

The government response to this discovery was to cancel the contracts of 12 squatters and their families and evict them from the Highlands. Their huts and gardens were bulldozed over. Eliud Kiberenge, a leading activist from Njoro who was in charge of the oathing ceremony at Ngata, was arrested and sent to prison for three months for complicity in the assault on the three squatters.[19] Later he recalled: 'On Ngata farm we made the mistake of oathing people who could not keep a secret. They were men who were too close with the Europeans.'[20]

The oathing campaign was in full swing by mid-1948. To achieve unity the activists were not inhibited from using violence. But at this time the need to use force to coerce Kikuyu squatters to take the oath was minimal.[21] The general discontent among squatters provided a fertile terrain for the oathing campaign. The consolidation of squatter support behind the activists is clearly brought out in the boycott of Asian traders.

The boycott of Indian shopkeepers in Nakuru District demonstrates the willingness of the radical wing of the KCA to take action on particular issues to defend the interests of the squatters.[22] This boycott was supported by most shades of African opinion but its organization was led by the militant wing of the KCA.

Asian traders played a central role in the commercial activities of Nakuru District. The family-run Asian *duka* was in evidence in all the trading centres and on many farms. Asians had a double role vis-à-vis the African squatters: they sold them most of the products which squatters brought and they often also bought the surplus agricultural produce of resident labourers. As middlemen, the Asian traders were natural objects of hostility for the squatters. In particular, African traders felt thwarted by the monopoly that Asians had over wholesale and retail commerce.

The small group of African traders tried to compensate for their economic weakness by exerting their political muscle. The general unrest among squatters provided a ready audience for their agitation. In 1948 the growing squatter movement turned against Asian traders. Earlier in the year, the government had decontrolled the price of potatoes. Hitherto, the potato crop of squatters had been sold at a fixed price of 12 shillings a bag, but when squatters in Elburgon and Molo brought their crop to market they were infuriated to find that Asian traders were now only offering 4 shillings a bag.[23] The squatter activists responded by initiating a boycott of all Asian shopkeepers.

The boycott, which began in Molo and Elburgon, soon spread to other parts of the White Highlands and leaders of the KCA/Mau Mau from Elburgon travelled around the settled areas to spread the boycott. The existing KCA farm committees provided the organizational bases for the campaign. Squatter participation in the boycott was widespread and farm committees often took the initiative themselves. Thus for example on one farm in Nakuru the squatters demanded that their employer transfer her custom from the local Asian trader.[24]

In most parts of the White Highlands the boycott lasted until December – in Elburgon and Molo it continued well into 1949. The monopoly of Asians over trade meant that any boycott against them could only be of a limited duration, but it nevertheless demonstrated a capacity for unified action. This united front remained solid despite appeals from the KAU national leadership to abandon it.[25] The strength of popular feeling and organization came as a surprise to local officials. The District Commissioner of Nakuru observed: 'There is reason for believing that this was a trial of strength and had it been more successful throughout the District as a whole it might have had more serious developments'.[26]

The Ngata affair and the boycott of Asian traders were seen as a warning of things to come by the colonial government which stepped up administrative control and police activity to curb the squatter movement. Strike leaders on the farms and those suspected of KCA affiliations were dismissed on the spot and sent back to the reserves.[27] The extensive use of repression forced the activists to operate underground. Thus during 1949 there was little overt manifestation of squatter unrest. Occasionally squatters went on strikes or go-slows, or refused to hand over their maize to the government-appointed buyer or sign their contracts.[28]

Beneath the surface the squatter movement was gathering force. Government officials were aware that something was happening but could not pinpoint the problem. Thus, after touring a number of estates in October 1948, the Senior Labour Officer noted: 'There is something very evil going on in this area.'[29] Considerable resources were devoted to intelligence gathering and for organizing a network of informers and the administration had fairly accurate information of the dimensions of underground activity. But police officers and labour inspectors saw these activities as merely the continuation of the past and failed to assess their significance. Even some of the more astute Special Branch officers such as Ian Henderson looked upon the underground activity as more of the same. In September 1949 a number of African informants reported the growing scale of squatter activity: according to their estimates 80 per cent of the Kikuyu squatters were 'either members of the KCA or ready followers and supporters'.[30] Yet neither the informants nor the Special Branch commented on the fact that such widespread oathing was a deviation from past KCA practices.

The inability of the administration to evaluate the political situation is surprising. Although there were no squatter-related outbursts, the appearance of religious sects and the sharp deterioration of labour relations should have provided sufficient warning. For example the Senior Labour Officer of the Rift Valley reported in August 1949:

I would like to put on record that in the space of 8 months since I have been in Nakuru, the Labour situation, both farm and domestic, appears to have deteriorated considerably. The African employee seems to be getting more lazy everyday, more and more insolent to his employer.[31]

The District Commissioner of Nakuru had a more realistic appraisal of the existing malaise on the farms:

Despite the absence of overt incidents, a consciousness of political disaffection was always present and there can be little doubt that were there necessary stimulus forthcoming, the vaguely discontented masses of Kikuyu might erupt without notice into open antagonism.[32]

One reason why the Administration failed to heed the warning signals was its preoccupation with religious sects. Indeed Mau Mau was seen by Government officials as another 'politico-religious sect'.[33] This outlook was reinforced by the growth of the *Dini ya Msambwe* sect in the

European settled district of Trans Nzoia. In 1949, members of this sect carried out a campaign of arson against European property when Bugishu squatters burned down government offices and settler-owned buildings.[34] The unpredictable and apparently irrational force of religion rather than the more mundane squatter movement preoccupied the police.

The network of police agents and informers provided the administration with a fairly accurate portrayal of events. However, since European officials were not inclined to view the 'backward' squatters as capable of rational action the intelligence was often misinterpreted. Thus as late as 30 June 1951, a record of a meeting of district commissioners and police officials at the office of the Provincial Commissioner in Nakuru Town discussed the '*Dinis*' in the forest. Mau Mau was perceived as simply a more powerful *Dini* than the rest.[35]

In fact, although forced to operate in secret Mau Mau had emerged as a radical force combining some of the characteristics of militant nationalism and an underground peasant movement. It was motivated by specific local grievances and at the same time led by a group of activists who were becoming increasingly national.

The emergence of Mau Mau

The transformation of a loose network of militant activists into the movement known as Mau Mau came through a process of experimentation and adaptation to the external environment. The breakdown of the uneasy alliance with the moderate wing of the KCA was a result of frustration with its lack of effectiveness. Since it appeared that the colonial government was in no mood to compromise, the militant option seemed the only way forward to the younger generations. The split with the moderate elements was consolidated through the establishment of separate committees of militant activists, an initiative that came from Nairobi. Their spread to the White Highlands in early 1950 indicated the close links forged with activists in Nairobi. Until that time the squatter movement had operated through area branches loosely linked together through the KCA. Now the formation of separate committees provided the organizational foundation for more militant forms of action.

The new separate young men's committees reflected the grassroots pressure for action. The function and aims of these committees were not clearly worked out and they evolved in response to events. Unlike the old KCA, the committees had a limited paramilitary dimension, such as providing guards for oathing ceremonies. From the outset the activists demonstrated a determination to use force, if necessary, to achieve their aims. The Forty Group in Nairobi – an organization that sought to adapt the role of the warrior to the demands of political

resistance – provided a rough model for the committees. The committees had a direct if informal link with Nairobi. In Kariobangi, one
of the strongholds of the Forty Group, resided many ex-squatters from
the Highlands.[36] These ex-squatters, who had friends and relations on
the European farms, served as ideal go-betweens.

Like the Forty Group, the young squatters' committees were prepared
to resort to the use of force. Thus in 1950, for the first time, squatter
resistance went beyond civil disobedience to begin deploying force and
sabotage against Europeans and Asians in the Highlands. This campaign
of direct action was prepared for through the mass introduction of the
oath of unity. As Eliud Kiberenge pointed out: 'Before the end of 1949
very few people took the goat's meat oath, only the ones who were
intelligent and trustworthy. We started giving this oath to a large number
of people since we needed greater unity for more struggle'.[37] The decision taken in late 1948 and implemented in March 1949 to expel all the
Kikuyu settlers from Olenguruone was closely linked to the new oathing
campaign. The eviction operation had an unsettling effect on squatters in
Nakuru. Money and supplies were collected for the Olenguruone settlers
throughout the district. And the rise of popular sentiment led the
administration to take special precautions to avoid a squatter invasion of
Olenguruone.

The reorganization of the squatter movement and the adoption of
more far-reaching methods of protest provided the basis for the escalation
of activities. By the end of 1950, the hitherto little known 'anti-European
movement', Mau Mau, had become a frequent topic of conversation
among European settlers.[38] During the year attacks on European-owned
property became frequent. Road blocks and stones were placed on isolated roads at night. In October, telephone wires were cut down in
Marashoni Forest near Elburgon. Several European farmers had their
machines and equipment sabotaged. On Selle Farm near Njoro, for
example, over £500-worth of damage was done to farm machinery.[39]
But these relatively minor attacks on European property were over-
shadowed by the manifest strength of the movement on the farms. Intelligence reports observed that Mau Mau was very strong in Ol Kalou,
Naivasha and the Elburgon–Njoro areas.[40]

The scale of the oathing campaign made the detection of Mau Mau
unavoidable. On 12 May 1950, 39 Africans were arrested in connection
with an oathing ceremony in Naivasha. A government official commented: 'It is apparent that considerable agitation by KCA members is
being carried out in the vicinity . . . One old man was beaten up by 11
Kikuyu (including one woman) because he refused to take their oath'.[41]
The same month the Labour Officer for Nakuru discovered five cases of
assault on reluctant oath-takers on five different farms.[42] In September, a
police informer disappeared from a farm in the Elburgon area.[43]

The Split: The Emergence of Mau Mau

The discovery of the mass oathing campaign in April–May 1950 came as a major shock to government officials and settlers. For the first time there was an awareness that the so-called Mau Mau represented a threat that went way beyond that posed by the KCA. Since the discovery of mass oathing was followed by strikes in sympathy with strikes in Nairobi, officials were forced to review their attitude towards the squatter movement.[44] Mau Mau, which local officials still regarded as a squatter version of the KCA, was now perceived as a special threat to security. A high-level government conference in Nakuru Town on 27 November 1950, attended by the Provincial Commissioner of the Rift Valley, the Attorney-General, the Chief Native Commissioner, senior police and labour officers and representatives of the European settler community, indicated that the administration was ready to take far-reaching measures. The Senior Labour Officer of Rift Valley Province asked for the introduction of communal fines, floggings, power to summarily evict suspects from the settled areas and the introduction of a vigorous propaganda campaign. Most of the officials present agreed with these demands and plans for a new system of pass rules in Nakuru District were also discussed.[45] Anti Mau-Mau meetings organized by the Labour Department in the early part of the year were substantially stepped up during the year.[46]

The fear of discovery and repression led to a change of emphasis by the Mau Mau activists. Attacks on European property ceased and instead Mau Mau concentrated on the consolidation of its position among the squatters. This emphasis paid off in the growth of grassroots support. The rise in the cost of living, particularly food prices, hit squatters harder than ever before and gave impetus to the growth of the squatter movement. The unrest on the farms is illustrated by the sudden rise in requests from European settlers for assistance from the Labour Department to sort out problems with squatters.[47]

By this time the movement had acquired a momentum of its own, and committees were established throughout the White Highlands. In 1951, police officials noted that Mau Mau had spread from Nakuru to Uasin Gishu and Trans Nzoia districts.[48] The extension of the movement coincided with the establishment of a paramilitary section. This wing of the movement was established sometime in late 1951. It consisted of a select group of militant young squatters whose main task was to enforce the security of the movement. The *Kiama Kia Bara* (the fighting group), as this body was called, provided guards for oathing ceremonies, messengers and other personnel for the movement. They also accompanied oath administrators to deal with uncooperative squatters.[49] A number of these warriors had had military experience during the Second World War.

During this period the *Kiama Kia Bara* was under the supervision of the area committees. The area branch co-ordinated the collections of funds and the administration of oaths. In late 1951, preparations for emergency situations were undertaken and food and medical supplies were obtained, mostly from contacts in Nairobi by way of traders travelling between Nairobi and the Highlands.[50]

Towards armed resistance

Unrelenting pressure from European settlers and the inflexibility of the government created the basis for a spiral of violence. In 1952 district councils were again busy drawing up new rules for squatters, limiting the size of their plots and in some areas eliminating the right to own stock altogether. The implementation of the harsh new rules coincided with the intensification of conflict in Nairobi and the Kikuyu Reserves. In all these areas repression became extensive.

The rise of political violence and the militarization of the squatter movement cannot be understood outside the context of the European response to it. During the summer of 1950, European settlers consolidated their position and assumed complete control over squatter affairs.[51] Most squatter activists saw this move as the first step towards a new offensive against Africans living on the farms. Indeed from this time onwards, repression increased in scale. During this period eviction of troublemakers for Mau Mau offences became prevalent. The crackdown had a double motive. For the settlers it was at once a deterrent and a way of changing their economic relations with the squatters.

This crackdown on squatter activists, which paralleled the state attacks on militants in Nairobi, was orchestrated through newly established district intelligence teams. By December 1950, district intelligence teams were established throughout the White Highlands. The team in Uasin Gishu consisted of the District Commissioner, the Assistant Superintendent of Police, the local labour officer, 'responsible farmers' and European representatives from each of the wards of the district council.[52]

Through the close collaboration of local officials, the police and European settlers an increasingly harsh climate of law and order was imposed on squatters. Security and economic motives converged in the drive to destroy the influence of the troublemakers. Many of the repressive measures that were formally enacted under the declaration of a State of Emergency in October 1952 had already been given serious consideration by the joint settler-administration committees.[53]

State and settler repression forced the Mau Mau movement in new directions. In the spring of 1952 it entered into its phase of armed resistance. This step, which was far from systematically worked out, was symbolized by the introduction of the *batuni* oath. The *batuni* or platoon oath was administered to young squatters of warrior age in Nakuru District and committed the oath-taker to fight the enemies of Mau Mau.

It was seen as a first step to participation in a future revolt.

It is almost certain that the *batuni* originated in the Thomson's Falls – Ol Joro Orok areas of Laikipia district,[54] from where it moved towards Nakuru and Naivasha districts. The geographic origin of the *batuni* oath is very significant since the Thomson's Falls – Ol Joro Orok area had very close contacts with militants in Nairobi. Two famous Mau Mau leaders, Dedan Kimathi and Stanley Mathenge, were both well known in the Thomson's Falls area and Mathenge had close connections with the Forty Group. Consequently the links between the Nairobi militants and the Rift Valley squatters, reinforced by the *batuni* oath, were of key importance for the preparation of armed action.

The *batuni* oath was at first given to a select group of trusted militants. Those oathed were taught the mechanics of the ritual and they in turn began administering oaths in other areas. Francis Mucherere, who was in charge of administering the oath in the Elburgon area, was elected from a committee of seven Kikuyu who were responsible for organizing the ceremonies.[55] The members of this committee had previously undergone training in administering the oath and in elementary fieldcraft in the forests of the Aberdare Range near Thomson's Falls. According to accounts the officers who trained them came from Nyeri.[56]

The aim of the *batuni* oath was to prepare the younger squatters for physical resistance, and it also served to strengthen organizational links between different regions and for the first time imposed a broader orientation on the squatter movement. While the movement's aims remained diffuse, the growing importance of the Nairobi leadership meant that the squatter movement would have an important anti-colonial dimension. The squatter movement always retained its organizational independence but it was now a detachment of a wider movement.

The relationship between the warrior's committees and the area branches was partially modified with the introduction of the *batuni* oath. The Kikuyu squatters were divided into sections or platoons and it appears that the prestige attached to these platoons gave them a degree of independence. In Elburgon, the area branch under the leadership of Kinanjui Mutegi collected money, food and arms for the future confrontation.[57]

The growth of the new military wing created considerable tensions within the Kikuyu community. African businessmen and other professionals for whom the way forward was through KAU and constitutional change looked with disquiet at the rising tide of militancy. One KAU official recalled: 'Mau Mau was started by the ordinary people and when we the leaders of KAU found out about it we were very surprised. I didn't like people being forced to join an organization that they didn't want to join'.[58] But the pressure on the better-off Kikuyu in the townships to join the movement was hard to resist. Businessmen who refused to join were boycotted and sometimes physically assaulted. One activist noted: 'many businessmen in the towns did not want to join us. We told them that you are like Europeans, you are oppressing us by not joining, so you must join. They moved with the Indians too much and that is why they did not want to join'.[59]

A test of strength between Mau Mau and the moderate KAU officials never materialized. Popular pressure forced most of the KAU branches to yield and in Nakuru, Naivasha and Laikipia they came to adopt a more radical posture. Indeed towards the beginning of 1952 many local branches were taken over by squatter activists who used KAU as a convenient cover for their activity. This proved quite useful for organizing a series of political meetings throughout the Highlands in June 1952. In June, leading KAU personalities led by Jomo Kenyatta made an extensive tour of the Highlands. Huge crowds of squatters attended meetings in Nakuru, Njoro, Elburgon, Gilgil, Thomson's Falls and Ol Joro Orok. The Commissioner of Police reported: 'the leaders of KAU have just returned from the most extensive crowded and successful tour that has ever been carried out in the Rift Valley Province.'[60] Kenyatta told the crowds just what they wanted to hear and his militant speeches were received with great enthusiasm. He raised his audience's expectations when he told a meeting in Naivasha that he could become the Prime Minister of Kenya, as Kwame Nkrumah had done in the Gold Coast.[61]

Kenyatta's rhetoric had the effect of strengthening the local KAU branches. During the period leading up to the Emergency the KAU branches in the Rift Valley became among the most active in the colony.[62] But Kenyatta could control neither these KAU branches nor the squatters' movement. Indeed everyone took Kenyatta's words about becoming prime minister as a call to action. Thus the tour was followed by a wave of Mau Mau activity that was distinctly unconstitutional in character. One activist recalled: 'We started talking about moving into the forest after Kenyatta's big tour of the Rift Valley. He was talking about how we would get freedom. We held many secret meetings. In these meetings we decided to fight the colonialists'.[63] Many government officials blamed this tour for the subsequent outburst of violence. The police reported a number of incidents right after Kenyatta's departure.[64] In Nakuru the Resident Labour Inspector observed that 'the area seems unsettled and I have great difficulty in getting resident labourers to sign on.'[65] The District Commissioner of Nakuru complained that after Kenyatta's rally 'all information regarding Mau Mau ceased to flow'.[66] The tour was important in demonstrating the unity of purpose of the squatter community, but it did no more than bring to the surface the underlying bitterness.

The elimination of Kikuyu who were collaborating with the government was the first priority of the Mau Mau movement. On 30 June 1952 an attempt was made on the life of a Crown witness in a Mau Mau case in Laikipia district.[67] A similar pattern of events was discernible in Naivasha and Nakuru. By the end of July a number of police witnesses had disappeared from the farms.[68] Law and order had broken down in Laikipia. A Kisi farm headman was assassinated and Mbugwa Karioki, a Kikuyu Crown witness, was found dead. Another witness returned home to find his hut burned to the ground, and it was discovered that at a Mau Mau meeting 'police witnesses were suspended from the roof by squatters semi-hanged'.[69] The point of no return had been reached; army troops moved into Laikipia 'to carry out routine manoeuvres'.[70]

The state counter-offensive

The growth of Mau Mau in the White Highlands was not only the product of squatter grievances. It was also shaped and provoked by the policies pursued by the administration. Initially the administration sought to temper its policy of repression through the promotion of a campaign to win the hearts of the squatters. To counter the influence of Mau Mau new African Advisory Councils were started at Elburgon, Njoro, Molo and Ol Kalou. In 1951 a Community Development Officer was appointed in Nakuru District to improve relations between the Government and Africans. The instructions issued to him reveal a degree of administrative naivety:

Broadly your duties will be:-
a) to secure the co-operation of the African people of the District with Government and other official bodies.
b) to assist in preparing a balanced public opinion, and
c) to help in the formation of a public conscience.[71]

'To influence public opinion', the Community Development Officer reorganized the boy scouts, set up football teams, citizens' advice bureaus and women's organizations.[72]

These token measures were greeted with scorn. The mobile unit established to disseminate propaganda throughout the district proved entirely ineffective. The Community Development Officer described a typical meeting, complaining that:

The crowd was composed almost entirely of people who would agree with anything said and very few were prepared to voice opinions. (It was in this area that a rumour had been spread, on a previous visit of the Information Unit, that machine guns hidden by Europeans in surrounding trees were trained at the audience).[73]

These propaganda exercises proved fruitless from the government's point of view. Inevitably the only option available was more repression.

From early 1952 onwards the European settlers had begun to agitate for firm action. In April, the Ol Kalou District Association expressed concern at the 'apparent growth of the prescribed Mau Mau Society and at the large scale desertions from labour forces'.[74] Its members demanded increased protection and stronger punishment for Mau Mau offenders. In May, the Kenya Police embarked on a major campaign against Mau Mau in the Rift Valley. In the Subukia area of Nakuru District, 150 Kikuyu squatters were detained and ten Kikuyu were arrested in Thomson's Falls.[75] The objective of this exercise was to isolate the militants from the rest of the population. Squatters were told that those who were 'forced to take a Mau Mau oath' could clear themselves 'by reporting to the Police or the D.C. within five days of having taken the oath'.[76] These appeals met with little success.

The serious view that the government took of the security situation is illustrated by the enactment of new powers which gave the district commissioners of Kiambu, Fort Hall, Meru, Nyeri, Nanyuki, Nakuru, Naivasha and Laikipia 'the equivalent of Supreme Court powers of punishment for certain offences which are commonly committed by adherents of the Mau Mau Society'.[77] These powers could not stem the tide and after June 1952 officials began to fear a total breakdown in law and order in the settled area. Police attention was particularly directed towards Laikipia. In August a curfew was imposed on Ol Joro Orok, Marmanet and Narok wards of Laikipia. Nakuru and Naivasha were declared Special Districts and enhanced powers were given to local officials.

During September, the police attempted to restore order through initiating a mass campaign of arrests. In the first week of September, 547 Kikuyu were placed under preventive detention. This wave of arrests resulted in a large flow of Kikuyu from the Lower Rift to the upper Rift Valley'.[78] Prominent Kikuyu chiefs from the Reserves toured Laikipia district, condemning the Mau Mau and administering cleansing oaths. Army detachments were moved in to Laikipia to back up the police.

Police operations only served to exacerbate tension and strengthen support for Mau Mau. In early October the maiming of European-owned cattle served to heighten tension still further.[79] The campaign of terror and sabotage coincided with similar operations in the Kikuyu Reserves and in Nairobi. This phase of armed activity saw the assassination of such prominent collaborators as Nairobi councillor Tom Mbotela and Senior Chief Waruhiu. The assassination of Waruhiu represented an important blow against the colonial regime. For the government it provided the pretext for a new offensive – on 20 October a state of emergency was declared.

The strategy pursued by the government during the years 1950–52 sought to contain unrest with a minimal amount of change. The central administration correctly saw that there was little room for reform and therefore refused to develop a strategy that could have extended its base of support among the Kikuyu. It relied on the old tactic of co-opting individuals and isolating troublemakers.

The Government tended to underestimate the strength of feeling among the squatters, but this was not because of lack of information. The colonial intelligence apparatus was quite able to provide the administration with the relevant facts, but these were poorly assessed. There were a number of reasons for this. First, civil servants had a predilection for seeing danger signs from conventional nationalist quarters. Thus they paid close attention to KAU. Once they realized that KAU could be easily domesticated the government became complacent.

The emerging squatter movement was not perceived as a political problem. It was rather portrayed as a labour issue that would eventually sort itself out. Even when police intelligence began to report widespread underground activity on the farms the administration refused to see it as a political problem. From the administration's point of view squatters were primitive, traditionalist and uneducated, not the stuff from which nationalist movements are made. When the administration turned its attention to the squatters, it remained under the assumption that it was dealing with irrational traditionalists or a religious sect. Thus at a meeting held at the headquarters of the Provincial Commissioners of the Rift Valley on 30 June 1951, the Provincial Commissioner stated that 'he wanted to investigate the secret societies and various "Dinis" which seemed to flourish amongst the Kikuyu both in the forest and on the farms'.[80] This focus on the wrong target meant that government officials tended to underestimate the strength of the forces they would face in the post-Emergency revolt.

The policy of repression, which first acquired a recognizable shape in late 1950, became less and less selective with the passing of time. As a result preventive detention and evictions served only to strengthen support for Mau Mau. With repression being the other side of the coin of economic impoverishment more and more squatters joined the camp of the militants. Nevertheless the government was a step ahead of its opponents. No one expected the scale of the crack down in the post-Emergency years. The government evolved a relatively thoroughgoing and sophisticated counter-insurgency programme. Its objective was to isolate the militants and to neutralize their grassroots base. The Declaration of Emergency was a step towards destroying the leadership of the movement. In the short run it provoked support for Mau Mau, but with the introduction of internment and communal punishment it ensured that the activists would be cut off from their supporters and that eventually they would become isolated.

In declaring a State of Emergency the administration raised the stakes and seized the initiative. It closed all avenues of protest other than that of armed rebellion. In a sense it had always been so; the existence of a powerful stratum of European settlers meant that there was no scope for constitutional reform. The Emergency sought to deal with Mau Mau before the institutions of the colonial regime were really placed under threat. Thus the revolt was as much the product of the government's strategy as of the determination of Mau Mau activists to fight for their future.

Revolt and repression

The Declaration of Emergency on 20 October 1952 was followed by 'Operation Jock Scott'. This military operation resulted in large-scale arrests of prominent Kikuyu throughout Kenya. In the White Highlands many KAU officials were detained, but most of the Mau Mau activists managed to evade the net of the authorities. The wave of arrests and the declaration of war on Mau Mau directly sparked off armed resistance. Before 20 October many young militants already had in mind the prospect of armed action, but this was seen as something for the indefinite future. The fear and confusion precipitated by the Emergency was an important factor in pushing the movement towards armed revolt. Thus whereas before the Emergency Nakuru District 'was virtually immune from serious incident', after October 1952 armed confrontations began to escalate.[81]

In many ways the move of Mau Mau towards guerrilla-type action in the forests can be seen as a direct response to the State of Emergency. A number of Kikuyu found themselves to be outlaws on the morning of 20 October. One such man was Dedan Kimathi, an official of the Thomson's Fall's branch of KAU and later to be one of the leaders of the revolt. To evade arrest, Kimathi became one of the first Kikuyu to move into the forest. The Provincial Commissioner noted the significance of this move: 'in Laikipia the local leaders, among whom was Dedan Kimathi, had disappeared, with the result that while assaults on loyal Kikuyu continued to take place, terrorist activities, were extended to the European population'.[82]

The arrests of individual Kikuyu were accompanied by a series of police raids on forest villages and farms. These operations had a dislocating effect that generated a heightened sense of insecurity among squatters. Certain government measures, such as the concentration of squatter villages, reinforced the anxiety that squatters had regarding their future.

The response of the settler community to the Emergency was also an important factor in provoking armed resistance. As Donald Barnet notes: 'A significant sector of the European settler community tended to interpret the emergency declaration and legislation as promulgating a sort of 'open season' on Kikuyu'.[83] The beating and harassment of Africans on farms was quite common. One man recalled: 'I was going to Dundori, when two young settlers stopped me and asked if I was Mau Mau. I said no I wasn't. One of them hit me and said there will be more of this if the Mau Mau continues on the farms'.[84]

The settlers often took the law into their own hands and in a number of cases pressured the government to remove certain Kikuyu from their own areas. The ruthless measures taken by the settlers and the government had the effect of uniting the squatters behind the young militants in the forest. During the weeks following the Declaration of Emergency about 150 Kikuyu left the farms in Nakuru District for the forests.[85] Most Mau Mau supporters remained on the farms to ensure that the movement had a strong presence in the area.

The move to the forest, like armed resistance, was very much a reaction to the Declaration of Emergency. As noted in Chapter 2, the forests had long served as hide-outs and no-go areas for Kikuyu squatters and many forest communities had survived for years outside the reach of the forces of law and order.[86] Thus for many militants disappearing into the forest was part of the community's tradition. What was new and a major departure from past traditions was that as a result of circumstances squatters did not merely disappear into the forest but also organized armed resistance. It was from the forests that the first armed actions were launched in the White Highlands. In response, the colonial forces concentrated their fire on the forest squatter villages.

During the last two months of 1952 the fighters in the forest initiated a number of small-scale actions in Nakuru. European property was burned down in Solai and Subukia. An African informer at Ndoswa village near Njoro was assassinated and another at Bahati narrowly escaped the same fate.[87] In Laikipia the movement was much more active, as there was a large concentration of fighters in the nearby forest. On 22 November the first European settler was killed in the Highlands by Mau Mau, in the Leshau ward of Laikipia District.[88] The government responded with great force to stamp out the revolt. In the Thomson's Falls area, 2,200 Kikuyu were rounded up, and Kampi ya Simba, a forest village near Leshau, was burned to the ground and all the squatters were removed.[89] The most important step taken by the government was the decision to introduce communal punishment. In cases of serious Mau Mau incidents whole communities of Africans in the vicinity were to be evicted from the Highlands. After the killing of the European in Leshau, 4,324 Kikuyu were evicted. In Ndoswa village, 300 Kikuyu were evicted and after a case of arson in Solai 80 people were sent back to the Reserves.[90] On 15 December the Provincial Commissioner of Rift Valley Province put into effect the following plan of communal punishment:

a) On any farm where a serious incident such as a murder has occurred total evacuation of squatters and seizure of crops and stock.
b) In neighbouring farms within, say a 3 mile radius of the farm in which the serious incident took place, 50% evacuation and the seizure of stock and forfeiture of crops of those 50% evacuated. In cases where less serious incidents have occurred such as a Mau Mau meeting, a 25% cut of the cultivation of the squatters concerned and the confiscation of their stock and crops.[91]

The great number of squatters evicted created problems of transportation and accommodation for the government. A temporary detention centre was set up to deal with sorting out the evicted squatters.[92] The punitive measures had an enormous impact on Africans living on the farms. The mass evictions reinforced the insecurity that was already prevalent and contributed to a sense of general despair. This feeling of desperation gave the revolt much of its future impetus. Hundreds of young Kikuyu squatters joined the fighters in the forest in the early months of 1953.

Our information on the organization of the struggle in the forest is impressionistic and sketchy. In particular it is difficult to separate the motive of fleeing from repression from that of organizing guerrilla warfare. According to most accounts the struggle in the forest was coordinated by militants from Nairobi.[93] In the early period of the revolt the government was concerned with controlling the settled areas and the reserves and this gave the fighters the breathing space to organize their forces. In 1953, this organization enabled them to carry out a number of successful raids, both in the Kikuyu Reserves and in the European settled areas. By the middle of 1954, the Security Forces had established their control of their areas, and the forest fighters became increasingly isolated in their sanctuaries. With the destruction of the Nairobi wing of the movement in April 1954, the forest fighters were deprived of their main source of supplies. From this point onwards, the forest fighters were forced to struggle for their own survival and their impact on the reserves and the settled areas was restricted to sporadic raids for food. One by one the various guerrilla units were destroyed and by the end of 1955 the revolt was more or less over.

The break-up of the squatter community

On the farms the evacuation of large numbers of squatters had an intensely unsettling effect on the Kikuyu. Violence against Europeans, which hitherto had been restricted to Laikipia District, spread to Naivasha and Nakuru districts. During the first week of 1953 European farms were raided in Nakuru, Laikipia and Trans Nzoia districts.[94] On the night of the first day of 1953, two European settlers were hacked to death in Ol Kalou.[95] Delegates of European settlers in the area warned the Provincial Commissioner 'that unless some drastic action was taken the local farmers would start shooting up the stock of the Kikuyu labour and possibly the Kikuyu themselves'.[96]

Local Europeans raided the farms and confiscated 5,000 sheep and other squatter property and the government followed this up by ordering the evacuation of all Kikuyu living in the Ol Kalou area.[97] This evacuation was part of a general flood back to the Reserves which occurred in February and March 1953. The return of large numbers of squatters was becoming a major political headache for the administrators of Kikuyuland. The District Commissioner of Kiambu reported that he was 'seriously perturbed by the large numbers of squatters being returned to this District . . . Already there are signs that the repatriated squatters are (not unnaturally) extremely sour and that they may become focal points for strong opposition to the Government'.[98]

In early 1953, resistance on the farms was focused on two government measures: the concentration of squatter villages and the compulsory photographing of Kikuyu on the farms. Large numbers of Kikuyu opted to go to prison rather than have their photograph taken.[99] The Assistant Labour Officer of Nakuru reported one such revealing incident: 'Arrangements were made on the 7th of March for me to take the photo's of all Kikuyu employees . . . when I arrived only a few men were present. When I had taken 14 photos a large party arrived carrying blankets and stated that they wanted to go to jail'.[100] Rumours were circulating to the effect that if the Kikuyu submitted to having their pictures taken, 'they will never be allowed to return to the Reserves and will be forced to work on European farms for life'.[101] As the rumours spread, hundreds of Kikuyu fled from the farms to avoid being photographed. The Provincial Commissioner reported:

> In general and in all the Districts of the Lower Rift, e.g. Nakuru, Naivasha and Thomson's Falls, the attitude of the Kikuyu has hardened against orders to concentrate villages and to be photographed in spite of a number of prosecutions, this attitude has been the result of intensive propaganda by the Mau Mau and I think that these measures can no longer be driven through.[102]

The campaign of disobeying new government regulations was virtually unanimously supported by the Kikuyu on the farms. In the Subukia area of Nakuru district all Kikuyu were removed for refusing to be photographed.[103] The eviction and voluntary migration of Kikuyu reached major proportions; during the first three months of 1953 around 60,000 Kikuyu left the Highlands for the Kikuyu Reserves.

In the Reserves, ex-squatters from the Highlands were active in escalating the struggle, spreading the *batuni* and other oaths in those areas of the Reserves where they had not yet been introduced. According to Boro Gicheru: 'When the squatters had to leave the farms and went back to Kiambu, they found that many of the people there had not taken the goat's blood oath. Many squatter oath administrators were busy in those days'.[104]

Many young squatters went from the Reserves straight into the forest. One such man was Karioki Chege, later to be known as General Kago.[105] The Lari massacre of 97 Kikuyu collaborators on 26 March 1953 was carried out by a force composed largely of Rift Valley squatters. The Loyalist camp at Lari in Kiambu had an odious reputation for treating the refugees from the Rift Valley with cruelty and disdain. One of the leading participants in the attack on Lari recalled: 'We decided to attack Lari because there were many guards who were punishing their fellow Kikuyu and killing them. They were signing away our land'.[106]

The attack on Lari precipitated an anti-squatter campaign in the Reserves led by the Loyalist elements. A delegation of chiefs from Kiambu told the Governor that Mau Mau criminals, 'together with discontented Rift Valley squatters are planning and organizing the thuggery and killings'.[107]

The attack on Lari coincided with a raid on the Naivasha Police Station. The success of this raid and the campaign of civil disobedience on the farms led the Government to form Provincial and District Emergency Committees. CID teams were set up in Nakuru, Naivasha and Thomson's Falls[108] and these teams screened an average of 3,000 Kikuyu a month. The teams were assisted by the appointment of a number of temporary 'chiefs' from the reserves. Throughout 1953 most of the Mau Mau activity in the Highlands took place in Laikipia district by units operating out of the Aberdare Forest. The operation of the forest fighters was actively supported by the farm labourers. The D.C. of Thomson's Falls noted in May:

> There has been considerable Kikuyu gang activity in part of the district in the past two weeks, involving the plundering and devastation of a European homestead in Leshau, the theft of four firearms, and a double murder of two loyal Kikuyu in the Ol Joro Orok area, as well as other incidents. It appears to be clear that these gangs are being formed by Kikuyu still resident in the district.[109]

The support that the forest fighters had on the farms is demonstrated by the hundreds of prosecutions of Africans for giving food to terrorists.[110]

By the end of 1953, however, the Kikuyu mass movement had suffered greatly from the evictions and the voluntary migrations back to the Reserves. Over 40,000 Kikuyu left Nakuru District in 1953 and the Laikipia Kikuyu population of 30,000 was reduced to 6,000 by the end of the year.[111] The European settlers faced an acute shortage of labour, which they tried to remedy by hiring seasonal labour from other ethnic groups. Large numbers of Baluhya, Kipsigis and Kamba were recruited to replace the Kikuyu squatters.

The Kikuyu were greatly restricted by the various emergency regulations operating in the Highlands. There was a curfew, regulations preventing them from leaving their locality and they had to carry special identification papers and photographs and often faced the possibility of arbitrary police arrest.[112] Kikuyu on the farms had become reluctant to fight not only because of their fear of the security forces but also because of the danger of being evicted to the already overcrowded Reserves. Life in the reserves was becoming intolerable for squatters. Many of them were unemployed or landless and they were made to feel unwelcome guests. As Boro Gicheru recalled: 'In Kiambu the people from the Rift Valley were called theives and were treated badly. The Chiefs and the Home Guards blamed us for the war and made life hell for us'.[113]

Thus the fear of being returned to the Reserves in itself had a debilitating effect on Kikuyu resistance in the Highlands. In fact in 1954 the focus of Mau Mau on the farms turned to defending the position of Kikuyu in the Highlands. This orientation manifested itself in the increasing attacks on non-Kikuyu Africans who had replaced the evicted Kikuyu. One observer noted: 'It is clear that gangs have turned their attention to attack on labour lines with the intention of intimidating labour and scaring off members of other tribes who have replaced Kikuyu'.[114] Early in the year six Samburu herdsmen were killed in Laikipia.[115] Similar, though less spectacular incidents took place in the Lower Rift throughout the year.[116]

The defeat of the forest fighters in the Reserves led a large number of them to move to the forests in the settled areas to find refuge there. These groups began to raid the labour lines for food and money from April 1954 onwards.[117] These raids were clearly not supported by the local African labourers on the farms, many of whom resented the demands put on them by the raiders from the forest. By this time the Kikuyu who remained in Nakuru District were resentful if not hostile to the Mau Mau groups. The very presence of these groups could implicate them and threaten their livelihood on the farms.[118] This fear proved only too true when 5,000 squatters were evicted in February after a raid on a European farm in Nakuru.[119]

As the forests around the settled areas became the main sanctuary of the forest fighters life for the Kikuyu on the farms became increasingly precarious.[120] Not surprisingly a growing number of Kikuyu began to collaborate with the government. The *East African Standard* reported in March 1954:

Kikuyu in the Rift Valley are giving more information to the police about the movements of terrorists . . . during the past month . . .

about 5000/- was paid out by the Rift Valley police as rewards. . .

Senior Superintendent Griffiths has stated in Nakuru that the Kikuyu population is becoming heartily sick of being bled of money and food by agents of hard core terrorists.[121]

While the report exaggerated the extent of alienation from Mau Mau, it reflected the general trend.

The beginning of collaboration by Kikuyu with the government was a turning point, though by no means the general rule. Kikuyu labourers still often assisted the forest fighters. According to the District Commissioner of Nakuru: 'It was found towards the end of the year, that the Kikuyu in the Njoro/Elburgon area . . . who numbered 20,000 were showing no signs of wanting to give up their sympathies, in fact, they helped gangsters'.[122] This view was amply confirmed by the shooting of a police officer in Elburgon in September and a growing number of stock raids in the area.[123]

The persistent tendency of the forest fighters to rely on the settled areas as a sanctuary gradually eroded most of their former support in the farms in 1955. Assuming the role of fugitives, the units from the forest restricted themselves to minor raids for food. An intelligence report described the situation in July 1955: 'Once again the picture in the Lower Rift is that of raids by small gangs for the purpose of obtaining food. There have been an increased number of incidents in the Naivasha district, but on the other hand, there have also been an increased number of killings of terrorists.'[124]

Defeat had forced the forest fighters towards a desperate struggle to survive. Their raids had become a source of irritation rather than a threat to security. In desperation they turned on their former supporters, demanding to be fed. As was to be expected the Kikuyu farm labourers reacted and began to co-operate with the police. On one farm in Ol Joro Orok, the Kikuyu labourers killed a total of eight raiders in 1955.[125]

The State of Emergency can be seen as an attempt to destroy the squatter community once and for all. Although, as we shall argue, it did not succeed in its objective, it did lead to the containment of radical resistance. By forcing militants into the forest the administration was able to prevent the emergence of a more coherent national liberation movement. The phase of armed revolt was an episode that marks a break with the previous pattern. Whereas previously the movement was gaining in strength and coherence, the guerrilla struggle was primarily one of fighting for survival. But the government did not have it entirely its own way. The tenacity of the forest fighters ensured that there could be no return to a European settler-dominated Kenya.

The defeat of armed resistance represented a devastating blow to the squatter movement. By 1955 the Kikuyu squatter community was broken up and scattered throughout the Rift Valley and Central Province. And yet as events will show this defeat did not lead to the consolidation of European power in the Highlands. All the issues raised by the squatter movement were to be raised anew by the end of the decade.

Notes

1. Kenya National Archives (KNA), MAA 8/125, Monthly Reports of Principal Labour Officers, Report of Labour Officer, Nakuru, February 1947.
2. KNA, DC NKU 2/388, Labour Inspector's Report 1946–48, no. 79, Intelligence Report, March 1948.
3. Labour Department Annual Report, 1947.
4. KNA, DC, NKU 2/388, Labour Inspector's Report 1946–48, no. 46, Intelligence Report, January 1948.
5. KNA, MAA 8/125, Monthly Reports of Principal Labour Officers, Report of Labour Officer, Nakuru, September 1947.
6. Interview with Thuo Kigera, 19 March 1972.
7. KNA, MAA 8/8, Intelligence Reports Conf. – Information no. 16, Report of meeting at Njoro, 21 September 1947.
8. *ibid.*
9. Interview with John Karibe 25 March 1972.
10. PC, Nyeri, MAA 120/4 Movement and Resettlement of Kikuyu, no. 3, June 1949, Security and the Squatter Problem. This retrospective report notes the extension of oathing in the settled areas in late 1947.
11. KNA, Government House 3/71, Appendices of Corfield Report, Chapter 5, appendix H.
12. Interview with Thuo Kigera, 19 March 1972.
13. Interview with Stanley Macharia, 29 February 1972.
14. *ibid.*
15. African Affairs Annual Report, 1948, p. 64.
16. KNA, MAA 8/124, The Central Co-ordinating Committee for Resident Labour, no. 18, Report from L.O. to Labour Commissioner, 13 March 1947.
17. *ibid.*
18. KNA: DC, NKU/ 2/385, Labour Department – Monthly Reports, Intelligence Report, October 1951.
19. KNA, MAA 2/5/250, R.V.P. 1947–53 no. 32, DC, Nakuru to CNC, 5 October 1948. This is the earliest document that I have come across that mentions Mau Mau by name. More specifically it notes the existence of an association 'variously alleged to be either the Mau Mau association or the United Natives Association, probably connected with the KCA'.
20. Interview with Eliud Kiberenge, 1 March 1972.
21. In 1948, only two cases of intimidation were reported to the police in the settled areas.
22. See Furedi (1974b).
23. *East African Standard (EAS)*, 19 November 1948.
24. DC, NKU 2/386, Monthly Labour Reports, Report for October 1948.
25. Interview with Eliud Kiberenge, 1 March 1972.
26. Nakuru District Annual Report, 1948, p. 2.
27. KNA, DC, NKU 2/386, Monthly Labour Reports, November 1948.

28. *ibid.*, see reports for this period.
29. *ibid.*, October 1948. United Kingdom, 1960 Cmd. 1030, *Historical Survey of the Origins and Growth of Mau Mau*, p. 82 refers to the 'the squatter unrest still simmering in 1949'.
30. KNA, DC, UG 4/1, Monthly Labour Reports, October 1949.
31. PC, RVP: Lab 27/5, Squatters and Squatter Stock no. 6, SLO's monthly report, August 1949.
32. Nakuru District Annual Report, 1950, p. 27.
33. Nakuru District Annual Report, 1948, p. 4.
34. Trans Nzoia and Uasin Gishu Districts Annual Report, 1949.
35. DC, NKU, 27/6 II, Squatters and Resident Labourers (Barazas Anti-Mau Mau, no. 317, Record of meeting held in the office of the PC RVP on June 30, 1951.
36. Interview with Dominic Gathu, 9 June 1972. On the concentration of ex-squatters in Kariobangi see KLO L.O. 41512, PC Nyeri, Adm. 18/1/1/10; Monthly Intelligence Report, Nairobi District, January 1950 indicates that a significant number of ex-squatters were picked up during a raid in Kariobungi.
37. Interview with Eliud Kiberenge.
38. Nakuru District Annual Report, 1950, p. 31.
39. KNA, DC, NKU 2/386, Monthly Labour Reports, October 1950, and *ibid.* November 1950.
40. *ibid.*, contains relevant reports for the period.
41. *ibid.*, May 1950.
42. *ibid.*
43. *ibid.*, September 1950.
44. *ibid.*, see reports, April to December 1950.
45. *ibid.*, November 1950.
46. Many government officials were pessimistic about the efficacy of administrative intervention as long as settlers maintained their attitudes towards Africans. 'The present tendency of Kikuyu labour to intrigue and subversive activity is attributable partly, it must be conceded to lack of administrative supervision but principally to an entire lack of understanding and appreciation of the African and his mental processes by the majority of employers who must be brought to realise that they, by force of circumstances, are directly responsible for all that happens on their farms'. See Nakuru DAR 1951, p. 3.
47. See correspondence in KNA, DC NKU 2/385, Labour Department – Monthly Reports.
48. Rift Valley Province Annual Report, 1951, p. 94.
49. Interview with Francis Mucherere, 6 March 1972.
50. Interview with Kimani Muchohio, 25 March 1972.
51. Throup (1983), p. 174.
52. KNA, DC, UG 4/1, Monthly Labour Reports, Intelligence Report by Labour Officer, December 1950. Throup's argument that the government failed to take the necessary measures against Mau Mau conflicts with our evidence. See Throup (1987), p. 227. If anything it can be argued that it was state repression which forced Africans to adopt the road of armed revolt.
53. The November 1950 meeting of top administration and settlers, previously discussed, anticipates the emergency legislation of 1952. See KNA, DC, NKU 2/386, Monthly Labour Reports, no. 8, 27 November 1950, Mau Mau meeting, Provincial Commissioners' Offices.
54. This was the opinion of virtually all those interviewed who had taken the oath.
55. Interviews with Francis Mucherere, Kinanjui Mutegi, Kimani Muchohio.
56. The relationship between Nyeri and the squatter movement has not yet been explored. According to the limited material consulted by the author, there was a strong cross-fertilization of ideas and organization between the two areas. The strong anti-squatter sentiment which prevailed in Kiambu did not have much resonance in Nyeri.

57. Interview with Michael Waweru.
58. Interview with Onesmus Gachoka, 10 May 1972.
59. Interview with Njoroge Nganga, 2 February 1972.
60. KNA, Govt House 3/71, Appendices. Corfield Report, 'Top secret letter no. C/349/1 addressed by the Commissioner of Police to the Member for Law and Order', 4 July 1952.
61. *ibid.*, Appendix General Biographies.
62. On 26 July 1952 at a rally in Nyeri, Kenyatta stated that the Thomson's Falls and Elburgon branches were the biggest subscribers to KAU. See *ibid.*, 'Report by Assistant Superintendent of Police, Nyeri'.
63. Interview with Francis Mucherere.
64. KNA, DC NKU 2/387, Monthly Labour Reports, June 1952.
65. *ibid.*
66. Nakuru District Annual Report, 1952, p. 3.
67. Rift Valley Province Annual Report, 1952, p. 65.
68. KNA, Govt House 3/71, Appendices, Corfield Report, Extracts from the Kenya Police Intelligence Summaries for 1952. August 1–15, 1952.
69. *EAS*, 15 August 1952.
70. *EAS*, 29 August 1952.
71. DC, NKU, L.G. 5/2/5/9, Social Welfare Centres Instructions . . .
72. Nakuru District Annual Report, 1951, p. 2.
73. DC, NKU, L.G. 5/2/5/9, Social Welfare Centres Safari report by C.A.A. Hayes D.O. November 1951.
74. *EAS*, 4 April 1952.
75. *EAS*, 9 May 1952.
76. *EAS*, 16 May 1952.
77. KNA, Govt House 3/71, Appendices. Corfield Report Extracts from the Kenya Police Intelligence Summaries for 1952. May 1952.
78. *EAS*, 5 September 1952.
79. *EAS*, 10 October 1952.
80. PC, RVP, Lab 27.6/3, Illegal Squatting, no. 317, Resumé of meeting 30 June 1951.
81. Nakuru District Annual Report, 1952, p. 3.
82. Rift Valley Province Annual Report, 1952, p. 66.
83. Barnett and Njama (1966), p. 71.
84. Interview with Njoroge Kagunda, 1 April 1972.
85. This estimate is calculated from interviews.
86. See discussion in Chapter 2 above.
87. Nakuru District Annual Report, 1952.
88. Rift Valley Province Annual Report, 1952, p. 66.
89. *EAS*, 26 November 1952.
90. KNA, PC NKU 2/846, Squatters and Squatter Stock, no. 58, PC, Rift Valley Province to CNC 23 December 1952.
91. *ibid.*, PC.RVP – to all district commissioners, 23 December 1952.
92. *ibid.*
93. Rosberg and Nottingham (1966), p. 307.
94. *EAS*, 2 January 1953.
95. KNA, PC, NKU 2/846, Squatters and Squatter Stock, no. 88, PC, Rift Valley Province to Governor, 7 January 1953.
96. *ibid.*
97. *EAS*, 6 February 1953.
98. KNA, PC, NKU 2/846, Squatters and Squatter Stock, no. 104, DC, Kiambu to PC, IP, 3 April 1953.
99. By the end of February 1953 there was no more space in the prisons in the Rift Valley.
100. NLO, Single File titled Kikuyu Prisoners Discharged, Report 26 March 1953.

101. *EAS*, 6 February 1953.
102. KNA, PC, NKU 2/846, Squatters and Squatter Stock, no. 156, PC, Rift Valley Province to CNC 2 February 1953.
103. Nakuru District Annual Report, 1953, p. 26.
104. Interview with Boro Gicheru, 31 March 1972.
105. *EAS*, 2 April 1954.
106. Interview, confidential.
107. *EAS*, 3 April 1953. The Chiefs were not popular with the squatters. A group of visiting chiefs were shouted down and stoned by a crowd of 3,000 squatters, whom they came to address in Thomson's Falls. See *EAS*, 20 March 1953.
108. African Affairs Department Annual Report, 1953, p. 61.
109. KNA, MAA 7/786, Movement and Resettlement of Kikuyu DC Thomson Falls, Report for May.
110. See *EAS*, 12 June 1953.
111. See Annual Reports for the districts concerned, 1953.
112. Nakuru District Annual Report, 1953, p. 26.
113. Interview with Boro Gicheru, 31 March 1972.
114. See *EAS*, 15 January 1954, 12 February 1954.
115. Laikipia District Annual Report, 1954, p. 1.
116. *EAS*, 5 March 1954, 12 April 1954.
117. Nakuru District Annual Report, 1954, p. 1.
118. *ibid.*
119. *ibid.*, p. 4.
120. The District Commissioner of Nakuru noted that 'by the end of the year it was evident that terrorist groups from as far as Kiambu had used the East Mau area as a resting place'. See *ibid.*, p. 2.
121. *EAS*, 26 March 1954.
122. Nakuru District Annual Report, 1954, p. 41.
123. KNA, DC, NKU 2/387, Monthly Labour Reports, January 1955.
124. KNA: PC, NKU 2/846, Squatters and Squatter Stock, Extracts of situation report, July 1955.
125. Laikipia District Annual Report, 1955, p. 1.

Five

The Revolt in Perspective

The transformation of militant protest into open revolt was the unexpected product of two mutually reinforcing forces at work. Repression and an inflexible system of administration appeared to close the avenue of constitutional reform and the absence of tangible progress undermined the credibility of moderate nationalists who were urging caution. At a time when activists in Nairobi and elsewhere faced state coercion the moderate option was bound to create suspicion. This suspicion was fuelled by manifest evidence of close collaboration between the Kikuyu establishment and the colonial administration. These loyalists had become powerful both politically and economically at the expense of the Kikuyu masses and although strictly speaking the moderate nationalists were not yet part of the Kikuyu establishment, in the eyes of the militants they were veering in that direction.

The political differentiation of the Kikuyu community into three fairly distinct camps – the establishment, moderate/constitutionalists and militants – had become evident by the late 1940s. This differentiation was most evident in Nairobi, where the political environment was particularly polarized. Thus in 1947 Jomo Kenyatta, the president of KAU, dissociated his party from the proposal for a general strike in Nairobi by trade union militants.[1] By the end of 1947, the lines between moderates and militants were firmly drawn in Nairobi. The squatters were drawn into this political conflict during their return to Kiambu in 1946–47. The hostility they experienced from the Kikuyu establishment and the lack of decisive support from the moderates tended to drive the squatter activists towards the militants. For squatters, as for the militant activists from Nairobi, moderate solutions did not correspond to experience. Given the far-reaching problems they faced they were drawn towards more militant solutions. In the pursuit of such solutions they were able to win the sympathy and support of the have-nots throughout the Kikuyu Reserves.

Social differentiation provided the potential for class conflict and for militant action. The realization of this potential was speeded up by government repression, which continually forced the militant activists to raise the stakes. In the European settled areas, the steady escalation of repression is evident from 1950 onwards. From the spring of 1952 this repression had the character of forcing the hands of the squatter activists in order to crush and isolate them. Bruce Berman's thesis that sections of the Kenya administration welcomed the Emergency as a way of destroying its militant opponents is very much borne out by the Rift Valley experience.[2] European settlers welcomed repression as it facilitated the reorganization of their relations with their squatters. The subsequent break-up of the Kikuyu squatter community was approved as a final solution to an age-old problem.

Repression did not cause resistance but it did speed up its escalation and forced the squatter activists and their allies on to a violent collision course. It pushed the squatter movement into a confrontation for which it was not ready. From this perspective the struggle in the forest and the general militarization of resistance is more the product of repression than of any dynamic inherent to the squatter movement. It can be argued that the move to the forest represents a break with past development. At least in the Rift Valley it forced activists to take on prematurely the might of the colonial state. Thus the move to the forest was only an extension of previous forms of resistance in a limited sense. The impulses of survival and defence were the key determinants rather than the conscious desire to escalate the struggle.

Of course it can be argued that those who revolt are never ready for it. And certainly the relation between the colonial system and the Kikuyu establishment on the one hand and those excluded from a stake in society on the other was fraught with tension. Social upheaval was on the agenda in any case, and state repression served to telescope its development. There are two important social factors that gave Mau Mau its peculiar identity. The Kikuyu establishment was a powerful and threatening force but not strong enough to impose its authority on the rest of Kikuyu society. It simply lacked the social base necessary for the establishment of real authority. As a result this powerful group had only a fragile hold over Kikuyu society. Class relations were thus inconclusive and relatively unstable. Secondly, in this polarized environment the nationalist movement found it difficult to reconcile conflicting interests and eventually it split. With the moderate option compromised, the militants could pursue their objectives unhindered by the legacy of constitutional reform.

The significance of the split

One of the peculiarities of Mau Mau was that it was a product of a split with the moderate nationalist movement. In most struggles for national liberation in Africa the have-nots have rarely been able to evolve their own independent organizational voice. In general the more moderate middle class leadership was able to retain control over its more radical rank and file. Where the nationalist movement fractures, as in Zimbabwe, it is usually divided along ethnic/regional lines or between groups of competing personalities representing the same social interests.

The significance of the split is apparent when compared to developments in Ghana at the same time. In the late 1940s, many of the tensions evident in Kenya came to the fore in the nationalist movement in Ghana. The Convention People's Party (CPP) led by Kwame Nkrumah faced difficulties in holding back the militant sections of the mass movement. In January 1950 the militant Trades Union Congress forced the issue by rallying for a general strike. Nkrumah at first attempted to get the strike called off but could not control the militant activists, and on 8 January 1950 he announced his support for it and ensured that the nationalist movement would remain united.

The British Governor at the time, Sir Charles Arden-Clarke, later recalled that Nkrumah and the CPP leadership had been forced into supporting the strike by the threat of political isolation.[3] Nkrumah's ability to give leadership to militant action ensured that even the most radical elements retained a loyalty to the CPP. Four months later, in May 1950, when faced with a similar decision, Jomo Kenyatta opposed the call for a general strike in Nairobi on the grounds that it was inconsistent with the main strategy of the Kenya African Union (KAU).[4] By this time Kenyatta had lost influence among the leadership of the militants. Unlike the CPP, which was able to reconcile conflicting interests within its organization, the KAU lost ground to the movement of radicals. The colonial administration thus faced a mass movement that could not be integrated into its framework of political rule.

The different directions taken by the CPP and KAU cannot be reduced to the character of their leaders or their policies. In settler-dominated Kenya, the colonial administration had little room for manoeuvre. It could not make the concessions to the nationalist movement that were available to its counterpart in Ghana. In such circumstances moderate nationalism was not able to gain credibility. In comparable situations, such as Zimbabwe, resistance was also forced to go beyond its moderate phase. But unlike in Kenya, the nationalist movement did not split along class lines, because social differentiation was more restrained. Mau Mau, an authentic voice of the Kikuyu have-nots, represents a unique response to colonial domination above all because of its *organizational independence*. The relationship of KAU to the squatter community will help situate Mau Mau in perspective.

The KAU and the squatter movement

The KAU was the first African political organization to operate openly in the White Highlands. Emerging out of the Kenya African Studies Union (KASU), an organization formed by a group of educated, middle class moderates 'for the advancement of African interests',[5] KAU spread to the White Highlands and by 1946 branches were established in most of the townships of the European-settled areas. While many KCA activists joined KAU, in the White Highlands it drew into its ranks the more established sections of Kikuyu businessmen and the salaried.

Most of the leaders of KAU were on the verge of economic and social success and looked forward to improving and consolidating their position through constitutional reform. In inclination KAU activists were drawn towards the course of advancement through reform rather than fundamental social change.

In terms of education and life-style KAU supporters were sharply marked off from the majority of Africans. A number of second-generation squatters who had moved to Nakuru town and other townships were active in KAU. Some had obtained missionary education and had gone on to become successful businessmen. A typical representative of this group was Onesmus Gachoka. Brought up on a farm in Naivasha, Gachoka went to study at the Africa Inland Mission School in Kijabe in 1916 and after leaving obtained a job as a milk clerk. By the late 1930s he had become the owner of a hotel and shop in Thomson's Falls and became a part-time assessor to the native court in Rumuruti. After the Second World War he emerged as a leading businessman, with connections throughout the settled areas. As a man of considerable local importance, he was invited to be one of the delegates to the founding conference of KASU. He recalled: 'I went to this the first meeting of KASU. It was held in Pumwani Memorial Hall in Nairobi. When I came back from this meeting I started registering people immediately'.[6]

Onesmus Gachoka was a representative of a class of educated small businessmen, who saw the KAU as the vehicle for the articulation of their interests. M.C. Benson, the secretary of KAU in neighbouring Ol Kalou, was a trader in hides and skins.[7] Daniel Mbugwa, the vice-treasurer, and Mwaura Kinyanjui, the treasurer, were both businessmen. In the Molo branch, Mirala Ndungu, the treasurer, was a trader, Stanley Macharia the vice-chairman, was a shopowner and Thuo Kigera, the chairman, owned a shop and a hotel. A number of KAU officials worked as clerks for European and Asian enterprises. Millington Mlala, a KAU official in Molo, worked for the Kenya Farmers Association. Duncan Wainana, treasurer of the Elburgon branch, was a clerk in a European run sawmill. Dedan Kimathi, secretary of the Thomson's Falls branch, was also a clerk. A list of the local KAU branch officials reads like a who's who of Africans in the White Highlands.[8] Or, as the District Commissioner of Laikipia put it: 'Most of the more advanced Kikuyu of the District are members of KAU'.[9]

In an indirect way KAU served as an African businessmen's club. A number of KAU officials stated that they joined the organization because of business considerations. One of them, Mirala Ndungu, said: 'I was forced to join; that is if you live here you have to join because of the people . . . if you are a businessman you have to join it so you can talk in front of that group of people'.[10]

The activists of the KAU were generally oriented towards the presentation of the grievances of Africans living in the townships to the colonial government. Despite the characterization of KAU as a nationalist organization, on the local level up until 1950 the nationalist perspective of the group was almost totally absent. The demands of the KAU were for moderate reforms, the elimination of particularly irritating forms of discrimination and the extension of trading privileges.

Thus Joel Kuria, Chairman of the Eldoret branch at a meeting proposed resolutions to the effect that this meeting:

> requests our kind Government to grant the Africans with plots for their own use and their families . . . [in the Township] . . . as soon as possible . . . [and] . . . asks the kind Local Government to survey and erect a building for market for the African's use.[11]

Other demands of the KAU were for the setting up of African Advisory Councils and the appointment of an African to the Legislative Council to represent Africans living in the European settled areas.[12] KAU members were irritated by the wide-ranging restrictions placed on their talent and ambitions by the racist social structure of the White Highlands. They sought to prove themselves as worthy representatives of African opinion. In response they went out of their way to demonstrate their respectability to the government. KAU meetings were started and terminated with prayers and the virtues of hard work and honesty were constantly emphasized at their public rallies. The following account of a KAU meeting in July 1946 in Thomson's Falls is typical of many other such assemblies:

> The meeting took place in the open near the location market hall and Mr. Johnson Keiya opened the meeting at approximately 11 a.m. with a call to prayer to all present . . . Those that were sitting down stood up and all present 'doffed' their hats while Mr. Lubin Mwangi, . . . recited a prayer to the meeting asking God to help them in their cause and that all would serve King George and the British Empire for the betterment of all races within the Colony of Kenya.[13]

Many KAU officials saw their role as leaders of their community and valuable intermediaries between Africans and the government. Hence they sought official recognition of their 'valuable' roles. The secretary of one KAU branch wrote to his DC in May 1950: 'At a recent meeting of the KAU, it was requested that Africans be allowed to meet with the Official Distinguished guest when they are on tour up here. For many a time this request has been put up by Africans but it does not seem to be entertained'.[14]

The KAU leaders occasionally attempted to expand their activities to the farms and to act as the spokesmen for the African squatters. This enterprise was not very successful as most squatters were inclined to distrust the well-to-do Africans in the townships. Many squatters saw KAU as being very much under the influence of the government. One KCA activist stated: 'The Government told people to make KAU. Mathu, Thuku and Gichuru made KAU at the Government's advice. It was the party of the educated and the rich'.[15]

The commonly held view that the KAU officials were collaborating with the government is not entirely unfounded. The intervention of KAU during the mass campaign of disobedience in 1946 sheds light on the relationship between squatters and KAU and between the government and KAU.

In the Thomson's Falls area, Johnson Keiya, the chairman of the local KAU branch, volunteered his services to intervene on behalf of the Labour Department to attempt to convince the squatters to sign their new agreements and travelled round the farms to do this. The Labour Officer for Thomson's Falls wrote to the Labour Commissioner at the height of the 1946 squatter agitation: 'I feel that the fact of my working with the local representative of the KAU may be producing some effect. I have just heard that all the squatters of Mr. Van Rensburg who refused to re-attest yesterday have now all agreed to do so'.[16] The Labour Commissioner replied: 'I think that, where assistance has been given by the local representatives of KAU, as in this case, that everything possible should be done to assist him in return'.[17]

A KAU meeting in Subukia in August 1946 clearly shows the KAU officials' intervention against the squatters. According to an intelligence report:

> Mr. Moses Njoroge of Thomson's Falls KAU next spoke. He told the meeting not to be afraid of the Labour Officer as he was there on their invitation and he would be glad to hear their *shauris* [complaints] . . . He told them they were well off in Subukia both as regards crops and grass and that they would be mad to let wicked people persuade them to go back to the crowded Kikuyu Reserve, as refusing to attest would mean that. The speaker had a very convincing manner.
>
> Mr. Charles Kamau from Njoro then spoke on work. He said many were very lazy and told them as long as they remained so they would never get on . . .[18]

KAU's intervention on behalf of the Labour Department was far from effective. It compromised the KAU leadership, who lost all credibility on the farms. Thus we saw in Chapter 3 how the Sosyambu squatters shouted down a KAU representative who spoke on behalf of the government. Similarly at a meeting of squatters in Naivasha in November 1946 only six out of 300 farm delegates supported Johnson Keiya's call for moderation. The other speakers rejected Keiya's advice as 'not good'.[19]

The administration recognized that the local KAU officials could serve as useful collaborators. Thus when Keiya applied for a plot of land at Olenguruone settlement for his father, Meredyth Hyde-Clark, the Labour Commissioner, wrote on his behalf: 'Johnson Keiya has been most helpful to this Department in Thomson Falls district'.[20] The Labour Officer responsible for Uasin Gishu also looked upon KAU officials as useful collaborators. In a cynical vein he reported: 'The Chairman of the local branch of the [KA] Union, a G.W. Kuria has already proved to me that he is a bad employer of Africans. He is a local building contractor. I think that he may be helpful to me if handled carefully'.[21] Although KAU officials were more than willing to 'prove' their worth to government officials they lacked the credibility necessary to influence the squatter movement. Their activities only confirmed their predilection for collaboration and weakened further their influence amongst the masses.

Throughout the 1940s the political impact of KAU in the White Highlands remained minimal. It lacked a mass base and the orientation of KAU activities reflected the interests of a very small social group. While the administration regarded the KCA as a threat to security, it had no such fears about KAU. The Nakuru District Commissioner reported in 1948 that although 'there are several branches of KAU in the District', they 'evoke little interest and fewer subscriptions'.[22] A year later, he described KAU as 'inactive'.[23] To all intents and purposes KAU remained a paper association; its activity was restricted to drawing up resolutions for the attention of the government.

The revitalization of the KAU and the Kenyatta phenomenon

As noted previously, the KAU was revitalized in 1950, and by 1952 it assumed a degree of political influence. This change in KAU's fortunes came about as a result of the shift in emphasis of KCA strategy. Many moderate KCA activists followed Kenyatta's advice and joined KAU. This move was justified on the grounds that the KCA could work openly through KAU. By 1950 most of the KAU branches in Nakuru, Laikipia and Naivasha districts were under the domination of the KCA activists.

The KAU politicians for their own part were pleased to see the influx of new members. Their experience had shown that on their own they were an insubstantial force. To win recognition as the leadership of the African community they had to mobilize support from broader sections of society. A clear shift in emphasis is discernible around 1950. The KAU began to articulate rather than oppose the interests of squatters. The Senior Labour Officer of the Rift Valley complained that KAU officials ceased to take a 'constructive stance towards labour matters'.[24] KAU officials changed their language and began to advance nationalist claims alongside demands of an economic character.

Under grassroots pressure the KAU men were forced to take on a radical posture. In Elburgon and Thomson's Falls matters went further when the KAU branches were taken over by young militants in 1952 during the months leading up to the declaration of a State of Emergency.[25] In these areas at least the very character of KAU had changed as the old leadership lost control over the organization it had created.

The grassroots takeover of KAU branches in Elburgon and Thomson's Falls should not lead one to believe that the tension between the Mau Mau leaders and KAU officials was resolved. The moderate wing of the KCA, who had joined KAU, were opposed to the direct action and violence of Mau Mau. They were, however, not in a position to express these views publicly. Onesmus Gachoka felt that 'no good can come of violence'.[26] Dedan Kibe, secretary of the Ol Kalou branch, indicated that their 'hands were tied by the Mau Mau and one could not oppose them'.[27] Thuo Kigera, chairman of KAU in Molo, succinctly expressed the political orientation of his class:

> The KAU officials believed that change should come about constitutionally and they did not believe in violence. The government did not bother KAU, only Mau Mau. Although the people supported Mau Mau I believe that we were right. Mau Mau only delayed independence. It was KAU that played an important role in getting desirable change. Kenyatta also strongly advocated constitutional means of change. And at the last conference of KAU . . . this line of action was approved . . . It is true that some spoke in favour of violence but they were a minority.[28]

It is necessary at this stage to note the ambiguous but significant role played by Kenyatta in relation to the squatter movement. There is no doubt that Kenyatta was held in high regard on the farms, but to draw the conclusion, as many local administrations did, that Kenyatta was in some sense responsible for the resistance of squatters is off the mark. In fact, whatever Kenyatta did or said at his meetings in the Rift Valley made little difference to subsequent developments. The squatter activists simply interpreted Kenyatta's words to accord with their objectives and to endow their actions with legitimacy.

Kenyatta was seen as the leader of the Kikuyu people, a fierce opponent of the *status quo*. He thus became the symbolic leader of the squatter movement. George Rudé has drawn attention to the phenomenon of 'involuntary leaders' in peasant societies:

> . . . the leader-in-chief in whose name the crowd riots or rebels may be an involuntary leader, whose leadership has been quite literally thrust upon him. Louis XVI of France, for instance . . . claimed no more personal responsibility for the activities of the peasants who burned down *châteaux* in his name than Luther did for the rebellious German peasants.[29]

In the same way one finds Kenyatta's name directly connected with a number of cases of unrest on the farms.

The typical colonial official believed that there was a shadowy conspirator lurking in the dark behind every instance of unrest. Upon discovering that 20 squatters refused to work for the fuel contractor that employed them in June 1951, a labour inspector conveyed in all seriousness the following intelligence: 'I was informed by Abdulla's personal boy that the trouble here was caused by Jomo Kenyatta's visit to the forest one night when he held a meeting and is alleged to have told the men not to work unless they got bigger *shambas*'.[30] If all such reports are to be believed Kenyatta must have spent a lot of sleepless nights moving about and agitating on the farms.

Kenyatta himself found it expedient to refrain from taking a clear stand. He recognized that if he publicly broke with Mau Mau, his hold over the Kikuyu people would be severely undermined. Pressure from below forced him to exercise discretion in his public pronouncements. The leading activists in Nairobi had a profound mistrust of Kenyatta but nevertheless used his name to justify their actions. As his biographer noted: 'KAU was now virtually in the hands of the younger men in Nairobi . . . They used Kenyatta's name freely in their propaganda, which included a stepped-up programme of oathing'.[31] Kenyatta, despite his opposition to the stepping up of resistance, had no option but to remain ambiguous. Thus he was all things to all men and as his biographer recorded 'Friends as much as enemies now found Kenyatta's position equivocal'.[32]

In reality Kenyatta sought to cool the situation rather than stir up unrest. There is a distinct note of moderation and conservatism in the speeches he addressed to meetings in the White Highlands. In July 1948 the following account of his speech in Thomson's Falls was made:

> He stressed the importance of unity amongst Africans and Education. He stated that the African is accused of being lazy, irresponsible and a thief. He appealed to them to show the foreigner that these allegations were untrue by working hard and not tolerating or giving refuge to thieves and bad characters. He spoke at length about the dangers of prostitutes and said they must be eliminated.[33]

Kenyatta's moderate public speeches did not compromise him because it could always be claimed that in private he meant something else. In a sense it didn't matter what he said or what he did because the different sections of Kikuyu society could interpret his actions according to their own objectives. However, not even Kenyatta's authority could reverse the moderates' declining influence. In the Rift Valley KAU remained marginal to the preoccupations of the squatter movement.

The revitalization of KAU indicated that Mau Mau was confident of challenging the moderates on their own ground. The takeover of KAU branches was not restricted to the Rift Valley. A similar pattern is discernible in Nairobi and the reserves. What would have occurred if the Emergency had not intervened is a matter of conjecture. But it appears that a movement consisting of a legal public front and an underground was in the making.

The ambiguous position of Kenyatta reflected the ambiguity of the situation. Although the militants were deeply suspicious of Kenyatta they never publicly challenged him. This reluctance to discredit Kenyatta as the public figurehead of the Kikuyu people reflected one of the central weaknesses of Mau Mau. While organizationally independent, Mau Mau was ideologically indistinguishable from KAU and moderate constitutionalists. Although representing a distinct social base, Mau Mau never expressed a point of view that ideologically conflicted with the standpoint of the moderates. The conflict of interest did not assume a political form despite the tension between those who wanted change and those who wanted to improve their position within the existing social structure.

The basic objective of freedom and land could be supported by all sections of Kikuyu society from the elite to KAU moderates, through to Mau Mau militants. There were differences of emphasis, but in ideological terms there was little to separate the most moderate KAU official from the Mau Mau militant. The differences of motive and class interest were not articulated through political objectives but through the means to be used to realize them. What separated moderates and militants were the tactics to be deployed in the pursuit of what were perceived as common objectives.

Of course the difference over tactics reflected profoundly conflicting interests within Kikuyu society. Those who had something of a stake in the status quo decided on a moderate course of action and in the end looked upon the eruption of armed resistance as a greater threat than that constituted by the colonial system. Those who had little to lose were drawn towards radical solutions and many were prepared to fight. But militant resistance was not translated into a coherent political perspective. As a result the organizational independence of Mau Mau coexisted with an ideological convergence with the more moderate elements. The history of nationalist politics shows that without an independent ideological perspective militant plebeian nationalists are inevitably outflanked by the moderate middle-class wing of a movement. The Irish civil war, leading to the defeat of those who wanted to carry on the fight, provides an instructive point of reference for the subject of our study.

The ambiguous relationship of Mau Mau leaders with Kenyatta is clearly reflected in the memoirs of Bildad Kaggia, one of the most far-sighted of the militant nationalists. Kaggia emphasizes the independent role of Mau Mau but at the same time concedes that 'although it was not under Kenyatta's control "the Mau Mau" movement looked upon Kenyatta as the national leader'.[34] Kaggia and his comrades certainly looked upon Kenyatta with contempt. But, although they put pressure on him behind the scenes they failed to challenge him in public. As a result it was Kenyatta's political authority that influenced the Kikuyu masses even when others were doing the fighting. Kenyatta may have lost control but he continued to personify the common objective of freedom for the Kikuyu people. This was a fatal weakness of Mau Mau.

The weakness of political coherence should not obscure the important achievements of the Mau Mau leadership. In contrast to general experience in colonial Africa the mass movement emerged with its own plebeian leadership. This represented a major innovation in the history of Kenyan nationalism. With Mau Mau, for the first time the mass movement acted independently of the educated middle-class leadership. Consequently, here was a mass movement not susceptible to cooptation. The colonial administration had no choice but to destroy it. The growth of Mau Mau can be seen not merely as the result of the strength of the mass movement but also as a symptom of the *weakness* of the middle-class moderate nationalists. A central theme of colonial policy in the subsequent period was to make sure that this would never happen in the future.

Maina-wa-Kinyatti has referred to Mau Mau as 'the peak of African anti-colonial politics in Kenya'.[35] In one sense this is obviously true. From our perspective it is not only the peak but more significantly the only period during which the middle-class politicians lost control over the mass movement. However, since the mass movement never developed its own distinct political perspective it was always possible for someone like Kenyatta to re-establish control at a later date. How that was realized is the subject of the next three chapters.

Reflections on Mau Mau

Considerable controversy surrounds the discussion on Mau Mau. Unfortunately the debate is often devoid of empirical research and rigorous analysis, often consisting of abstract counterpositions of different 'models' of the movement. As noted previously, there has been a dominant tendency

to read history backwards and to transform a contradictory social movement into a coherent institution with procedures and ideology. This
approach permeates Donald Barnett's work, which endows Mau Mau
with a sophisticated system of organization and a hierarchy of control.[36]
All that is missing is a constitution and a book of accounts. Our discussion of the Rift Valley shows a different picture. The movement was
essentially an ad hoc response to changing conditions. There are discernible patterns of organization but the movement was *influenced* rather than
controlled by leaders from Nairobi or elsewhere. Communication was
based on a network of informal ties rather than on a formal system.

Interpretations which portray Mau Mau as a centrally organized institution find their strongest support on the level of ideology. All sections of
the movement articulated a similar ideology. Public pronouncements
and petitions used similar language and put forward shared objectives
whether from Nairobi, Nyeri or Elburgon. This was not the product of
centralized leadership but rather born of a common experience of economic insecurity, land hunger, a feeling of frustration born of racial
oppression and resentment of the Kikuyu establishment. These sentiments developed spontaneously; nobody had to teach a Kikuyu squatter
or a shantytown dweller to hate the colonial police or the Kikuyu
authorities.

However, an emphasis on shared ideology risks obscuring the differential element in the experience. The main catalysts behind the explosion
were the unmediated tensions that prevailed in Nairobi and the European settled areas in the Rift Valley. In these regions tensions were
always liable to boil over into conflict. There were important sources of
tensions in the Kikuyu Reserves too, the study of which lies outside the
focus of this study.

The central weakness of existing interpretations of Mau Mau is a
crude fascination with institutional and cultural continuity. Colonial
officials persistently sought clues about Mau Mau in traditional Kikuyu
religion. This emphasis was carried on by scholars in the 1960s and
1970s. The colonial administration can be excused its obsession with
rituals and oaths, but serious scholars should be expected to look beyond
surface appearances and examine the forces beneath. The rituals and
oaths used by the movement had similarities with past customs. This is
only to be expected; established cultural idiom tends to become part of a
system of communication and mobilization in most political movements.
However, it is unlikely that an investigation of the cultural idiom can
unravel the social relations that have come to shape political developments. Mau Mau cannot be seen as a more extensive or even more
radical use of past oaths and rituals. To develop our understanding of the
subject matter we have to pinpoint the situations in which these oaths
were used. And even a limited knowledge of the key events shows that the

context in which the rituals were applied marked a fundamental departure from the past. Elements of continuity in cultural form are subservient to dislocation and disruption.

The significance of oathing lay not in the ritual but in the existence of a widespread social consensus. As long as this consensus prevailed the oath could symbolize a unity of purpose. It was not the oaths that drove squatters into battle but a determination to fight. Behind the ritual lay an entirely secular purpose. While the social consensus persisted, the government's counter-oath campaign was doomed to failure. Its mistaken premise was the need to fight some mystical power and not the hatred that was a response to social injustice. R. Buijtenhuijs seeks refuge in the other world when he argues that the 'Mau Mau initiates aimed at a revival of Kikuyu culture'.[37] The peasants and workers who fought and died did so not for the sake of culture but to cement a unity of purpose. Buijtenhuijs confuses the symbol of unity with the social consensus that was forged in the heat of a real life struggle. Inevitably, when the movement was defeated, no one had any inhibitions about breaking past oaths. Not because the oaths had lost their mystical force but because the social consensus behind the movement had broken down!

The preoccupation with Kikuyu values is based on the simplistic formula that because Mau Mau was primarily based on the Kikuyu it had something to do with that people's culture. This procedure is scrupulously followed by Bethwell Ogot in his study of Mau Mau songs. Not surprisingly Ogot discovers that Kikuyu songs express Kikuyu values.[38] Recently the approach has been used by Kenyan historians to dismiss Mau Mau as a narrow tribalist affair.[39] The aim of this school of thought is to dismiss the nationalist dimension of Mau Mau. Its reasoning is shallow and superficial. No nationalist movement develops evenly among all the constituent peoples of a nation. Mau Mau can no more be dismissed as non-nationalist because it was based on the Kikuyu than German nationalism can be caricatured as a Prussian affair.

Although Mau Mau was primarily Kikuyu, it was not a tribalist movement. The emergence of Mau Mau was restricted to certain sections of Kikuyu society. Colonial society had stimulated the development of social differentiation, as the following report of the Kiambu District Commissioner in 1941 makes clear:

> It is a fact that hundreds possibly even thousands, of acres have changed hands by 'irredeemable sale' during the past 15 or 16 years, and that most of this has gone into the hands of a very few people, including Chiefs, Tribunal Elders and the educated minority . . . the landless class is springing up in the reserve at a far greater pace than is healthy.[40]

Even in the Highlands, where the Kikuyu community was far more homogeneous than in the Reserves, social differentiation had marked political effects. Support for the movement was concentrated on the farms, most of the Kikuyu in the small townships stayed on the sidelines. And as we have argued the activist core of the movement had a clearly defined social background.

But if Mau Mau was not tribalist, was it a nationalist movement? Maina-wa-Kinyatti is the main exponent of the thesis that Mau Mau was an anti-imperialist nationalist movement. Unfortunately his arguments are a mirror-image of the culturalist/Kikuyu nationalist thesis. Whereas they see only continuity of culture, Kinyatti depicts Mau Mau as the culmination of resistance movements stretching back to the nineteenth century, arguing that: 'It is evident that resistance movements since the 19th century progressed from lower to higher levels of organization and political awareness culminating in the Mau Mau armed confrontation'.[41]

If Mau Mau is simply more of the same, then the distinct character of the movement is lost. And the act of 'resistance' abstracted from specific social experience does not on its own make a movement nationalist or anti-imperialist. In the end Kinyatti cannot sustain his argument except by pointing to statements and songs of Mau Mau teachers. Whereas Ogot uses songs as evidence of cultural continuity, Kinyatti uses the same procedure to prove a continuity of anti-imperialist resistance. Before protest could turn into an anti-colonial movement it had to go through important experiences. In the Rift Valley, the Olenguruone affair politicized and nationalized the perspective of the squatter movement. The squatter agitation of 1946–47 brought squatters into close proximity with urban militants, a process that transformed what was hitherto an agrarian movement. Through this interaction the nationalist movement also changed. The squatter constituency exerted a radical influence upon it. The decisive development was of course the split with moderate nationalism. This was a major break with past forms of nationalist politics and endowed Mau Mau with its radical impulse.

With Mau Mau, a truly radical nationalist movement emerged. Because of its sudden break with middle-class nationalism, Mau Mau failed to develop a distinct political programme and an ideology. Even nationalism as a principle remained diffuse and ill-defined. The aim of most activists was winning access to land. Kikuyu squatters fought and died for land and not for some abstract conception of nationhood.

Although overwhelmingly Kikuyu in composition, Mau Mau cannot be construed as a tribalist project. Certainly the evidence in the Rift Valley shows that Mau Mau was able to win support from other ethnic groups. The authorities, and particularly the police, were rightly concerned that Mau Mau would gain adherents among non-Kikuyu inhabitants of the forests around the European settled areas. The involvement of Maasai and Dorobo in Mau Mau shows that what was important was not tribe but the common experience of life in the forests in the European settled areas.

G.A. Skipper's November 1951 report on the Shabaltarakwa Forest Area ('the place of many cedars') adjoining Olenguruone Settlement provides evidence that ex-forest squatters dismissed for Mau Mau offences from the Elburgon area were able to find a haven with Maasai residents.[42] In 1953, a report of the Londiani Forest Division Intelligence Committee shows that Mau Mau had mixed ethnic support. Thus on 16 March 1953, a mixed force of Kikuyu and Maasai freed eight prisoners held by the Forest Department at Kiptunga.[43] According to the report, 'the Dorobo of the Likia area are not to be trusted'. One Dorobo man, Chertue arap Serembu, was arrested for collecting funds which were obtained from Nandi and Dorobo residents in North and South Tinderet. The report notes that Mau Mau has 'spread into the Maasai tribe'.[44]

In the end the colonial authorities succeeded in preventing the spread of Mau Mau in any significant sense to non-Kikuyu ethnic groups. That is a testimony to their strength rather than the inherent Kikuyuness of Mau Mau. Certainly the evidence for Nakuru District shows that Mau Mau had considerable potential for gaining support among non-Kikuyu people in the forest. The common experience of being part of an outlaw community in the forests overrode ethnic suspicion. The concerted government policy of breaking up this community of interest shows that the colonial authorities had something very real to fear: that was the transformation of a radical nationalist movement into one that operated on a truly national scale.

Notes

1. See Central Province Annual Report, 1947, p. 1.
2. Berman (1976), p. 171.
3. Arden-Clarke (1958), p. 50.
4. Rosberg and Nottingham (1966), p. 267.
5. *ibid.*, p. 214.
6. Interview with Onesmus Gachoka, 10 May 1972
7. DC, Nyandarua, T.C. 6/10, Meat Control Laikipia. Butcheries, M.C. Benson to D.C. Rumuruti, 16 July 1944.
8. It is interesting to note that the majority of KAU officials interviewed were educated at the Africa Inland Mission School at Kijabe.
9. Laikipia District Annual Report, 1949, p. 10.
10. Interview with Mirala Ndungu. It appears from reports that business related matters were often discussed at KAU branch meetings. The following report of a KAU meeting held at Eldoret is typical: 'A man called Samuel Kimothio from Nairobi was introduced. He said that he was Chairman of the Kenya African Livestock Association and

that a meeting was to be held at Eldoret to attract members to the Association'. At a subsequent meeting of the branch, ten Kikuyu members paid 50 shillings each for shares in this business venture. See KNA, DC, UG 4/1, Monthly Labour Reports, Intelligence Report by Labour Officer. November 1950.

11. KNA, DC, UG 5/1, Associations no. 48, J. Kuria to DC Eldoret, 1 December 1947.

12. PC, NKU: DO Molo. Associations (no file number), Monthly Report October 1947.

13. KNA, PC, NKU 2/840, Labour Officers' Reports, no. 1, Labour Department, Thomson's Falls to Labour Commissioner, 22 July 1946.

14. KNA, DC, UG 5/1, Associations no. 131, Demesi, Secretary KAU to DC Eldoret, 25 May 1950.

15. Interview with Njoroge Kagunda, 6 April 1972. Mathu, Thuku, and Gicheru were all prominent moderate Kikuyu politicians and members of the Kikuyu 'establishment'.

16. KNA, Lab 9/320, RLO. Aberdare District Council, no. 30, Labour Officer, Thomson's Falls to Labour Commissioner, 22 August 1946.

17. *ibid.*, no. 33, Labour Commissioner to Labour Officer, Thomson's Falls, 19 September 1946. A year later Johnson Keiya was appointed to the newly established African Advisory Council.

18. KNA, Lab 5/1, Intelligence Reports 1945–48 no. 64F, Report of meeting of KAU at Subukia, 25 August 1946. That this KAU intervention was not an isolated case can be gauged from the following observation in the Nakuru Labour Officer's Intelligence Report for August 1946: 'The Labour Officer is in constant touch with Mr. Johnson Keiya . . . he appears appreciative and understanding and much may be achieved in labour conditions generally in this district by working with this organization'. See *ibid.*

19. KNA, Lab 3/41, Squatters Complaints no. 77A, KAU meeting at Naivasha. Police report, 17 November 1946.

20. KNA, Lab 9/340, R.L.O. Standstill Order no. 25, Hyde-Clark to F.W. Carpenter, DC. Nakuru, 30 October 1946.

21. KNA, DC, UG 4/1, Monthly Labour Reports no.1, Monthly Labour Report of Labour Officer Eldoret, February 1944.

22. Nakuru District Annual Report, 1948.

23. Nakuru District Annual Report, 1944.

24. Molo Labour Office (Molo Lab. O.), File on Associations 12/5, Summary of Intelligence Reports, May 1950.

25. One sees a parallel takeover of the Nairobi branch. See Furedi (1973).

26. Interview with Onesmus Gachoka, 10 May 1972.

27. Interview with Dedan Kibe.

28. Interview with Thuo Kigera, 19 April 1972.

29. Rudé (1970), p. 20.

30. KNA, DC, NKU 2/385, Labour Department – Monthly Reports, Report of Labour Officer, Nakuru, June 1951.

31. Murray-Brown (1972), p. 242.

32. *ibid.*, p. 243.

33. DC, Nyandarua, Lab 27/3 vol. 3, R.L.O. 1937. Attestation of Squatters. Monthly Report. July 1948.

34. Kaggia (1975), p. 113.

35. Maina wa Kinyatti (1977).

36. Barnett and Njama (1966).

37. Buijtenhuijs (1982) p. 80.

38. Ogot (1977).

39. See Kipkorir (1977).

40. Kimabu District Annual Report, 1941.

41. Maina wa Kinyatti (1977), p. 309.

42. PC, RVP, For. 13/5/20/1/Vol. 1, Forests. Mau Forests. Chapaltarakwa no. 192, C.A. Skipper, D.O. Special Duties to PC, RVP, 3 November 1951.
43. KNA, DC, NKU 2/454, Intelligence Reports, C.H. Creswell D.O., Londioni Forest Division Intelligence Committee, Summary for fortnight ending 25 March 1953.
44. *ibid.*

Part II

Part II

Introduction

It is customary to separate the pre-1955 period of Kenya's history from the subsequent phase, which is usually labelled 'the road to independence'. The first period is usually treated as a matter for history while the post-Mau Mau era is discussed as a subject for politics. But although the defeat of the revolt represents a major disruption of previous trends, there is no fundamental break with the post-Mau Mau era. The Emergency and the campaign of repression could not, on their own provide the solution to the issues raised by Mau Mau. Its long-term effect was to create the conditions in which the colonial administration could implement a strategy for stabilization.

As argued in Chapter 6, the British Colonial Office understood that after Mau Mau there could be no return to the past. The question was no longer whether Kenya would become independent but when, and under what conditions. It was clear that changes had to be made in the forms of political relations through which the colony was governed. It was also evident that British socio-economic interests could not for long be preserved through white minority rule. The declaration of a State of Emergency can be seen as a first step in the construction of a system of political institutions through which the existing social relations could be perpetuated in the post-colonial era.

The key element in the government's post-Emergency strategy was to provide the conditions for the emergence of a moderate nationalist leadership. The crushing of Mau Mau provided an opportunity for the emergence of a moderate nationalist option. But that option had first to be created. The nationalist parties that arose in the post-emergency period owed their existence above all to the colonial regime. These parties had no historical roots, nor did they evolve from any manifestation of grassroots pressure. It was on the initiative of the colonial administration that the new political system was born.

To be sure there existed a mass constituency for nationalist politics.

The Emergency could repress but not eliminate the yearning for national independence. However, the new political parties did not emerge in response to these sentiments. Rather they can be seen as external impositions on the African population. These were ready-made parties and ready-made representatives. With the destruction of the Mau Mau alternative, such ready-made representatives were to enjoy a monopoly over the African political constituency.

The evolution of African political representation was carefully regulated and monitored by the colonial administration. The emphasis was on piecemeal change through which individual African leaders could be trained into their role. Under the Emergency all African political parties were banned. The suppression of parties allowed the government to work on individual Africans, who through cooptation could be groomed as worthy representatives. This focus on individual leaders was part of the policy of creating an African political elite, an elite whose allegiance would be to the prevailing institutions rather than to any mass constituency. This individualization of African politics was seen as a way of insulating politicians from the popular aspirations of change.

The promotion of individual political leaders coincided with the construction of a framework of regional representation. The elevation of local, regional and ethnic representation was rightly seen as a powerful antidote to radical nationalism. Thus the foundation of the new political system was a parochial one and the new African leaders were encouraged to become regional representatives.

Since the 1920s the government had sought to restrict African political participation to the level of local politics. Africans could participate in and elect representatives to the Local Native Councils. However, participation and representation was denied on the national and even the provincial level. For a brief period after the Second World War African parties were allowed to operate on a national scale. With the ascendancy of the radical nationalism of Mau Mau, the government was forced to criminalize African political activity altogether. The Emergency put an end to this brief phase of national political organization.

With the military defeat of Mau Mau, the colonial government turned its energy towards the creation of a new system of African representation. In June 1955 it announced a partial lifting of the ban on African political activity. Africans were now allowed to form political associations, though only on a district basis. Such associations were not allowed in Central Province – here loyalist Kikuyu could only be nominated to an Advisory Council. Clearly, the aim of the policy was to consolidate regional/tribal affiliations and to isolate the Kikuyu people from the emerging political institutions. The blocking of the creation of a nationalist dimension was central to the administration's policy. When in December 1955, C.M.G. Argwings-Kodhek proposed to launch the Kenya African National

Congress, cutting across regional lines, the government refused to register the party on the grounds that colony-wide associations could not yet be permitted.

In 1957 elections of individual African leaders to the Legislative Council took place. This extension in African participation was carefully vetted to ensure that the administration remained firmly in control of the proceedings. The African elected members were essentially a collection of individuals with no national movement to back them up.

The 1957 elections were decisive in influencing the subsequent development of Kenyan politics. They acted as a catalyst for the establishment of district associations that were seen as vehicles for individual and group self-advancement. Consequently, local machine politics emerged, consolidating regional affiliations. It is at this stage that ethnic affiliations and a regional outlook became important influences on African politics. For the administration, district associations were relatively easy to control and district commissioners played a 'helpful' role in assisting their formation.

The administration's life was also made easier by the individualization of African politics. The new African members of the Legislative Council were a collection of individuals without connection to any mass movement and could thus be easily influenced and manipulated. In such conditions, personal rivalries among them could flourish and the adminstration had little difficulty in playing off one against the other.

By the time the ban on national parties was lifted a new system of African politics had been created. A new group of African elite politicians, whose position depended on regional links and their association with the colonial state, was ready to assume control of national politics in 1960. Many of those detained during the Emergency, such as Jomo Kenyatta, could now be allowed to return to politics. Their presence was necessary to endow the new political parties with legitimacy.

The two new national parties, the Kenya African National Union (KANU) and the Kenya African Democratic Union (KADU), represented contending regional alliances of African elites. The beneficiaries of the colonial system, joined by respected ex-detainees, ran the parties. KANU was based on the three largest ethnic groups – Kikuyu, Luo, Kamba – in the colony while KADU drew support from the smaller ethnic groups such as the Kalenjin and the coastal groups. As such, KADU had insubstantial African political roots, but the Asian and European communities helped get it off the ground. In their eyes KADU was an insurance policy against the more unpredictable KANU.

With the return of prominent ex-detainees, KANU was able to establish itself as the voice of the African masses. It was the only legal party with links with the pre-1952 nationalist movement and was therefore in a position to act as the natural voice of national independence. In a significant sense KANU was very different from the old nationalist movement. It did not emerge out of a popular movement. On the contrary, it was the product of the new colonial political system: a successful product in the sense that it became the acceptable vehicle for the realization of national independence or *Uhuru*.

It is generally conceded that KADU was very much a European creation. It became a useful instrument for pursuing the policy of divide and rule. In contrast to KADU, KANU is often portrayed as more or less the authentic voice of African nationalism. As we argue in Chapter 7, KANU was not immune from the influence of the colonial administration. The colonial state worked hand-in-glove with the KANU leaderships to contain any manifestation of radical nationalism. African politicians with radical credentials were isolated in an attempt to prevent them from winning influence inside KANU.

Thus Bildad Kaggia, an ex-detainee with strong links with Mau Mau, came under pressure when elected as chairman of the Naivasha branch of KANU in 1962. KANU headquarters refused to accept his election on the grounds that his home was not in Naivasha. A few weeks later the Assistant Registrar of Societies warned Kaggia not to call himself chairman of KANU. In the end Kaggia's national reputation forced his opponents to back down but other ex-detainees were not so fortunate.[1] The repression of radical nationalism coincides with the consolidation of the Kenyatta leadership. This, the main theme of Chapter 7, resulted in the creation of a new political balance of forces inside the nationalist movement.

When Kenya was granted independence on 12 December 1963, the new African nationalist leadership was well placed to deal with radical opponents of the post-colonial system. In November 1964, KADU voluntarily dissolved and merged with KANU. By March 1966 Kenyatta was ready to crack down on those who still upheld the radical nationalist tradition, and KANU was purged. A group of radical nationalist politicians formed the Kenya People's Union (KPU) and until it was banned in October 1969 it attempted to build an alternative movement. As we argue in Chapter 8, the KPU was easily contained, and its demise marks the end of the era initiated by the Mau Mau revolt.

The creation of the new African nationalist movement in the 1950s was paralleled by the stabilization of the economic position of the indigenous capitalist class. Land consolidation in Central Province benefited the landowning collaborators. As M.P.K. Sorrenson argues, the colonial administration hoped that this class 'would be too interested in farming to be seduced by Kikuyu politicians into further subversion'.[2] In other parts of Kenya the same process was under way. By the time *Uhuru* had arrived it was clear that the African nationalist leadership would fiercely resist any attempt to change the prevailing socio-economic institutions.

The ethnic factor

Ethnicity or tribalism is one of the most widely discussed topics in the literature on the sociology of African politics. Although the administrators of Kenya were consummate practitioners of the policy of divide and rule, ethnicity only emerges as a political factor in the 1950s. In the White Highlands, an area of heterogeneous ethnic mix, there is evidence of ethnic identification throughout the period under consideration. However, it is only in the late 1950s that tribalism emerges as an important political influence.

The evidence from our investigation suggests that tribalism is not the natural or inevitable consequence of ethnic identification. In the case of Kenya, a tribalist consciousness was strengthened through the implementation of policies designed to fragment nationalist politics. The expulsion of Kikuyu squatters became an invitation for other ethnic groups to take their place. When Kikuyu squatters returned to the White Highlands they were portrayed as intruders on the welfare of other ethnic groups. These local tensions were part of a national pattern. What colonial policies achieved was to create the impression that the interests of one ethnic group could only be enforced at the expense of another.

The transformation of ethnic consciousness into a divisive regional outlook required the intervention of the new breed of nationalist politicians. The foundation of the new African political elite was the district.

The advancement of political careers now depended on the promotion of local claims. Increasingly such claims took precedence in a free for all for the control of scarce resources. As we suggest in Chapter 8, the tribal appeal became the strong card played by the Kenyatta regime in the attempt to prevent ex-squatters from lining up with the KPU. Tribalism, like the new nationalist leadership, did not spring from below. It was imposed on African society and required the destruction of radical alternatives before it could become a powerful force.[3]

Notes

1. Kaggia (1975), p. 192.
2. Sorrenson (1967), p. 201.
3. Throup places an exaggerated emphasis on the ethnic factor in history. He writes that only 'a few administrators, such as Askwith, recognised that most Nairobi Africans were still enmeshed in ethnic rivalries and were not yet ready to enter the democratic multi-tribal future espoused by the Kenya African Union and the African Advisory Council'. See Throup (1987), p. 175. According to Throup's analysis ethnicity is an original sin rather than a product of colonial history. From this perspective, the 'tribal particularism' of Africans is the obstacle to the emergence of a nationalist movement

Introduction

and the colonial government is a neutral observer.

Ethnic rivalries among Africans in Nairobi did not emerge spontaneously. For example during the first mass protest movement in Nairobi in 1922, the East African Association was able to mobilize Africans across ethnic lines.

During the trials that took place after the 1922 disturbances, we find that the composition of those arrested corresponded to the ethnic make up of the African communities in Nairobi. See *East African Standard*, 1 April 1922. Writing of Harry Thuku, the leading figure in the protest, one missionary noted: 'Thuku has created tremendous enthusiasm, not only in Kikuyu but in Kavirondo and amongst Mohammedans as well as Christians'. See *Oldham Papers*, Box 236, Hooper to Oldham, 4 March 1922.

To prevent the emergence of an African nationalist response in Nairobi the government encouraged the ethnic fragmentation of the population. Nevertheless even in the late 1950s Luo politicians were able to win the support of Kikuyu activists. It is from the late 1950s onwards that ethnicity emerges as a dominant influence in Kenyan politics.

154

Six

The Administration Takes & Loses the Initiative

In the short run the military defeat of Mau Mau allowed the colonial administration to take the initiative. More specifically, in the Rift Valley, the European settler appeared to be the master of the situation. The eviction of the Kikuyu community from the Rift Valley had destroyed the squatter movement. As far as the European settler was concerned the problem of the squatter had been solved. European farmers could now run their enterprises as they pleased – they could ignore past traditions and hire agricultural labourers on terms of their own choosing. At least this was the theory. In reality matters were more complicated. The special conditions created through Emergency regulations allowed for the strict implementation of European interests. However these conditions could not last for ever. Sooner or later Emergency regulations would have to be rescinded and the question was, would stability prevail in the post-Emergency period?

The defeat of Mau Mau could not obscure the underlying problems raised by the revolt. The explosive character of Mau Mau had shown that changes had to be made. As a European settler-dominated colony, Kenya had no future. Nor was Kenya viable as an independent white-minority dominated country along South African lines. Even in the midst of the Emergency, far-sighted officials knew that Kenya had to be decolonized. The Report of the East Africa Royal Commission in 1955 confirmed the necessity for change and argued that the maintenance of racial land barriers was incompatible with the development of a modern economy.[1] The attention of the colonial government turned towards implementing a form of change that would cause minimal disruption to the existing social order. This required cultivating moderate African negotiating partners who could be trusted with preserving Kenya's socio-economic institutions.

Mau Mau had shown that moderate African leaders lacked credibility with the masses. To reverse this trend the colonial administration had to neutralize militant nationalists and construct a viable moderate African leadership. It was these political considerations that motivated the colonial government's policy of controlled decolonization.

The controlled reconstitution of the Kikuyu community

The eviction of the Kikuyu squatter was a short-term expedient essential for the establishment of law and order. The colonial administration knew that it needed a longer-term strategy for the maintenance of stability. The solution to unrest in the White Highlands was seen in terms of 'closer administration' of Africans living in the European settled areas. Under the guidance of the Provincial Commissioner of the Rift Valley Province, a new system of administration was established that relied on a group of African intermediaries who would establish a line of communication between the people and government.

The screening camps, which had hitherto been used to interrogate Kikuyu suspects, were turned into chiefs' centres. The Kikuyu staff of the screening camps were given new roles as chiefs, elders and tribal policemen. By April 1956, chiefs' centres were established at Subukia, Dundori, Bahati, Njoro, Elburgon and Londiani in Nakuru District.[2] As the Administrative Instructions to Chiefs in Settled Areas make clear, the main emphasis of the administrative network was law and order:

> The primary purpose of Chiefs in settled and Urban areas is, in conjunction with the Administration and Police to maintain law and order and good government and generally to keep the African population contented and law abiding.
>
> In order to do this Chiefs will . . . Get to know all Africans and employers in their areas and encourage them to report the presence of strangers or anyone about whom they have any suspicions. Any irregularity detected by a chief should be reported to the employers in the first instance . . .[3]

In fact the policy of closer administration was a euphemism for closer control and intelligence-gathering.

The speedy establishment of the chiefs' centres reflected the concern of the administration for the future. They were instituted with the knowledge that many of the ex-squatters would have to be re-employed on the farms since non-Kikuyu agricultural workers had not proved a satisfactory substitute. During the years 1952–56, European farmers were faced with a serious shortage of agricultural labour. In 1955, there was a shortage of 10,000 agricultural workers in Nakuru and Naivasha alone. The Labour Commissioner noted that 'the difficulty in obtaining labour, coupled with a general dissatisfaction over its quality, resulted in a growing demand for the return of Kikuyu workers'.[4] And, he minuted:

It is doubtful whether Naivasha and Laikipia will ever have enough farm labour until Kikuyu are allowed to return. Certainly the higher altitude farms of the Kinangop must have Kikuyu. If the security authorities are confident that sufficient safeguards are practicable in the return of screened Kikuyu, I can from the labour point of view only welcome the project.[5]

European settlers echoed the Labour Department and urged the return of Kikuyu labourers.

The government was prepared to allow the return of ex-squatters under a strict programme of security surveillance. In 1955, pilot schemes to resettle Kikuyu workers in the White Highlands were started. Every Kikuyu had to be checked and cleared by Special Branch,[6] their daily activities in the European areas were severely restricted, and they could only be employed on monthly contracts. These measures could only work so long as Emergency regulations were in force and only so long as a relatively small number of Kikuyu were resettled. In August 1955, the War Council instructed the Provincial Commissioner to develop a longer-term policy for controlling the flow of Kikuyu into the Rift Valley. The establishment of chiefs' centres was only one aspect of the new long-term policy of control; a system of permits and labour exchanges designed to curtail the movement of Kikuyu was also put forward.[7]

In 1956, the 'Return of Kikuyu' schemes were stepped up. The large influx of ex-squatters – up to the end of March 1957, 10,000–12,000 Kikuyu entered Nakuru alone – had a stabilizing effect on the labour market.[8] By September 1957 the Labour Department noted that 'there are . . . signs that the demands for Kikuyu labour are easing'.[9] It was also noted that the settlement of Kikuyu ex-squatters had created a degree of unemployment among workers from other ethnic groups. Six months later, in March 1958, the problem of unemployment among Africans could no longer be ignored. Swiftly, the Labour Department moved to end the further importation of Kikuyu labour into the Highlands.[10]

The creation of a community of migrants and vagrants

Despite all the precautions taken, the administration lost control over the process of resettlement because it had failed to appreciate the massive changes brought about by the Emergency. The Emergency did not provide the foundations for long-term social stability; on the contrary it intensified the previous patterns of social conflict. The mass eviction of Kikuyu from the Highlands had an unforeseen effect on the labour market: a potential reserve army of labour had always existed in the colony, but in the 1950s this potential became actual.

The consolidation of land in the Kikuyu regions increased the number of landless peasants. They were forced into the labour market and joined by evicted squatters and Africans from other parts of Kenya. At the same time, Emergency conditions and subsequent labour shortages speeded up the mechanization and rationalization of European agriculture. Many European settlers invested capital in machinery and tried to operate with a reduced labour force. As the Labour Commissioner remarked in 1958, there were few new openings for the unemployed:

> The surplus of labour helped employers to exercise greater selectivity in engaging workers; at the same time labour forces were reduced and increased output was often achieved from the smaller and better supervised, number of employees. In agriculture, particularly, there was a trend to longer working hours . . . the level of productivity was usually maintained with the smaller labour forces employed and in some cases even increased through better supervision and incentive schemes. Mechanization also played its part in increasing productivity.[11]

The falling labour requirement of European settlers was not the only problem. The Emergency had destroyed the balance of labour between the settled areas and the African land units. Thousands of Africans were recruited to replace the evicted squatters – thereby expanding the labour force – precisely at a time when the number of unemployed was about to escalate. It is ironic that the administration remained largely oblivious to the long-term problems reflected in this trend. There were a few officials who saw the danger signs. J. Webster, Secretary of the War Council, warned the Provincial Commissioner of the Rift Valley in May 1957 along the following lines:

> Almost the greatest security danger in the Colony at present is the large number of Kikuyu living in a discontented state in the Kikuyu Reserve. The trouble which would arise if these Kikuyu remained unemployed would inevitably spread to the RVP. It is therefore important to the security of the Colony as a whole that as many unemployed Kikuyu as possible be placed in employment so long as local security conditions are not thereby damaged.[12]

Webster's solution was unrealistic – the limit of the European farmers' labour requirement had been reached.

The growth of unemployment, particularly among the Kikuyu, destroyed the calculations of the administration. There could be no smooth process of resettlement in the post-Emergency period. By 1958, large groups of Kikuyu were travelling from farm to farm looking for work. The response of the colonial administration was to arrest them and send them back to the Reserves. Nevertheless the flow of Kikuyu migrants continued unabated. The administration reacted by stepping up the eviction of jobless Kikuyu. When labour officials in Kiambu complained about the indiscriminate deportation of Kikuyu from Nakuru District, the Provincial Commissioner retorted:

> The answer is quite clear. No unemployed Kikuyu, Embu and Meru (or members of any other tribe) can be classed as a *permanent resident of any Settled Area District*. If such a person is convicted of vagrancy he can be repatriated to his Native Land Unit regardless of how long he has lived away from it.[13]

Detention and eviction were not effective deterrents to the flow of Africans into the Rift Valley. The Emergency had in effect created a permanent group of migrants or, in official terms, vagrants.

Matters came to a head with the lifting of Emergency Regulations in 1960. Tens of thousands of landless and unemployed Africans flooded into the Rift Valley searching for work. An intelligence report for Molo in January noted that 'some farms report as many as 25 persons per day calling in search of employment'.[14] By this time the reaction of local officials was little short of panic. A circular issued by the District Commissioner of Nakuru in February 1960 told all employers about the gravity of the situation. In order to reduce the floating population of Kikuyu, farmers were told to refuse to employ anyone seeking work on their premises and to hire only through labour exchanges. Employers were also advised that the Vagrancy Ordinance, the Trespass Ordinance and the Control of Africans By-law (within Townships) 'would no doubt be of great assistance in preventing unemployed persons from remaining in the District.'[15]

The circular represented a vain attempt to impose order on an inherently unstable situation. Any remaining illusions regarding administrative consolidation in the post-emergency period were shattered. The frustrated District Commissioner of Nakuru wrote, mixing his metaphors: 'It would seem, to the cynical, that the ball has gone round full circle and that we are back to where we started, a large surplus landless, unemployed population in the Central Province and even the most Micawber-like of us can hardly expect that this, in terms of time, does not spell trouble'.[16] The District Commissioner's sense of cyclical development betrayed him in one important respect – this was no return to 1952. Rather, the time had come for a complete overhaul of the colonial system.

The proletarianization of the squatter community

The Kikuyu ex-squatters who returned to the Rift Valley found that life on the farms had changed for the worse. The resident labour system, the

159

official term for squatting, was in decline. According to the 1958 agricultural census there were only 21,000 Africans on squatter contracts.[17] While this underestimates the numbers of hired squatters, it is indicative of the trend. The squatting system had become peripheral to agricultural employment in the Highlands. European farmers had no need for tenants – they wanted a steady pool of agricultural labourers. Only a handful of skilled men and old retainers were kept on squatter contracts. As one Labour Inspector reported: 'Inspections show there is little difference between wages paid to Resident labour and non Resident labourers as a rule farmers give Resident Labour contracts to their key men in the wish to attach them to the farm for a definite period.[18]

The majority of the Kikuyu ex-squatters who returned to the Highlands were put on monthly contracts. The large number of unemployed migrants restricted the bargaining power of monthly labourers. Their wages were low and the small plots of land they received in return for their work could meet only a small part of their subsistence requirements. Even the Labour Department was shocked by the low level of real wages. The Senior Labour Officer argued that the persistence of the existing wage structure was bound to have negative political consequences. He wrote in May 1960:

> I consider . . . the question of introducing machinery for minimum wages in rural areas is now becoming more urgent as the present position can be exploited by agitators and politicians, and in view of the distorted picture that employees have of the political situation there will certainly be an increase in labour unrest.[19]

Economic misery was compounded by racial oppression and the arbitrary application of European power. European farmers took advantage of the Emergency regulations and the threat of unemployment to reduce wages and to discipline their workers. An official of the Labour Department reported in February 1958:

> I was extremely perturbed and somewhat shocked at disclosures by the Police regarding labour conditions on a number of farms . . . Amongst the allegations made by the Police were that employers were guilty of malpractices in regard to squatter cultivation, that wages were not being paid when they were due, that gratuitous thrashings were being administered by employers, that in one instance the employer used a *posho* measure with a false bottom, and that in one case an African had been locked up with the employers dogs in a dog kennel when he had a difference of opinion with the employer.[20]

Officials were also concerned about wage reductions and the non-payment of wages. In 1959, the Labour Department was forced to initiate a campaign in Laikipia District to force European farmers to pay their labourers' wages.[21]

As the pressure of unemployment increased, wage reductions became the norm. One Labour Officer noted that in Ol Kalou, 'since Kikuyu have been returning to the district . . . there has been a gradual decline of the starting rate for labourers. At one time during the early months of the Emergency, the rate stood at 50/- per ticket, it is now 30/-'.[22] The steady process of impoverishment of the ex-squatters inevitably created resentment and discontent. Despite the threat of evictions, many of them felt they had no choice but to resist. They did not have much to lose by going on the offensive. From late 1958 onwards intelligence reports regularly note labour unrest on the farms.[23] In 1959 a spate of strikes broke out on the farms in Nakuru District and the District Emergency Committee (DEC) drew up contingency plans to deal with the threat of a general strike.[24] The spread from Kiambu into Nakuru District of the *Kiama Kiu Muingi*, a recently formed secret society, was a cause for further administrative alarm. Government *barazas* were held throughout the district and several suspects were swiftly repatriated.[25] The battle for the White Highlands resumed yet again.

Decolonization and counter-reform

The eruption of mass unrest in the Rift Valley threatened the orderly process of decolonization that had been worked out by the British Colonial Office. Although Mau Mau had been defeated militarily, the scale of the resistance had shown that a European settler-dominated Kenya was not viable. It was clear that the existing form of state structure could not guarantee stability; on the contrary it itself contributed to the build-up of tension and disaffection. Even at the height of the Emergency, plans were drawn up to share political power with African representatives. The Secretary of State for the Colonies, Oliver Lyttelton told Europeans at the time:

> Sixty thousand Europeans cannot expect to hold all the political power and to exclude Africans from the legislature and from the government. The end of that will be to build up pressure which will burst into rebellion and bloodshed. You are suspicious and critical of what you term in a pejorative sense 'Colonial Office rule'. When as a result of over conservative and traditional policies you provoke an explosion, you are not slow to ask the British Government and the Colonial Office . . . for troops; aeroplanes and money to suppress a rebellion. I warn you, that one day you will be let down and therefore besides force, which must be used and which we will provide, you must turn your minds to political reform and to measures which will gradually engage the consent and help of the governed.[26]

Through a series of constitutional arrangements stretching from the Lyttelton Constitution of 1954 to the Lancaster House Conference of 1960, a policy of gradual transfer of power was evolved. During this period of transition, the Colonial Office pursued the twin objectives of giving the European community sufficient time to adjust to African political advancement while grooming a moderate group of African politicians to run the future government.[27]

The opening-up of the White Highlands to Africans was one of the main concessions made to public opinion at this time. For the administration the opening up of the White Highlands was essentially a political problem. The resistance of the squatter movement and Mau Mau had forced the issue. But the administration could not be seen to make any concessions to this quarter. The government also had to assure European settlers that their future would not be threatened and obtain the cooperation of leading African politicians. In the end the government embarked on a policy of keeping concessions to a minimum – offering token gestures as a way of indicating that collaboration would be rewarded.

In 1958, Governor Sir Evelyn Baring was thinking in terms of allowing two or three 'exceptional' Africans to own land in the White Highlands. As he wrote to the Colonial Office, outlining the proposal, they would be:

> Exceptional non-European farmers capable of farming up to a European standard and perhaps capable also of maintaining a standard of life not far off that of many Europeans. Harry Thuku in the Kiambu district is an example, and there is a single Elgeyo in the edge of the Uasin Gishu Plateau.[28]

The Colonial Office encouraged this line of action, as the 'granting . . . [of] . . . a lease or two to non-Europeans would do more to see change to Africans than anything we can say.'[29]

However, this policy soon became difficult to 'sell', as African politicians could not afford to compromise themselves by a public acceptance of such token measures. Leading African politicians demanded more concessions regarding land policy and a faster pace of constitutional advance. The Kenya government was reluctant to announce officially its new land policy, to avoid crediting radical African pressure with extracting this concession. In contrast the Colonial Office wanted the announcement of the new policy to be made as soon as possible so as to maintain political initiative. In September 1959 J.L. Buist of the Colonial Office wrote:

> Frankly I think I would find it hard to advise any delay . . . If we leave it till January, there is the risk of our all being preoccupied with the constitutional issue; and the further risk that Mboya may refuse to bring his people to the table until some 'concession' of this kind is made. It would be very unfortunate to announce a new land policy, which could be interpreted as the result of pressure; it is much better to do so now and maintain the political initiative. . . If we are to try and

bring this off before the conference (thus strengthening African moderate opinion at a crucial time) we must act at once . . .[30]

A number of officials in Nairobi argued that the announcement should be delayed until the politicians around Tom Mboya (the most prominent politician not in detention) had moderated their demands. One official wrote to the Colonial Office:

> This is probably one of the most important policy decisions that has been made since Kenya was made a colony and it is important from the political point of view more than from any other . . . I believe that to publish the White Paper at the right moment might have the effect of reducing political tension and retaining some hope of survival of African and European Moderates . . .[31]

The vacillations over the announcement of the new land policy reflected the instability of the situation. The objective of political stability required that the colonial government maintain control over the whole process of transfer of power. To this end the government was prepared to take initiatives so as to pre-empt the emergence of radical opposition. The Governor of Kenya put the principal motivations behind the opening up of the White Highlands thus: 'We are encouraging change in order to forestall the type of sudden revolution which might do great economic harm to a country which must attract capital if it is to provide a livelihood for its large and growing African population'.[32]

This approach could only work if the Administration won the collaboration of African politicians. But too close an identification with the administration would have had the consequence of compromising the African negotiators. This put a degree of constraint on the subsequent negotiations.

The negotiations over the opening up of the White Highlands were restricted to a small circle of government officials, a few prominent African politicians, and representatives of European settlers. Although each group had its own particular objectives, all had a common interest in arriving at an arrangement that would keep the existing economic institutions intact. The agreement that was reached entirely excluded the Africans who worked in the Highlands from any future benefits. An ordinance introduced in October 1959 removed racial barriers to land ownership in the White Highlands and established 'good husbandry' as the sole criterion for land purchase. A Land Control Board was established to oversee inter-racial transfer of land. The criterion of 'good husbandry' and the procedures of the European-dominated Board meant that only a handful of rich Africans could have any hope of buying land in the Highlands.

Institutionalization of discontent

The proposed constitutional changes and the opening-up of the White Highlands provided a framework for decolonization. But whether this framework would prove viable depended on the ability of the state to contain mass unrest. During the years up to 1960 the existing Emergency regulations had sufficed to maintain political control. Political initiative and control were exercised through District Emergency Committees (DECs). These bodies, composed of local officials and settler representatives, sought to maintain social order and to ensure that once the Emergency was lifted stability would still prevail.

In Nakuru District, the progress of the recently established Nakuru District Congress Party was closely monitored by the DEC. This party, formed by Africans from Nakuru Town, projected a moderate constitutional perspective. The DEC noted that this party was 'responsible' and 'moderate' but nevertheless was anxious that it should not become active on the farms. It feared that political unrest there might throw the Nakuru District Congress off course. The influence of this party was insignificant until the second half of 1959. However, as the problems of unemployment and impoverishment began to preoccupy the Africans on the farms, many of them turned to the Congress.

In February 1960, the Congress carried out a successful recruitment campaign on the farms and was thus able to demonstrate the considerable influence that it had established outside Nakuru Town.

The sudden growth of the Nakuru District Congress on the farms was due to the need of African agricultural labourers for some sort of organization to defend them from wage reductions and growing unemployment. The involvement of a political organization in what the administration saw as the arena of 'industrial relations' was viewed by local officials with concern. The senior labour officer of the Highlands wrote in May 1960:

> The Nakuru District Congress and the Eldoret District Congress are taking an increasing interest in farm labour and are certainly persuading considerable numbers to lodge their complaints and alleged grievances with them. Despite the fact that the employees have to pay for this privilege they are reporting to these political organizations in increasing numbers and as a result are extremely truculent when returning to their employers and very often refuse to leave the farms.[33]

Local officials knew that they had nothing to fear from the Congress. However unrest on the farms was more unpredictable. The response of the administration was to establish an institutional framework for resolving conflict, the first of a number of attempts to contain class conflict. The administration at this time saw the answer in the establishment of moderate trade unions for agricultural workers. Ever since the early 1950s, Labour Department officials had been preparing for the eventual establishment of an agricultural union. In a circular issued by the Labour Department in January 1958 to European farmers, it was noted that the Plantation Workers International Federation had drawn up plans for the organization of agricultural and plantation workers in Kenya.[34] This circular was the prelude to a carefully orchestrated campaign designed to sell the union to European settlers.

The Senior Labour Officer more or less created the new union leader. He handpicked the union leadership and even took it upon himself to instruct the future General Secretary of the General Agricultural Workers Union (GAWU) on how to run a 'legitimate trade union'.[35] The Labour Commissioner was enthusiastic about this initiative and wrote:

> Thank you for this most interesting report which indicates how labour relations are liable to be bedevilled by current misconceptions on political issues. The sooner the interests of farm labour are represented by a registered trade union the better, and you should closely watch the intrusion of the Nakuru and Eldoret District Congress into labour matters and, if things are getting out of hand ask the P.C. to find out if the Registrar of Societies can do anything about it.
>
> Once the GAWU has obtained registration, you will stand more chance of prevailing upon its officials to give the correct advice to farm labour.[36]

The Labour Commissioner, Ian Husband, met with the leaders of the European farming community to ensure that the new union would be speedily recognized. By July 1960 he had received the consent of the employers. The recognition of GAWU by the employers was one of the fastest in the trade union history of Kenya if not of the world. The collaboration between employer and trade union was manifest by the end of the year. European farmers were busy collecting subscriptions for the union even though there was no formal agreement on the 'check off' system in existence.[37] The Special Branch was enthusiastic too – in September 1960 it reported that GAWU, the largest union in Nakuru District, had refused to join the countrywide strike of workers.[38]

The challenge from below

Herman Oduor, the General Secretary of GAWU, did his best to establish class peace. But the growing tide of unrest could not be held in check. Many workers took the objectives of the union at face value and began to demand action. By the end of 1960 the Nakuru District Commissioner had come to consider GAWU something of a mixed blessing:

> The formation and rise of the GAWU was a help in some ways but a hindrance in others. Under the wise leadership of Mr. Herman Oduor

it helped to bring home some of the economic facts of life to the workers, but on the other hand it tended to make the workers believe it was a repository for all their complaints, both real and imaginary.[35]

The growth of unemployment and of social tension simply overwhelmed GAWU and the local officials.

The debate on constitutional issues and decolonization had a strong impact on the consciousness of Africans living on the farms. Despite the carefully worded documents and the moderate phrases, they identified the new changes with opportunities for a better life. The discussion taking place in Nairobi was interpreted as a simple equation; freedom means land and jobs. The Lancaster House Conference of January 1960 was the first time the British government publicly declared its intention of handing over power to an African majority government. This announcement sparked off a massive flow of Kikuyu into the Highlands. Thousands of landless Kikuyu were establishing their claim for land after independence. Officials were surprised that large numbers of Kikuyu went so far as Uasin Gishu and Trans Nzoia, 'which are not traditional areas of employment for Kikuyu'.[40]

This great number of Kikuyu migrants only added to the already considerable reservoir of unemployed. The employment situation markedly deteriorated in 1960 as the Lancaster House discussion created a minor panic in the European community. Many European farmers ceased development activities on their farms and often reduced their labour force. Towards the end of the year a number of farmers, especially those from the Afrikaner community, decided to abandon their farms and leave Kenya. A special committee on this matter received information to the effect that by November 1960, 38 farmers in the Uasin Gishu, 28 in Trans Nzoia and 20 in the Ol Kalou area 'were either intending to leave after harvesting or had already left'.[41]

On the farms, the Kikuyu labourers tried to re-establish the way of life that they had known before the Emergency. Many ex-squatters returned to the areas in which they had resided before they were evicted from the Highlands. In this manner some of the old relations among squatters were resumed.[42] The rapid adjustment of the Kikuyu to life on the farms enabled them to maintain some degree of continuity with the squatter communities of the past. The significance of this process can be seen by the fact that many Kikuyu, who could not obtain any employment on the farms, were taken in and assisted by their ex-neighbours and relatives. The S.L.O. in his report for 1960 noted: 'The unemployment situation in the Province would have been more serious but for the custom of the African in providing hospitality to unemployed friends and relatives.'[43]

The growth of the nationalist parties

The success of decolonization depended on the normalization of political life. Africans could not be indefinitely excluded and the legitimacy of British strategy depended on the active participation of African politicians. Emergency regulations were lifted in the beginning of 1960 as a prelude to establishing a framework for political transition.

But political relations were far from normal. British strategy defined politics narrowly. The rules of the game catered for a small group of 'legitimate' politicians who could be relied on to run the post-colonial system. The success of a political settlement depended on containing the mass movement and crushing the 'troublemakers'. This was particularly essential in the Rift Valley where instability was widespread. In February 1960, a month after the termination of the Emergency, the administration was forced to hold public meetings throughout Nakuru District 'to counter the impression that the revocation of the Emergency regulations has led to the relaxation of other laws as well'.[44] These meetings were backed up by a number of raids carried out by the paramilitary General Service Unit (GSU) in the Molo–Elburgon areas in April 1960.[45] Three months later repression was stepped up in the Ol Kalou area and many 'instigators' were arrested. And Operation Milltown, launched to crack down on unrest on the farms, demonstrated the fragility underlying the process of political transition.

Most discussions of this period concentrate on the Lancaster House Conference and the subsequent growth of nationalist parties. It is our contention – and this argument will be developed in Chapter 7 – that the growth of party activity cannot be seen in its own terms. The political parties grew in influence because they could operate publicly while the more direct forms of political action were repressed. Even party politics were not immune to repression – whenever local parties came under grassroots influence and went beyond the strict rules of the game, administrative reaction was swift. The first party to operate in Nakuru District in the post-Emergency period was the Nakuru District Congress. Despite its moderate image this party, according to the estimates of Special Branch, had a membership of 2,000 by February.[46] In May, the Congress opened its first offices outside Nakuru town, one in Elburgon and one in Njoro.[47]

The Nakuru District Congress did not win mass support from Africans living on the farms. Its image was too moderate and lacked the radical appeal of other parties. Most Kikuyu on the farms looked to the Kenya African National Union (KANU) to represent their interests. KANU's popular rhetoric was more in tune with the sentiments that prevailed on the farms. A Special Branch officer observed that in Nakuru District 'the Kikuyu were not joining the Nakuru Congress but were waiting for the formation of a Nakuru branch of KANU'.[48]

In a sense it was not KANU's programme that was attractive but rather the meaning that the Africans on the farm attached to it. Independence was seen as land for the Africans. The Senior Labour Officer reported to his superior in May 1960:

> I feel that it is now appropriate to bring to your notice the effects of the present political situation on labour in the Rift Valley Province. The general impression of employees is that notwithstanding the precise date of independence, there will soon be changes in the matter of land and farming in the White Highland. Employees consider that quite shortly farms in the RVP, will be subdivided into small holdings which will be handed over to the Africans.[49]

Land was the burning question which defined the political climate. And KANU managed to convey the impression that it stood for free land for all.

The widespread hope that *Uhuru* would mean the subdividing of European-owned land among African labourers provided the political direction for further action. These rumours surfaced in May 1960, which was also the month in which unrest on the farms took on a concrete and general character. The District Commissioner of Nakuru noted that throughout the month there were numerous go-slows and strikes on the farms and that Africans who were discharged often refused to leave the premises.[50] The Labour Officer reported increasing unrest among farm labour mainly from Kikuyu and to a certain extent Kissii: '. . . many farm workers . . . firmly convinced that the land would be partitioned and distributed free to them when *Uhuru* was achieved'.[51]

In Nakuru District political activity clearly accelerated after May 1960. In June, the Congress transformed itself into a new branch of KANU. This organization was able to mobilize widespread political support from those Kikuyu who had hitherto remained inactive. The District Commissioner of Nakuru reported in June 1960: 'The most important event politically during the period was the marked increase in the amount of money being collected legally and illegally and particularly from Kikuyu . . .'[52]

Attempts by the administration to counter the growing politicization of farm labour in Nakuru District failed. Government *barazas* on the farms tended to be ignored. The following warning had little effect on the Kikuyu audiences:

> Those who used the word 'Uhuru' should think carefully what they mean. Even now every person has freedom of expressing his views and of criticising the Government (so long as he does not incite people to break laws). 'Freedom' must not deteriorate into disrespect for law. Respect for the law is the basis of all good government . . .

> Rumours that everyone will get free land when self-government comes . . . are nonsense . . .[53]

At the government-sponsored *barazas* held at Elburgon and Molo, the administration was dismayed when Harry Thuku, the prominent Kikuyu loyalist was heckled down.[54]

The most important political development in Nakuru District was the increasing presence of KANU. In October 1960, police officials noted the formation of a KANU ginger group under the guise of the Women and Youth Wing. The militants of the youth wing were able to extend the popular base of KANU through their activities on the grassroots, as the District Commissioner noted:

> Outside Nakuru . . . [town] . . . their technique is to tour the Townships or other centres of population with a loud speaker van; political slogans are shouted, a crowd gathers and singing takes place before the van moves on. These activities were due to lead up to a 'social dance' of the 'Women and Youth League' . . . apart from their political significance these activities are a potential menace to law and order since high feelings and large crowds can be whipped up in a very short time.[55]

The administration attempted to check the growth of KANU within Nakuru District. Licenses for meetings and for collecting money were often delayed and a number of KANU activists were prosecuted for trespass on European farms.[56] In November, the social dance of the Youth and Women's League referred to above was raided by the police. The administration maintained that political singing took place without a licence and arrested three KANU committee members.[57] In December, a crowd of KANU supporters at a meeting in Njoro stoned the police, who wanted to arrest members of the audience. Eventually, with the aid of police reinforcements, 20 KANU supporters and the branch chairman were arrested.[58]

The most important source of administrative concern was not the increasing influence of KANU, but the growth of illegal squatting. The farmers reducing their labour force were met with a novel response. 'This will be our land soon and we will not go'.

This fundamental challenge to law and order created new problems for local officials. In December 1960, the Labour Commissioner was ordered by the Council of Ministers to estimate the scope of the problem of illegal squatting. To his dismay he found that in 1960, 171 cases of mass illegal squatting were reported in the White Highlands.[59]

With the growth of illegal squatting, the Kikuyu on the farms, this time often as unemployed and illegal squatters, had again become a political force to be reckoned with. The developments of 1960 in the farms gave the administration little cause for optimism. Large numbers of Kikuyu migrated into the settled areas only to increase the ranks of the unemployed. Political organizations were active and growing in strength. Labour unrest was widespread and illegal squatting had become a major political problem. The administration had failed to utilize the possibilities offered by the Emergency and saw political initiative slip from its hands. The ground swell of protest on the farms threatened to destroy the carefully arranged transfer of power.

Notes

1. United Kingdom 1955 Cmd. 9475 *East Africa Royal Commission, 1953-55: Report*, Chapter 6, paragraph 19.
2. DC, NKU, Adm/15/14/1, Post Emergency Administration Circular, Administrative Instructions to Chiefs in Settled Areas, 14 April 1956.
3. DC, NKU, Adm/15/4/3, Meetings with Chiefs and Headmen, Instructions to Chiefs in Settled Areas, 26 January 1956.
4. *Labour Department Annual Report, 1955*, p. 5.
5. KNA, Lab 3/124, Re-employment of Kikuyu in RVP and Nairobi no. 5, Minute of Labour Commissioner, 18 March 1955.
6. *ibid.*, no. 3.
7. *ibid.*, no. 45, MAA to Minister for Labour, 1 April 1955.
8. KNA, DC, NKU 2/154, Nakuru Monthly Intelligence Reports, March 1957.
9. KNA, PC, NKU 2/840, Labour Officers' Reports no. 151, Report of the Acting Senior Labour Officer. RVP, September 1957.
10. *ibid.*, no. 162, March 1958.
11. Labour Department Annual Report, 1958, p. 9.
12. Lab Molo, Conf. 3, Labour Confidential and Secret, JLH Webster, Secretary War Council to PC.RVP, 28 May 1957.
13. KNA, DC, NKU 5/2, Labour Nakuru 1947-61, no. 95, PC, RVP to DC, Kbu, 30 August 1959.
14. DC, NKU, Adm 15/3/4, Molo Reports, no. 31, Monthly Report, January 1960.
15. DC, NKU, Lab 27/1, Unemployment, Supplement to Employers, 14 February 1960.
16. KNA, DC, NKU 5/2, Labour Nakuru 1947-61, no. 92, DC, NKU to PC, RVP, 15 August 1959.
17. Colony and Protectorate of Kenya; *Kenya, European and Asian Agricultural Census 1958*, p. 34.
18. NLO, Monthly Reports, February 1966.
19. NLO, C.21, Labour Unrest, no. 15, SLO, RVP to Labour Commissioner, 13 May 1960.
20. Lab Molo, Conf. 2, Labour Confidential and Secret, Acting Senior Labour Officer to Labour Officers, RVP, 15 February 1958.
21. NLO, no file cover, See Monthly Reports, for Thomson's Falls, 1959.
22. NLO, Monthly Reports, Thomson's Falls, August 1959. Wages were to fall further in 1960. In March it was reported that in Nakuru District starting rates were as low as 15/- per month. See KNA, DC, NKU 2/154, Nakuru Monthly Intelligence Reports,, March 1960.
23. See reports in *ibid.*
24. DC, NKU, Adm 15/3/8, Intelligence, Njoro Reports, September 1959.

25. KNA, DC, NKU 2/154, Nakuru Monthly Intelligence Reports, April 1958.
26. Chandos (1962), p. 348.
27. Harbeson (1973), pp. 25–74.
28. KNA, L&S 1/64, Land Tenure and Control outside the Native Lands, no. 5, Governor to Right Honourable A Lennox-Boyd M.P., 19 December 1958.
29. *ibid.*, no. 33/1, F.O. Webber C.O. to Baring, 4 January 1959.
30. KNA, L&S 1/65, Land Tenure and Control. Policy outside the Native Lands, no. 59, JLF Buist C.O. to WAC. Mathieson MELL, 9 September 1959. Towards the end of 1959 the Government took steps to end the racial exclusiveness of land ownership in the White Highlands. See Kenya, Colony and Protectorate, *Land Tenure and Control Outside the Native Lands*, Sessional Paper no. 10 of 1958–59 and no. 6 of 1959–60.
31. *ibid.*, no. 63, N. Harris, Office of the European Minister Without Portfolio to W.A.C. Mathieson, 14 September 1959.
32. *ibid.* no. 74, Governor, decipher telegram to Secretary of State, 24 September 1959.
33. NLO, C21, Labour Unrest, no. 13, SLO.RVP to Labour Commissioner, 13 May 1960.
34. Lab Molo, Conf. 2. Labour Confidential and Secret, Circular no. C16, signed by K.D. Harrap, Acting Senior Labour Officer, RVP, 21 January 1958.
35. Interview: Confidential.
36. NLO, C.21, Labour Unrest, no. 16, Ian Husband to SLO, RVP, 18 May 1960.
37. KNA, Lab 91026, G.A.W.U., File Note, 14 November 1960.
38. Lab Molo, Labour, District Security Committee, Minutes, 26 September 1960.
39. Nakuru District Annual Report, 1960, p. 16.
40. NLO (no file number) Report of the SLO for RVP March 1960.
41. NLO, C.15, Resident Labour Matters, no. 39, W.N.B. Loudon, Chief Executive Officer, Board of Agriculture, 3 December 1960. Confidential Abandoned Farms. Notes of a meeting held in the PC's Office, Nakuru on Wednesday 30th November 1960.
42. Interviews.
43. NLO (no file number), Senior Labour Officer Rift Valley Province, Annual Report, 1960.
44. KNA, DC, NKU 2/154, Nakuru Monthly Intelligence Reports, no. 56, Nakuru District Report, January 1960.
45. Lab Molo, Conf. 3, Labour, District Security Committee, Minutes, April 1960.
46. *ibid.*, Minutes, 23 February 1960.
47. KNA, DC, NKU 2/154, Nakuru Monthly Intelligence Reports, no. 65, Nakuru District Report, May 1960.
48. DC, NKU, Adm. 15/3/8, Intelligence, Nyoro Reports, May 1960.
49. *ibid.*
50. *ibid.*
51. Lab Molo, Conf. 3, Labour, District Security Committee, Minutes 28 April 1960. The Congress was eventually dissolved and reorganized into the new KANU branch.
52. KNA, DC, NKU 2/154, Nakuru Monthly Intelligence Reports, no. 66, Nakuru District Report, May 1960.
53. DC, NKU, Adm. 15/4, Official Barazas, Current Points to Africans for Barazas and other Talks. Progress to Self Government, June 1960.
54. KNA, DC, NKU 2/154, Nakuru Monthly Intelligence Reports, no. 67, Nakuru District Report, June 1960.
55. *ibid.*, no. 72, October 1960.
56. See reports for November 1960 in *ibid.*
57. *ibid.*, no. 75, November 1960.
58. DC, NKU, Adm. 15/3/8, Intelligence, Njoro Reports, December 1960.
59. KNA, Lab 9/305, Resident Labourers. General Correspondence, no. 104, Senior Labour Officer, RVP to Labour Commissioner, 18 December 1960.

Seven

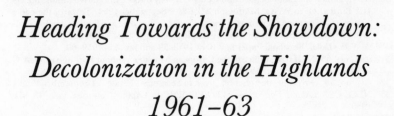

Heading Towards the Showdown: Decolonization in the Highlands 1961–63

Discussions on the last phase of Kenya's colonial era, usually under the rubric 'The Road to Independence', have tended to focus on the formal negotiations between the representatives of the interested groups and the rivalry between the Kenya African National Union (KANU) and the Kenya African Democratic Union (KADU) in national politics.[1] But while the debates in the Legislative Council and the statements of African politicians in Nairobi were making the newspaper headlines, the White Highlands was the scene of a major political struggle. The issues were neither the new constitution nor African nationalism, rather they were land, jobs and a larger share of the wealth for the African living on the farms.

The Mau Mau revolt had set off a train of events that indicated that Kenya could not remain indefinitely under direct colonial rule. Protracted negotiations were initiated by the Colonial Office to ensure that the transfer of political power would be smoothly executed and that British interests would be defended. The main focus of the negotiations was the safeguards necessary for the maintenance of capitalist social relations and for the preservation of Kenya's links with Britain. The negotiations themselves were a phase in the institutionalization of anti-colonial sentiment. Through the process the African participants acquired the status of 'nationalist leaders', and 'statesmen' – men of legitimate authority. The negotiations not only resulted in an agreement but also in the creation of legitimate African politicians.

The African negotiators were negotiating not so much about the broad issues facing the country in the future as about their own role after independence. Thus they were much more concerned with jockeying for power than with making a strong stand against the British. The Colonial Office was able to turn the tension within the African camp to good advantage and played off one African politician against another with consummate skill. In particular, it encouraged ethnic divisions and provided behind-the-scene support for KADU so as to weaken the position of the African politicians as a whole. KADU, a creation of the colonial government, was able to acquire a measure of organizational coherence through promoting ethnic suspicions against the Kikuyu people.[2]

As indicated in Chapter 6, the Emergency was not simply about the repression of militant nationalists. It also provided the colonial administration with a breathing space to work out a strategy of controlled decolonization. One of its key concerns was to strengthen the credibility of its loyalist allies so as to establish an alternative African leadership. Initiatives like the establishment of the General Agricultural Workers Union (GAWU) aimed to create 'representative' African institutions under British tutelage. On a national scale, while militants were languishing in detention, a group of African public figures were being groomed for running the post-colonial state. Many handpicked Africans were sent abroad to education institutions in Britain and the United States to get the necessary training.

Moderate nationalists were able to consolidate their position through their connections with the colonial state. This position was also boosted through the strengthening of their economic position. During the Emergency the colonial administration actively encouraged sections of the African petit bourgeoisie to transform themselves into a class of capitalists. Although the new capitalist class was still weak, relative to its pre-Emergency position, it had gained considerable power. Collaborators throughout Kenya, and specifically in Kikuyuland, were rewarded, increasing the social basis for moderate nationalism. Consequently by the end of the Emergency the balance had shifted away from those who supported the Mau Mau perspective towards those inclined to compromise. The colonial administration knew that the problems that drove Kikuyu squatters and their allies towards militant resistance remained unresolved. But it hoped that with the help of its revitalized African allies an outcome satisfactory for colonial interests could be realized.

It could be argued that the very aim of political bargaining was to assist the ascendancy of moderate nationalism. The final settlement boosted the position of the African businessmen and middle class and effectively excluded the majority from participating in the benefits of independence. Most observers have tended to emphasize the rise of ethnic tensions during this period. To be sure this development, encouraged by the British, acquired important dimensions in political life. But the most significant feature of the three years leading up to *Uhuru* was the emergence of class divisions as the decisive factor in political affairs. This was the inevitable consequence of the drive of the African middle class to monopolize political influence so as to gain access to economic power.

Three years of negotiations proved to be good training for the future statesmen of Kenya. But while the Colonial Office was certain that it had the full cooperation of the leading African politicians, it was less certain of its capacity to contain mass unrest. During the years leading up to independence the colonial regime was fully stretched – not even the support of leading KANU and KADU politicians could guarantee the future stability of the Highlands.

The Highlands in transition

From every point of view the future of the Highlands constituted the greatest obstacle to the smooth transition to formal independence. This, the most prosperous region in the country, became the battleground for the contending interests: European settlers, African businessmen and the landless. The European settlers wanted to ensure that their way of life would be maintained with the minimum of disruption. For the emerging African capitalists the White Highlands represented an obvious sphere of investment, an economic asset essential for the consolidation of their economic power. For the landless the European farms meant the fulfilment of a dream: land and an independent economic existence.

The transition towards the Africanization of the Highlands coincided with growing class polarization in Kikuyuland. The government-engineered land reform had rewarded the loyalist elite of Central Province and established a stratum of capitalist farmers. But this land reform had also excluded thousands of Kikuyu from access to land and led to an increase of landless peasants. This stratum of newly proletarianized Kikuyu joined the ex-squatters in a search for a new means of existence. Inevitably many of them headed for the Rift Valley, and in particular towards the areas that had always experienced Kikuyu migration. The intensification of migration was a major contributor to the exacerbation of social tension in the Highlands during the period under consideration. To make matters worse the flood of new immigration coincided with a period of economic uncertainty and stagnation in the European settled areas.

Economically, 1961 was disastrous for the White Highlands. Severe drought, flood and pests hit hard the already ailing agricultural sector. Famine conditions in the African areas bordering the farms brought thousands of work-seekers on to the labour market. Most of these men were forced to go back to their Reserves, as jobs were impossible to obtain. Indeed, the year saw the loss of at least 11,000 jobs in agriculture in the Highlands. European settlers reduced their labour force and limited the scope of their activities, adopting a wait-and-see attitude while the Lancaster House negotiations were in progress. As the Labour Commissioner reported: 'The policy of most employers was towards short-term development with the minimum of capital outlay and maximum cash return from the land, labour economies were affected'.[3]

The cumulative effect of unemployment and famine conditions forced the government to take emergency measures. Famine relief was provided for Africans living on the farms and soup-kitchens were established in the townships. The improved harvest of 1962 brought little amelioration in the economic situation. There were further redundancies in agriculture, with an estimated 10,000 jobs being lost in the Rift Valley. The number of unemployed substantially increased as many Europeans sold their farms.[4] The last year of direct colonial rule, 1963, saw a further deterioration in the White Highlands. Costs of agricultural inputs rose at a time when world agricultural prices remained low, and there were consequently further redundancies in agriculture. The Senior Labour Officer of the Rift Valley estimated that during the year the pool of unemployed increased by 10,000 to 30,000. He warned: 'It is obvious . . . that some unemployment relief measures must be introduced if a catastrophic situation is to be avoided'.[5]

Social unrest

The threat of economic catastrophe was only one side of the problem. Unemployment and land hunger stimulated political unrest and served to strengthen the climate of social instability. The fight for land involved thousands of Kikuyu on the European farms. In the tradition of Mau Mau an informal movement publicly referred to as the Kenya Land Freedom Army (KLFA) – popularly known as the *Kiama Kia Muingi* or the *Kiama Kia Hunya* – provided a degree of coherence to the movement of landless Kikuyu. Although oathing was widespread, this movement was more of an informal pressure group than the underground organization it was represented to be in the press. It was a spontaneous expression of determination to get free land by the ex-squatters and the newly proletarianized Kikuyu peasants.

Nakuru and Thomson's Falls were the main centres of land agitation. In 1961, the growth of unemployment in Nakuru District provoked a wave of oathing, strikes and other forms of protest. The flood of Kikuyu from Central Province during January and February only exacerbated the situation. The situation was particularly tense in the forests around Elburgon.[6] The District Commissioner noted in April that 'increasing anxiety was expressed at the uncontrolled movement of the growing number of unemployed. Thefts and robberies by young thugs are on the increase'.[7] In May, the settlers in Nakuru were shocked by the killing of a European farmer. The killing in the context of growing unrest provoked the administration to impose a night curfew in the Mau Narok, Njoro and Elburgon wards.[8] Every farm and forest village in the area was raided and by June over 200 Kikuyu were arrested for minor offences.[9]

By July, the sporadic unrest on the farms had acquired an overtly political expression. An administration report noted: 'A rise in the political feeling of the African population has become apparent during the month. The first open signs of this appeared at the Native Dances organized by KANU at Njoro on the 9th of July. Here before an audience of some 4,000 predominantly Kikuyu, political songs were sung and feelings started to run high'.[10]

Three days after this meeting, a 12-hour curfew was imposed on the population of the forest villages of Gichage and Ndoswa near Elburgon. This curfew, which lasted a week, was designed to assist police investigations of reports of illegal oathing. Opposition to this administrative response was clearly expressed at a meeting of KANU at Elburgon on 16 July. Intelligence reports 'estimated that 5,000 were present of which approximately 90% were Kikuyu . . . Disparaging remarks were made about Administration and the Police, and the measures taken in the Elburgon Forest Station following reported oathing ceremonies there . . .'[11]

In August 1961, Jomo Kenyatta was released from detention. The Kikuyu on the farms greeted this news with jubilation and hundreds went down to Kenyatta's home in Gatundu to greet him. In Molo and Njoro Divisions, Asian merchants were asked to lend their lorries for this journey. Two Asian merchants who refused to comply with this request had boycotts imposed on their businesses. The boycotts were only lifted a month later, on condition that the merchants made substantial political donations to KANU.

The belligerent attitude of the forest squatters continued in August. The D.C. of Nakuru reported that 'On 20th August, two Tribal Policemen at Naivasha Forest Village were badly beaten up whilst investigating a rowdy beer party . . . Reports have been received from Sabatia and Esageri Forest Villages of insubordination and subversive attitudes on the part of the villagers . . .'[12]

In September, unrest among forest squatters increased throughout Nakuru. Reports of assaults on Tribal Policemen were received from Naivasha, Elburgon, Sokeso Glade Camp and Sabatia.[13] Throughout the rest of the year, this pattern of unrest was evident on the farms and in the forest villages.

The growth of social unrest was neither organized nor coherent. It was shaped by the economic crisis and the desire to share in the fruits of independence. The local administrators failed to grasp the fluidity of the situation and tended to blame the unrest on the clandestine work of the KLFA. This was the theme of the Nakuru District Commissioner's report for 1961: he warned that the KLFA was 'run by ex-detainees who are extremists' who had been active in oathing farm labourers 'mainly in the Molo/Ravine/Elburgon/Njoro areas and lately also in Bahati'.[14]

Many ex-detainees were indeed active on the ground, but rather than being an organized plot it was a scramble to claim a stake to a part of the

Highlands. Since *Uhuru* was identified in the popular consciousness with free land, every landless Kikuyu shared the common aspiration of Land and Freedom. The activists went a step further and attempted to give this aspiration a political expression. The main tactic pursued by the ex-detainees and activists was to take control of the local KANU branches and to fight for their objectives through this party. In Nakuru District, the main inspirer of this tactic was Mark Mwithaga, a populist Kikuyu politician with a strong base of support among the ex-squatters.[15]

Through the Youth Wing, the KLFA activists were able to influence the local KANU branches and by the middle of 1961 most of the Nakuru District branches were under their domination. The KLFA met with similar success in the districts of Naivasha and Laikipia in 1962. This intervention set off a series of power struggles inside the party. The local government officials saw these disputes in terms of the 'moderates' versus the 'extremists' and as a matter of policy did its best to boost the position of the 'moderates'. The District Commissioner of Laikipia reported:

> The KANU branch continued under its Chairman, Stephen Macharia and Secretary General G.G. Kariuki. On the whole these officials just managed to keep the branch alive in the face of . . . takeover bids from the irresponsible Youth Wings. It was a hard year for them in which they begun to learn some responsibility in the conduct of their affairs. Four convictions were sustained by officials of the branch.[16]

The tension within KANU was mitigated by a common dislike for KADU. It appears that a number of Youth Wing activists were diverted towards engaging in anti-KADU activities. The political differences between the leadership of KANU and KADU were relatively insignificant but party rivalry had strong ethnic overtones and by the end of 1961 these had come to the surface.

The potential for ethnic conflict had existed ever since the evicted Kikuyu had returned to the White Highlands in considerable numbers. European farmers preferred Kikuyu labourers to others and many non-Kikuyu labourers found themselves without jobs. With growing unemployment the non-Kikuyu farm labourers found it difficult to obtain employment in Nakuru District.[17] The establishment of KANU and KADU along clearly defined ethnic lines expressed the emergence of new and significant divisions within the African community. For their own reasons, the colonial administration and the leading African politicians actively promoted ethnicity. Ethnic appeals found a mass resonance because the outstanding political question in the region was which ethnic group would get land in the Highlands after independence. This question was directly posed as a result of the Colonial Officesponsored policy of regionalism. Under the Lancaster House Agreement the independent African administrative structure was to become quasi-federal.[18] In 1962 the Regional Boundaries Commission looked into the details of defining the future areas of the Regions. Not surprisingly, the hearings of the Boundaries Commission greatly heightened ethnic tensions as the leaders of the different ethnic groups attempted to assign the Rift Valley within their sphere of influence.[19]

In Nakuru District as a whole, the Kikuyu were in a clear majority, with substantial pockets of non-Kikuyu living in Rongai, Subukia, Eldama Ravine and Nakuru Town. In the rural areas of the district, KADU was fairly weak and did not constitute an important political force. Ethnic tension flared up in 1961, generally as an outcome of heated political meetings and often on the initiative of outside speakers. It is interesting to note that ethnic clashes in the district started in Nakuru Town in January 1961, an area with a heterogeneous African population. The consequences of this clash were felt as far as Laikipia, where fights broke out between KANU and KADU supporters.[20] Throughout the year, a number of incidents took place between KANU and KADU youth wingers, culminating in a small riot in Londiani in December.[21]

To the delight of European settlers and local officials 'tribalism' had emerged as an important force in Nakuru District. This politicization of ethnic relations could not escape the notice of any observer. The Senior Labour Officer reported that KANU–KADU rivalry had made a major impact on Africans on the farms. He wrote: 'KADU tribesmen were reluctant to join GAWU as they considered it to be a subsidiary of KANU and a number of farmers reported that their employees divided into KANU and KADU groups when collecting their rations and pay. It was also noted that these groups did not support each other in a number of strikes that occurred on farms'.[22]

Competition for jobs and land acted as a divisive force on the Africans living on the farms. Many ex-squatters were drawn into this conflict and feared that other Africans would encroach on the land they had staked out for themselves. The recommendations of the Regional Boundary Commission in December 1962 were a major blow to the aspirations of the Kikuyu ex-detainees. The Commission ruled that most of the White Highlands was to be outside the Kikuyu Region.

Finding themselves a minority in the Rift Valley Region, the Kikuyu farm labourers were worried about the possibility of ethnic discrimination. The Provincial Commissioner noted some of the causes that gave rise to KLFA activity:

Kikuyu living in Rift Valley . . . are acutely aware that they are living outside the likely limits of any Kikuyu region that may be introduced under the new Constitution. They clearly see that unemployment is steadily increasing and nothing so far has happened to make them feel that the majority of them have any real chance of obtaining plots of land on settlement schemes for the foreseeable future.[23]

Although important as part of the national political pattern, ethnic issues were far from being the dominant problems facing the landless Kikuyu. The main questions that provoked unrest centred around land and the fear that what were seen as legitimate claims would not be realized. As a result, the landless Kikuyu concentrated their energy on holding on to the land they lived on, illegal squatting of available land and resisting eviction. Throughout 1962 hundreds of Kikuyu labourers and migrants squatted on European farms. Attempts to evict them during the first months of the year proved ineffective. Most of the evicted labourers drifted back to the farms and resumed their illegal squatting there. As the District Commissioner of Nakuru reported in April: 'Evictions from farms and forest areas is widespread and it is suspected that these people find refuge in abandoned and semi-abandoned farms instead of going back to the reserve'.[24] Police raids on farms had little effect on illegal squatting. In Thomson's Falls, those arrested 'defied the Magistrate and announced that they had no intention of leaving "their" land'.[25] The growth of popular resistance forced KANU and even GAWU officials to support the illegal squatters.[26]

As the policy of eviction proved ineffective, the administration changed its approach. European farmers were instructed to refrain from evicting Africans from their farms. This shift in policy represented an attempt to defuse potentially explosive situations and limit the scope for the growing radicalization of the landless. The administration was able to obtain the cooperation of most European farmers. The District Commissioner reported with relief that 'most of the farmers have been accommodating about keeping on labour that they do not require in order not to exacerbate the prevailing unemployment problem'.[27] The decision to allow illegal squatting on European farms was made as a concession to the Kikuyu labourers as a prelude to striking out against the local activists. During the spring of 1962, intelligence reports indicated that the KLFA, acting through local KANU branches, was behind the illegal squatting campaign.[28] Although these reports laid too much stress on conspiracy, they were not far off the mark. KANU activists were fully involved, but illegal squatting would have occurred regardless of their support.

From the administration's point of view the focus on KANU had the merit of identifying and then eliminating the leading radical activists. During the next two to three months a surveillance campaign was organized to identify the most articulate 'troublemakers'. The Special Branch in Nakuru was following the situation on the farm carefully, and through its network of informers was sifting out intelligence on the activities of the illegal squatters' movement. By July, so-called KLFA cells were identified in Molo, Elburgon and Marioshoni and kept under surveillance.[29] In September, Police and paramilitary units of the General Service Unit (GSU) went into action. Dozens of Kikuyu were arrested in Molo, Elburgon and Dundori, and home-made guns and ammunition were discovered during the course of the raids. The campaign continued until the middle of October.[30]

In October, the administration initiated its 'Follow-up Operation'. Under Eliud Mahihu, a well-trusted Kikuyu collaborator, special courts were established to screen KLFA suspects. The courts were mainly a propaganda exercise and failed to obtain a single confession. Nevertheless the government boasted that 'the back of the LFA had been broken'. In reality all that had happened was that a few activists were eliminated from the scene. As the Provincial Commissioner wrote to the Chief Commissioner: 'The back of the KLFA organization is now being rapidly broken by police action, but as regards the removal of . . . the main underlying causes that gave rise to the movement, the outlook is bleak'.[31]

The Provincial Commissioner's assessment of the situation was to be fully confirmed during 1963, the last year of direct colonial rule. The realization among Kikuyu that time would soon run out, and that this was the last chance for the landless to claim a stake in European land, led to the escalation of illegal squatting and unrest. In anticipation of a mass land invasion, the administration shifted its policy yet again, commencing with the eviction of redundant labourers. The evictions were selective; the prime targets were KLFA suspects and their relatives. One Labour Officer commented: 'A number of farmers in the District were once again replacing their Kikuyu labour with non-Kikuyu as more cases of implication in the LFA's activities, among their labour, came to light. During the month one farmer discharged the entire labour force numbering 30, and another instructed all his Kikuyu employees to remove themselves from the farm'.[32]

In practice, the campaign to evict illegal squatters never got off the ground. Resistance to evictions was widespread and only a major military operation would have been adequate to carry out this task. On the eve of independence this was not a viable political option. The administration was forced to acknowledge this and the Senior Labour Officer of Rift Valley observed that it was 'impossible for the forces of law and order to cope with this problem'.[33] Grassroots pressure forced the local KANU branches to take a sympathetic view of the illegal squatters' movement. And on the farms KANU spokesmen replaced GAWU as the representatives of Kikuyu labourers. This development is well captured in a report written by a local official in June 1963:

It is most unfortunate that the functions of the GAWU is being misunderstood or underestimated by some farmers because KANU Youth Wingers or officials have undertaken the responsibility of representing farm workers.

. . . A situation has arisen around this district where KANU Youths have incited or intimidated labour, abused farmers and made work for the officials of this department and the GAWU extremely difficult. Meetings are held in the labour lines at night and workers are told not to leave farms when discharged, refuse to work when certain conditions are not met by the employers and cultivate any land of their choice.[34]

The breakdown in law and order became more acute after the national elections. The victory of KANU at the polls and the realization that, after *Uhuru*, Kenya would be run by a KANU government boosted the hope that land seizures would be recognized by the future administration.

From June 1963 illegal squatting accelerated in a desperate scramble for land. The impact of this escalation of land seizures on European farms was considerable. According to the Provincial Annual Report, by the end of 'the year many farmers were finding it difficult and sometimes impossible to carry out their farming activities efficiently'.[35] The effect of the results of the General Election on the activities of the landless Kikuyu cannot be underestimated. According to a contemporary report: 'It was understood that after the General Election there appeared to be a feeling among the Public in the area that the Police no longer had power to maintain law and order and this led to the arrival of the GSU'.[36] Even the paramilitary forces drafted into the area could do no more than carry out the occasional much-publicized punishment raid.

The transition period to independence itself helped shape the illegal squatter movement. It raised expectations about the future and forced upon the landless the realization that this would be the last opportunity to get land. During these crucial years no senior African politician was prepared to publicly disabuse the landless of their dreams and the conviction grew that land was there to be seized.

The dilemma of decolonization

On the national plane the Colonial Office had little problem about selling its idea of an independent Kenya. Everything was going to plan and the main nationalist party, KANU, had been domesticated. The 1960 KANU *Manifesto* provided the necessary guarantees for continuity in post-independent Kenya. The *Manifesto* promised to resettle landless Africans but 'not at the cost of the high standard of agriculture already attained, and which must continue'. And it pledged that 'both public and private enterprise, local or from overseas, have a sure place in Kenya's development'.[37] By May 1962, with the entry of KANU leaders into the government, the colonial administration had realized its main objective: continuity of socio-political relations appeared to be assured.

The main obstacle to the successful implementation of Britain's decolonization policies was the unrest among landless Kikuyu in the Rift Valley. For this reason the central focus of administrative thinking turned towards the European-settled area of the Rift Valley. The main dilemma of the administration was that it had to contain the unrest on the farms without the application of brute force. A major military showdown in this delicate period could undermine all the effort that had gone into the achievement of the Lancaster House Agreement and wreck the plans for a smooth transfer of power. The response of the administration was to evolve a sophisticated counter-insurgency strategy that combined concessions with the selective application of coercion.

Repression was selectively aimed at the more articulate spokesmen of the radical wing of KANU. In addition, attempts were made to strengthen the reliable moderate wing. The administration, through the local district officers, actively supported the conservative wing of KANU in instances of factional struggles. A number of radical KANU officials were given prison sentences or put out of circulation by deporting them to Central Province. J.W. Howard, District Commissioner of Nakuru, wrote to his successor upon retiring in January 1962: 'most of the worst shifts have been put under restriction. Do not allow Mark Mwithaga out under any circumstances'.[38] Mwithaga and his colleagues found themselves under constant administrative pressure. Arrests, often on trumped up charges, were a regular feature of the period. In a number of instances the administration worked hand-in-glove with KANU headquarters to realize their shared objective of eliminating radical branch officials. One intelligence report observed:

> The main political interest continued to centre round the quarrel between rival KANU factions in Nanyuki and Kiganja. The official, and moderate faction receives support from KANU headquarters; but the unofficial and extremists faction continued to operate. The Police are investigating to see what can be done to prosecute them.[39]

The detention of radical KANU officials served to strengthen the control of the party leadership over the local branches. But it provided no solution to the continued problem of unrest.

The centrepiece of the administrative strategy was a programme of 'land reform' in the Highlands. The programme of resettlement was a direct response to agitation for land. In his study on land reform in the White Highlands, G. Wasserman characterized land settlement as a form of 'counter-insurgency'. As he correctly observed, land reform in the Highlands was pre-emptive, 'in that it was initiated largely to prevent the formation and mobilization of the mass nationalist base'.[40]

African land settlement in the White Highlands was part of the agreement reached at Lancaster House in 1960. The economic objective of the projected settlement schemes was to protect the existing socio-economic relations of capitalist agriculture. The political rationale of defusing mass unrest and strengthening the hands of moderate African leadership motivated the planners of this project. In its application to the International Bank for Reconstruction and Development, the administration spelled out the political considerations behind the settlement scheme. It argued that without financial assistance only a handful of Africans could acquire land in the Highlands. It continued:

> This situation can only lead to an increase of tension and to the build up of tremendous pressure by irresponsible Africans for forcible measures to expropriate land. Such a situation in short, would contain many of the ingredients of another 'Congo' debacle. It is clear that in order to avoid the floodgates of discontent building up behind the dam wall of the land issue, a spillway must be provided. This spillway is the settlement project.

and

> Until African entry into the Highlands becomes an accomplished fact . . . responsible African leaders are in a difficult position . . . But as soon as there is visual proof that the land barriers are down . . . The position of African leaders will be greatly strengthened and they should be able to pronounce sensibly and realistically on land issues without fear that such pronouncements could be used by extremists . . .[41]

To outflank the 'extremists' and strengthen the credibility of 'responsible' African leaders the government announced two types of settlement schemes in 1960. The Yeoman schemes were designed for affluent Africans with £200 of capital to invest. Under the so-called Peasant schemes, 60,000 acres (24,300 ha) were set aside for 4,500 poor African families.[42]

The Peasant schemes were totally inadequate to meet the needs of landless Africans. If anything, the establishment of the settlement schemes exacerbated the problem in the short run because farmers who sold their land to the Settlement Board simply discharged their labourers. The escalation of social unrest during this period was partially an outcome of the instability and insecurity created by the haphazard operation of the Settlement Board. Kikuyu farm labourers were reluctant to leave farms bought by the Settlement Board in the hope that they would thereby strengthen their chances of being included in the settlement scheme. Officials were all too aware that, despite the repression of militants, continued unrest could only be solved by obtaining more land for the landless Kikuyu.[43]

The unstable social climate in the Highlands was a central consideration behind the government's announcement in July 1962 that a one-million acre settlement programme designed to settle 25,000 to 30,000 African landless and unemployed would be established. Administrative reports from the White Highlands were unanimous in urging the administration to introduce the settlement schemes under the one-million acre programme as soon as possible.[44] In late 1962, the government initiated the 'Accelerated Kikuyu Settlement Programme'. Its objectives were made clear by the Permanent Secretary of the Ministry of Land and Settlement, N.S. Carey-Jones:

> The object of this is to prevent a flood of Kikuyu from other parts of the Central Region and the Rift Valley Region (driven by unemployment and pressures from other tribes) into parts of the Central Region west and north of the Aberdare Mountains, which could effectively drive out the Europeans, and replace them with squatters. This would destroy the economy of the area . . . [and] remove all prospects of orderly settlement either there or in other parts of Kenya.[45]

The accelerated programme of settlement did not contribute to the return of social stability. On the contrary it raised expectations that soon more land would be made available, and fuelled tension on the farms. The number of Africans threatened with eviction from farms sold to the Settlement Board rose, creating further complications for the authorities. In response, Africans defended themselves by illegally squatting on the Settlement Board's land. In the Kinangop area and in the Ol Kalou Salient the settlement programme was paralysed because of the activities of illegal squatters.[46]

The government viewed with alarm the breakdown of law and order. The sudden invasion by Kalenjin tribesmen of land at Menengai, in Nakuru District, during the summer of 1963 was seen by the administration as a prelude to similar grabs by Kikuyu. In late 1963, the government introduced the Kikuyu Crash Settlement Schemes to stabilize the situation in the Kinangop area. Within the space of a couple of months, 4,500 plots were allocated to landless Kikuyu. Wasserman explains the motivation behind the scheme thus: 'All the Settlement officials spoken with, viewed the crash programme as an absolute political necessity for the new Government without which a major land grab would have occurred shortly after Independence'.[47]

The successive modifications in the settlement programme were forced upon the government by the unyielding determination of Kikuyu farm labourers to get free land. The extension of the settlement scheme was a concession to this pressure and prevented the situation from getting completely out of hand. The success of this strategy was qualified by the persistence of land agitation and in the end only stored up problems for the future. The Senior Labour Officer of the newly established Rift Valley Region concluded his report for 1963 by warning that 'it is obvious therefore, that some unemployment relief measure must be introduced in the new year if a catastrophic situation is to be avoided.'[48]

The settlement schemes were a pragmatic short-term device designed to postpone the inevitable showdown. The African government was landed with the problem. The African District Commissioner of Nyandarua wrote in 1964, the first year of independence:

> The biggest problem in Nyandarua as I see it is what to do with the labour deposed and evicted from farms bought by the Settlement Board. The re-settlement programme will not absorb even half the local labour because for various reasons most of the plots now settled were given to people coming from outside the District. A recent survey has revealed that there are 17,969 unemployed/landless people in the District. They are known as 'illegal Squatters'.[49]

With the Colonial Office discreetly out of the way, it was left to its creation, the new African government, to deal with the problem of land agitation.

Class polarization within the nationalist movement

The institutions established to contain unrest worked effectively in the arena of nationalist politics. Through the Lancaster House negotiations collaboration with the African nationalist leadership was institutionalized and the prospects for the smooth transfer of power looked good. The implementation of this agreement depended on the ability of the nationalist leaders to sell it to the African population. In most parts of Kenya they had few problems in winning acquiescence for the deal. In the Rift Valley matters were different. The landless Kikuyu were not prepared to accept their exclusion from the fruits of freedom. At the same time they lacked the political motivation and outlook to organize against the nationalist leadership. In the end they tried to achieve their objectives through taking control of the local branches of KANU.

At the time the takeover of local branches by radical activists was referred to as the work of the KLFA. For convenience we can use the term KLFA as long as we are conscious of the fact that it did not exist as an independent organization. The common use of the term stems from the administration's policy of criminalizing protest. The authorities found it much more convenient to explain mass unrest as the work of a group of secret conspirators than the result of land hunger and discontent. It was not clever manipulation, but rather mass pressure that forced KANU branches in a radical direction.

Originally, KANU branches in Nakuru District were run by the Nakuru town establishment. Among the first set of office bearers of the Nakuru District KANU branch one finds two businessmen, two trade union organisers, two clerks and one dispenser.[50] These officials lacked a base of support and faced widespread suspicion from the landless Kikuyu on the farms. Almost immediately this suspicion was transformed into hostility and a number of militants emerged to fight for the leadership of KANU. During the period September 1961 and the spring of 1962 the so-called KLFA activists wrested control of the local KANU branches. The KLFA activists had strong popular support. Many of them had well-known connections with Mau Mau and a solid record of anti-colonial struggle.[51] KANU thus became an important organizational weapon in the hands of the landless Kikuyu.

The first casualty of the takeover of KANU was GAWU. KANU officials supported the initiatives of farm labourers as a matter of policy. They intervened on behalf of evicted Africans and encouraged direct action on farms. In this pursuit of militant tactics, KANU contrasted sharply with GAWU. The GAWU was encouraged and nourished by the administration from its inception. Labour Department officials viewed the union as a useful force for stability. According to the official who was responsible for its establishment, 'GAWU helped isolate industrial from political issues'.[52] From the outset, GAWU lived up to expectations: it followed a moderate course and always accepted official advice. However before long GAWU began to experience an erosion of its authority. African labourers became disenchanted when they realized that union membership did not bring any benefits. By the summer of 1961 GAWU organizers faced a major decline of support. The Labour Officer of Molo minuted: 'The GAWU Representative informed the Labour Officer that of his members very few paid up. He also stated that the reason for members refusing to pay their subscriptions was because they are not satisfied with the agreement made between their Union and the KNFU'.[53]

The collapse of paid-up membership was not merely the result of a lack of tangible gains. Earlier in the year, in February 1961, the General Secretary of GAWU, Herman Oduor, issued a statement claiming that the unemployment situation was not as bad as it seemed. This undiplomatic gesture provoked a wave of indignation and the local union officials felt obliged to repudiate it. As the District Commissioner Nakuru reported: 'Local officials of the union have made it known that they are in complete disagreement with the statement made by the General Secretary Mr. H. Oduor to the effect that he had admitted that the unemployment situation was not as serious as he had imagined.'[54] Oduor's statement confirmed Kikuyu labourers in their suspicion that he was the Europeans' dupe.

The prevalent view that GAWU officials did not always act in the interests of their membership is confirmed by government reports:

A large agricultural concern employing over seven hundred people which had encountered a certain amount of difficulty in dealing with union officials, decided to adopt the easy way out of their problem. A bottle of whisky and a few of beer is freely dispensed to visiting officials. In one instance the union was called in to assist in moving some recalcitrant Kikuyu from one area of the farm to another . . . with success.[55]

Corruption inside the union was widespread: 'one branch secretary after another was dismissed for mis-appropriating funds'.[56] But it was not corruption as much as the conservative approach of the union that accounted for its decline. The decision of GAWU not to defend its members who were convicted of KLFA activities is a case in point. GAWU did not oppose the evictions of KLFA sympathizers so as to demonstrate to the authorities its responsible attitude to law and order.[57]

In fact, GAWU went a step beyond sitting on the fence and joined in the police campaign against the KLFA. In September 1962 it 'declared its willingness to assist to stamp out subversive activities on the farm'.[58] But by this time GAWU was a spent force with little influence – its role in the police campaign was minimal and consisted of a few public denunciations of the KLFA.

By the summer of 1962, GAWU had lost contact with the Kikuyu farm labourers. They turned to KANU instead of GAWU to represent them in industrial matters. The Labour Office in Naivasha recorded that 'many employees lodged their complaints with the Secretary of KANU in Naivasha. Their reason for doing so has not been known.'[59] His colleague in Thomson's Falls was more precise in his assessment of this development:

> Because the Union refused to take up claims of their members who were convicted of subversive activities, it was fast losing its members. During the month there was a tendency, among the farm workers to take their complaints to a political organization rather than to the Union.'[60]

The radicalization of KANU had undermined GAWU as a representative union. Whereas KANU was responsive to grassroots pressure the dominant influence on GAWU was the administration. The growing popularity of KANU in Nakuru, Naivasha and Thomson's Falls threatened the very existence of GAWU.

In a last-ditch attempt to respond to the challenge from the local KANU branches, Herman Oduor pleaded for help from the General Secretary of KANU:

> We write requesting you advise all your branches not to take up labour disputes with farmers. It would be a good example for KANU head office to show a good example of discipline within its branches.
> Many farmers, who are aware of the party's constitution and the scope of its activities, do very much resent to [sic] some dogmatic,

abusive, threatening letters written to them over some labour issues which should be dealt with by our own Union. Often some complaints are grieved when their cases fail when discretion of the employer is not in favour of the complainant. Employers have certain rights just as the workers and for that reason, some cases may be to his discretion.[61]

The conservative orientation of the GAWU aroused the hostility of farm labourers. At a time of mass unemployment and political unrest GAWU proved to be an anachronism. In the months leading up to *Uhuru*, farm labourers turned to the organization which they had fashioned inside KANU. The administration could do little to counter this development except arrest a number of KANU militants for 'indulging in trade union affairs'.[62]

The new radical KANU officials aroused the hostility not only of GAWU but also of the KANU national leadership. Kenyatta and his colleagues were furious about the promises that local officials had made to farm labourers about distributing free land after independence. The Nairobi leadership was firmly committed to the maintenance of the socio-economic status quo. They had acquired a stake in this system and looked upon the KLFA's promises of free land as a direct threat to their own interests. Moreover the radical activists appeared as a potential opposition to the Nairobi leadership and a threat to the newly formed system of authority. Thus the Nairobi leadership had no hesitation about supporting the police campaign against the KLFA or, what amounted to the same thing, against illegal squatting.

The campaign of repression had limited success in weakening the hold of radical activists over local KANU branches. Among those detained were two KANU branch chairmen, the most prominent being Kinanjui Mutegi, from Elburgon, who received a seven-year sentence.[63] Despite the assistance of the police, the KANU national leadership could not maintain control over the White Highlands branches. This was confirmed by Sir Anthony Swann, the Minister of Defence:

> Thomson's Falls, Nakuru, Molo, Elburgon and Naivasha were sensitive spots in which the terrorists are gaining ground. KANU had made the Kikuyu in their reserves co-operate with the administration and security officials had no evidence linking KANU leaders with the KLFA.
>
> But it is considered certain that the lower ranks of KANU party's Rift Valley branches are thoroughly penetrated.[64]

Swann could not accuse the KANU leadership or the police of not trying.

In the last six months of colonial Kenya the KANU leadership joined the administration in a combined operation, ostensibly against the KLFA. The real target was the radical element inside KANU. KANU officials from Nairobi toured the Rift Valley to warn of 'so-called KANU

Youth Wingers, who are terrorizing the people'.[65] Jomo Kenyatta, now elected as the future Prime Minister, laid into the KLFA in Ol Kalou: 'Nobody should remember about being in the first Mau Mau and living in detention. I want to build a new Kenya not an old one . . . The Government does not want these oaths. You must leave this rubbish which is no good.'[66] But police action was more effective than Kenyatta's posturing. Eleven officials of the Naivasha and Gilgil branches were detained for their KLFA connections. *The Daily Nation* reported: 'So many KANU officials and members of the party's Naivasha and Gilgil branches, have pleaded guilty to being members of the KLFA that a reorganization of both branches is expected'.[67]

Using the excuse of branch reorganization, the KANU establishment attempted to parachute in its own candidates. Not surprisingly, a series of faction fights erupted in the branches. The focus of the struggle was in the newly established Nyandarua District. In August, the pro-Nairobi KANU chairman announced that the branch and those in Ol Joro, Orok, Ndaragwa, Dundori and South Kinangop were being reorganized.[68] Using the prestige of Kenyatta and the full resources of the party, the KANU elite tried to bribe or coerce its way into Nyandarua. This initiative was a failure. The District Commissioner admitted defeat when he reported the results of the election for branch officials in November 1963: 'any KANU official who did not support the KLFA was replaced'.[69] J.M. Kariuki, a leading Kikuyu politician, who represented Nyandarua District in Parliament, emerged as one of the main spokesmen of the landless Kikuyu.

The challenge to mainstream nationalism

The conflict that developed within KANU was an expression of the contradictory nature of decolonization. Social tension within the Kikuyu community had assumed a political form in previous periods. During the years leading up to the Mau Mau rebellion we saw how KAU and Mau Mau represented different social groupings. Since the early 1950s social differentiation had become accentuated. Indeed the very process of decolonization accelerated this process. Through the Lancaster House plans a section of the African establishment was integrated into the new system while the majority of the population was excluded from the benefits.

Martin Kilson has observed that 'there is no necessary harmony of interests between African elite groups and mass elements during colonial political change'.[70] He wrote:

> Far more than has been recognized by some observers of African political change, there are numerous circumstances in which the African elite may well have a greater harmony of interest with colonial

authorities or expatriate groups than with the common people. This is particularly the case during decolonization, whenever people challenge the authority of the governmental and social systems. These are after all the systems the new elite aspire to control once colonial authorities transfer power to them.[71]

H. Weiss noted a similar pattern of political relations in Zaire: 'The goals of the leaders and the masses were never really the same . . . the leaders wished to Africanize the existing system, while the masses appeared to wish its destruction.'[72] A. Astrow's analysis of decolonization in Zimbabwe goes a step further and shows that the sell-out of the aspirations of the masses is inherent to the process of transfer of power.[73]

From the outset the KANU establishment was on a collision course with the landless Kikuyu in the Highlands. The local KANU officials and the so-called KLFA were on a collision course with the Kenyatta leadership. A former official of GAWU expressed these differences clearly:

> Nakuru KANU officials were irresponsible. They incited the people and people absented themselves from work to go to meetings. They told the people that everyone will have land once we have *Uhuru*. We thought this was wrong. You cannot move the country too fast and even after *Uhuru* the law is the law.[74]

The struggle of the landless Kikuyu was fundamentally directed towards the realization of their concept of *Uhuru*. As the name suggests, the Kenya Land Freedom Army meant that land – access to a just livelihood – was intimately related to freedom. The landless Kikuyu did not set out to change the world. But the realization of their objective would have meant a major reorganization of the existing socio-economic constitutions and thus represented a threat both to the African establishment and the interests of Britain. There could be no compromise with the aspiration of the landless masses. As the Permanent Secretary of the Ministry of Land and Settlement recalled: 'The one thing that had to be prevented, if there was to be an orderly transition from European to African ownership, if the economy was to be preserved and a reversion to subsistence agriculture avoided, was effective seizure of land by squatters.'[75]

The landless Kikuyu were prevented from realizing their objective. But they were not defeated during the period under discussion. In this respect they constituted one of the most successful rural movements in Africa in the 1960s. The Mau Mau experience and the history of struggle provided the landless Kikuyu with a tradition for political action. Although the movement remained loose and informal it used the lessons it had learned during the 1950s. The movement kept a low profile to avoid attracting state repression. Only a limited level of organization was necessary for land seizures and most of these initiatives were organized through the framework provided by the local KANU branches. One activist noted: 'The only thing that the KLFA did was to give the oath and tell people that they will win and get their land.'[76] In the context of widespread unrest, this 'only-thing' was sufficient for endowing the movement of landless Kikuyu with clarity of purpose.

The pressure for change inside the KANU branches could not be ignored by the party leadership. The KANU establishment was forced to make a number of gestures so as not to lose credibility with the masses. It was due to KLFA pressure that the KANU bosses opted for supporting the extension of settlement schemes for farm labourers from the European farms. In January 1963, KANU representatives argued strongly for the policy of giving property to Africans living on farms for high-density settlement schemes.[77]

In another case, the so-called Mpanda settlement scheme, pressure on the KANU leadership proved decisive. The administration hoped to alleviate the effects of mass unemployment by settling landless Kikuyu in Mpanda in Tanganyika. The KLFA was opposed to this scheme for it rightly saw it as an attempt to undermine the claim of landless Kikuyu to land in the Highlands. In any case, the land on offer was of poor quality and infested with tsetse fly. Despite government pressure, KANU could not be seen to be supporting this scheme. In the end the KANU leadership gave tacit approval to the KLFA's campaign of boycott. The Mpanda Scheme thus never got off the ground. The Civil Secretary of the Rift Valley wrote in resignation: 'I confirm that it is not possible for me to find any volunteer families from this region to go to Mpanda'.[78]

The activities of the KLFA inside KANU only constituted one aspect of the movement's strategy. Land agitation took on more direct forms through illegal squatting and land grabs. These activities forced the administration to make a number of concessions, the most important of which was the granting of special priority status for farm labourers on high-density settlement schemes.

Land agitation

Illegal squatting and land invasions began in 1961 and reached their height in the months leading up to independence. While the police knew how to deal with individual politicians, they were at a loss as to what to do with a volatile mass movement. Early attempts at conciliation were ignored and the announcement of token settlement scheme places only added fuel to the fire. By the middle of 1962, illegal squatting had reached mass proportions. In Naivasha District, it had spread from the farms to the townships. According to a contemporary account, 'illegal cultivation in Kijabe, Naivasha and Gilgil has increased enormously.'[79]

The scale of mass squatting was responsible for wrecking the plans of settlement scheme officials. European farmers too were affected – in some cases they could not carry out their activities because of the presence of unwelcome squatters. The government's response relied on the old trusted methods of repression. Since illegal squatting could not be repressed it launched a drive against the KLFA. In many respects the KLFA was a creation of the propaganda-machine of Government House. The aim of government propaganda was to portray the KLFA as a subversive conspiracy given to violence and atrocities. Following the precedent of the criminalization of freedom fighters during the Mau Mau period, the media began to hint at the work of the 'forces of darkness' behind the scenes.

In September 1962, the Minister of Defence stated that the KLFA 'was engaged in a deliberate plan to provoke civil war after the country had attained independence'.[80] In line with the campaign of disinformation, the *East African Standard* ran the headline: 'Reds May Be Behind KLFA'.[81] Government stories about the threat to European lives posed by the KLFA were embellished by journalistic sensationalism. Publicity emphasized stories of oathings and illegal arms. The following news item captures the flavour of media reporting:

> Another large cache of homemade firearms and ammunition was unearthed by the police in the Rift Valley Province bringing the total found since July to 65 guns. At a meeting of . . . [European] . . . local associations at Molo the security position was discussed . . . a statement was issued . . . stating that it was considered that the KLFA had power to expand considerably after independence.
>
> There was widespread oathing in the area . . . if this continued . . . the association would unhesitatingly recommend that all Kikuyu should be discharged and replaced by members of other tribes.[82]

KADU politicians took their cue from the media and joined in the anti-KLFA and anti-Kikuyu hysteria. In September 1962 J.M. Shikuku, the General Secretary of KADU, urged stern action against the Rift Valley Kikuyu, demanding that the government 'declare the Rift Valley a disturbed area to bring the situation under control'.[83] A week later anti-Kikuyu demonstrations involving Nandi and Tugen people were organized by KADU.[84]

KADU politicians had their own motives for supporting the government's policy of criminalization. Between August and December 1962, the Regional Boundaries Commission was meeting to establish the spheres of influence of the various tribes in the post-independence Rift Valley. To compensate for their lack of influence over national events, the Kalenjin and other KADU politicians were determined to dominate the Rift Valley Region. KADU leaders had their own plans for the Region. In September 1962 a boycott was initiated against Kikuyu businesses in Kericho by KADU.[85] A month later this boycott escalated into a vocal anti-Kikuyu movement and hundreds of Kikuyu fled Kericho for

Nakuru District.[86] Many European farmers actively assisted KADU in this enterprise. During the autumn of 1962 and the winter of 1963 hundreds of Kikuyu labourers were made redundant for alleged connections with the KLFA.[87]

The escalation of ethnic rivalries was the main achievement of the government's criminalization policy. An atmosphere of ethnic rivalries and hysteria was conducive for launching policy operations against subversives. And should the situation get even more out of hand in the future, a pretext was established for military intervention.

A closer inspection of events shows that agitation for land was restricted to illegal squatting and civil disobedience. The movement of landless Kikuyu did not initiate any violent actions, much less did it engage in subversion. Large numbers of Kikuyu were oathed, but the KLFA had no perspective of armed struggle or 'civil war' as suggested in government propaganda. During the course of events a number of loyal headmen and newly established African landowners were assaulted but these acts were not part of any systematic campaign.

To ascertain the reasons for the arrest of nearly one thousand Kikuyu for KLFA activities in 1962, the Daily Crime and Incident Reports of the Kenya Police were consulted for that year. Of these reports only one, occurring on 15 September, deals with an incident which could be interpreted as the use of force against authority:

A Kikuyu tribesman who Police arrested for being a suspected member of the KLFA incited farm labourers to attack the police party. The labourers, mostly Maasai, surrounded the police party. One man was armed with a bow and arrow. An Inspector fired a shot in the air and the labourers dispersed. Accused, a Kikuyu is in custody.[88]

The next most serious offence took place in Molo on 29 September. Two arrests were made after a 'Kikuyu tribesman was beaten up and threatened for volunteering to go to Mpanda'.[89] The vast majority of the Kikuyu arrested were charged with being members of an illegal organization. This charge could be interpreted loosely and provided a useful measure for detaining suspected 'troublemakers'.

An examination of the reports shows that most of the offences were the creation of the policy of criminalization rather than of a secret movement. The absence of violent offences shows that the police measures were pre-emptive and, one could argue, provocative. Nor should we take seriously the hundreds of KLFA confessions reported in the press. The seven-month police campaign, which ended in March 1963, resulted in 8,762 confessions of taking an oath of allegiance to a prescribed society. In Nakuru alone, 1,708 people were arrested and the police claimed to have found 368 home-made guns and 767 rounds of ammunition.[90] On paper it looked like a major victory over a well-organized secret society.

In reality confession was a way to avoid a protracted period in detention. One statistic shows the spurious character of police claims: there were only two cases of resistance to arrest reported.[91]

Despite all the publicity, the campaign of repression failed to check the growth of land agitation on the European farms. On the contrary, during the remaining nine months of colonial rule the breakdown of law and order became the accepted norm. The Senior Labour Officer admitted that it 'clearly became impossible for the forces of Law and Order to cope'.[92] Civil authority was unable to enforce eviction orders against most cases of illegal squatting. Even when evictions were enforced there was no guarantee that the ex-farm labourers would not return.

The following description of events at Bondet Farm near Molo illustrates the prevailing social climate. According to the local labour officer:

> The position on this farm is that the discharged employees who numbered between 20 and 30 who had gone back to the farm were all removed by the Police in Police lorries and taken to Elburgon chief's camp, where I understand they have been placed under the care of the Administration.
>
> When I spoke to the Manager . . . he informed me that there was illegal cultivation going on and as he wanted to control it he had asked those remaining on the farm to identify their *shambas* but nobody has done so and for this reason he had given notice to another 27 women to leave the farm.[93]

Six days later the Labour Officer had a change of mind. He wrote: 'I visited the farm and after discussion with the Manager all notices which had been issued to 27 women were withdrawn and nobody is going to be discharged. The position on the farm is now quiet'.[94] The impossibility of controlling the farm labourers after they had been evicted forced the administration into a veritable impasse – or rather a wait-and-see policy. The eviction of illegal squatters would have required a major military operation, an option that was politically inexpedient four months before independence.

Settlement scheme officials faced problems similar to those of the European farmers. One official reported:

> You already know a great deal about the numerous problems which are now beginning to appear in this District as more and more landless Kikuyu are showing their fierce determination to obtain a slice of the settlement scheme cake. Of these problems clearing the non-qualifiers out of the way so that Settlement can proceed is without doubt our most difficult task.[95]

With the spread of illegal squatting on land designated for settlement schemes, the movement came to pose more of a direct threat to the government's hopes for a smooth transfer of power. The extension of illegal squatting and civil disobedience resulted in a number of important local struggles. We shall turn to examine them so as to indicate the dimension of this challenge to authority.

The defiance of the administration by the landless Kikuyu at Bahati Transit Farm reveals the determined stand taken by the movement at the grassroots. Bahati Transit Farm was opened in June 1962 with the objective of providing temporary domicile to approximately 650 unemployed African families. 'Those selected,' the administration stated, 'should be Kikuyu who have no ties with their Reserves or origin who are unemployed and yet are physically capable of work'.[96] The 'successful applicants' were hired as casual labourers and had to work four hours a day in return for ten shillings per month, plus rations for themselves and their families.[97]

Very few Kikuyu applied to move into Bahati. As they saw it, such a move would have been an admission that they had no claim to free land. In November 1962, the administration decided to evict a large number of Kikuyu from the South Kinangop area in order to make way for the new settlement schemes. It was thought that Bahati Farm could provide the logical outlet for these Kikuyu:

> By its very existence that Transit Farm meets an essential need. It provides an answer to Magistrates' objections to issuing eviction orders against illegal squatters and an answer to criticism by politicians . . . that landless families are being inhumanly evicted from farms without having any alternative place where they may lawfully reside.[98]

With the forcible eviction of thousands of Kikuyu from farms brought by the Settlement Board, Bahati Farm was soon filled to capacity. In April 1963, the District Commissioner of Nakuru issued a notice stating that no more admissions should be made to Bahati for the time being.[99]

The Kikuyu living at Bahati on a 'temporary' basis were discontented with the insecure status posed by their so-called temporary residence. They wanted land or secure employment. In January 1963, all the residents of the Transit Farm went on strike for two days in protest over their inadequate conditions.[100] Throughout the next three months, the residents constructed their own independent community structure and elected their own leadership. By March, the European manager had lost *de facto* control over the farm. Residents came and went as they pleased with little regard for the farm rules. According to a Special Branch report, between June and September, 'several reports of oathings and subversion were received, and their attitude towards authority and supervision of any kind was one of contempt'.[101]

By July, the situation in Bahati Farm could no longer be ignored by the administration. On 14 July, 40 families were instructed to send their wives for work the next day. The wives were to be paid a shilling per day for cleaning coffee or pyrethrum, for a European farmer. On arrival at Mr Williamson's farm, all the women refused to work unless they were paid Shs 2.50 per day plus a ration of *posho* (maize meal). Their demands were refused and the women were returned to the Transit Farm. The manager of Bahati Transit Farm reported:

> I told them that they were to report on Wednesday morning at 7 a.m. when a lorry would be ready to take them again to Subukia. All those that failed to report on this occasion would be regarded as not needing help from the Government and would be discharged from the scheme, together with the rest of their family . . . Following this they all started shouting a lot of abuse at me and my staff and demanded that they be signed off the scheme today.[102]

Instead of signing off or reporting for work, they decided to resist the manager. The husbands of the 40 Kikuyu women left for Nakuru Town in order to obtain the support of the KANU office. The response of the KANU office was a mixed one. Fred Kubai, a prominent KANU leader with past credentials as a Mau Mau activist, refused to back the cause of the Bahati residents. At a *baraza* held on 27 July at Bahati, Kubai put the manager's case:

> When Mr. Fred Kubai visited the farm he made it quite clear to the residents that they must obey the instruction of the manager and that no promises of further land or employment could be made. This attitude was resented strongly by the residents with a resultant loss of popularity for Mr. Kubai.[103]

Kubai, Kenyatta's troubleshooter in the area, and soon an assistant minister in the first KANU government, was not prepared to support such flagrant breach of authority. The reaction of local KANU officials was different. Several local KANU branches petitioned the Minister of Home Affairs demanding that conditions be improved at Bahati.[104]

The precise demands of the Bahati residents were clearly articulated at a meeting of residents and staff called by the local administration on 31 July. Muruti Njoroge, the spokesman for the Bahati residents, asked for improvements in rations, medicine and education. But his main emphasis was on the necessity for sending people to settlement schemes or alternatively providing permanent employment for the residents.[105] For the residents nothing less than land or permanent employment sufficed, hence their rejection of casual or part-time work.

Negotiations failed to bring the two sides closer. And with the passing of time the mood of the resident became even more intransigent. In September 1963 the residents began to organize visits to nearby farms to canvass support.[106] The Rift Valley Regional Secretary reported on this development: 'The discontented attitude of those on the farm is now affecting the morale of labour on the surrounding farms'.[107] In November the Bahati squatters raised the stakes and publicly declared that when independence came they would take over the farm and divide it among themselves. The Regional Secretary viewed this threat with apprehension. He wrote to the Permanent Secretary in charge of national security:

> We are faced with some 400 Kikuyu families who are in effect saying that they must either be settled where they are or they will cause trouble in the future . . . The District Administration and the Kenya Police are most concerned at the security situation and feel that there is an extreme likelihood on Independence of the residents forcibly taking over the farm. If this were to happen the repercussions would be of major significance in that the whole concept of the Government's ability to keep control of the landless and to ensure the sanctity of land rights would be brought into disrepute.[108]

During the last weeks before independence the mood of the Bahati residents took on a desperate character. This was due to the demoralization of the 400 Kikuyu families, who felt they had been let down by the KANU political leadership. However, this did not prevent the settlers from pressing their claims. One month after independence, the Special Branch reported: 'Latest reports indicate that unless Government take some positive action to assist the families, approximately 450, they will take over the farm, by force if necessary at the beginning of February, 1964'.[109]

The refusal of the Bahati settlers to obey government instructions was based on the belief that only through active protest could they defend their interests. If the government refused to give them land then they would take it. In December 1963, at a ceremony held by the Bahati residents, their intentions were symbolically made clear:

> Investigations revealed that the people from the Top Camp held some kind of ceremony at which a sheep had been slaughtered and evoked under a *Mugumo* Tree and that after the pieces of meat had been eaten the beads were distributed amongst the participants. The beads signified that wearers were entitled to land on the farm when, after Independence, it was said that it would be distributed amongst them.[110]

The cohesion and sense of purpose of the 440 families at Bahati illustrates the near total rejection of Lancaster House plans by landless Kikuyu on the farms. The social chasm between them and the KANU establishment could not be overcome, even by someone of the stature of Fred Kubai. This was not because of personal failings. In the Highlands, the local KLFA-dominated KANU branches spoke a different language from the KANU leadership. The Civil Secretary of the Rift Valley understood that in Bahati the nationalist leadership lacked legitimacy:

197

It is believed that there are persons who visit the Farm and encourage the residents to stay where they are with promises of free land in the future. It is possible that a leading politician from KANU might well disillusion them in this respect, but I fully believe that there will always be a hardcore of those who are determined to obtain land even in defiance of central Gov't.[111]

On the eve of the transfer of power, this 'hard core' expressed the dominant sentiment among the Kikuyu in the settled areas.

It was not only at Bahati that the KANU leadership failed to contain unrest. Control of the Londiani branch of KANU, which had experienced intense factionalism between its conservative and radical wings, was turned into a trial of strength by the KANU leadership. In August 1963, a number of senior party leaders, including Kenyatta, directly intervened in support of the 'moderates'. They received indirect assistance from the police, who arrested a number of alleged KLFA activists in the Londiani area.[112] Despite the outside pressure, the KANU leadership was rebuffed – the branch election resulted in the faction led by Benson Gichecha, a known supporter of the prescribed KLFA, gaining control of the branch.[113]

The setback of the Kenyatta leadership at Londiani was not an isolated incident. The greatest challenge to Kenyatta was the land invasion in Nyandarua District. During the last four months of colonial rule the landless Kikuyu launched a major campaign in defence of their claims. The creation of settlement schemes in Nyandarua district had resulted in the displacement of over 40,000 people.[114] The displaced Kikuyu refused to leave the district and illegal squatting in Nyandarua District increased massively. The main target of the illegal squatters was the 24 South African families who owned most of the 111,000 acres in Ol Kalou. As a result of a vociferous anti-Boer campaign and attacks on European property, the South African families were unable to continue their farming activities. The aim of the land-hungry Kikuyu was to drive out the farmers and take over the land after independence.

The dimensions of illegal squatting in Nyandarua created what the main civil servant dealing with the problem characterized as an 'intensely dangerous security situation.'[115] The government took this threat so seriously that it organized a crash settlement programme and settled 4,000 families in a record six weeks! It was left to the Kenyatta government to sort out the situation. It was forced to make concessions, initiating a new settlement programme, the Jet Schemes in the Ol Kalou Salient. The Jet Schemes were designed to forestall an upsurge in unrest and give the new government breathing space to deal with the problem. The political climate which led to the establishment of the Jet Schemes is graphically told by a local official:

The take over of farms within the area took place against the back-ground of thousands of unemployed living either legally or illegally on the properties. Theft was a regular but untraceable occurrence, illegal livestock in quantity had been introduced and malicious damage was not uncommon. (As for instance the deliberate burning of thousands of acres of grazing), illegal cultivations were rife and grew in volume daily. The general populace lacked direction, a sense of security and had no sense of purpose whatsoever other than a desire for land.[116]

For the first time in the post-Mau Mau period social unrest threatened to turn into widespread violent action.

In October a number of attacks on European farms was a prelude to the circulation of letters warning them to leave before *Uhuru*.[117] But it was not the European settlers who were to bear the brunt of the wrath of the land agitation. During the last months before independence, the agitation turned against the now visible stratum of newly arrived African landlords.

The turning point

With the arrival of the new African farmers the landless Kikuyu were confronted with the real meaning of *Uhuru*. One of the aims of the settlement schemes had always been to give prosperous Africans a stake in the existing economic structure. Collaborators were needed to oversee the transition to independence. The government's policy was to ensure that all settlement schemes should have this stable influence: accordingly, 'a small proportion of Civil Servants, Soldiers and employed persons should be allocated plots on each settlement scheme since they tend to provide political stability and leadership'.[118]

More generous grants of land were made to the leading collaborators. Special low-density schemes on high-potential land were established with the view to establishing the social foundation for a new African gentry. And with the assistance of agricultural extension service and credit it was envisaged that a class of African farmers producing cash crops could be constituted. The down payment for plots on these schemes was Shs 5,000, which effectively excluded most farm labourers. As the District Commissioner of Nyandarua remarked: 'These plots are not popular in Nyandarua because the bulk of the people cannot produce Shs 5000. The result is that these plots go mostly to successful rich men from other Districts of Central Province such as Civil Servants and rich farmers'.[119]

The arrival of rich carpetbaggers aroused the anger of the landless Kikuyu. Sporadic violence against low-density plot-holders prevented many from taking over the farms. Outsiders were threatened with violence if they settled on their newly purchased land. According to one local

KANU activist, 'the people became angry when all the loyalists obtained good land and forced our people away'.[120] Many former Mau Mau supporters were astonished by the quick promotion of Kikuyu loyalists into local civil service positions and were bitterly resentful that those who had 'sold-out' now got the best land: 'We did not want loyalists to be the party leaders. Especially we did not want the loyalists to steal our land. We had worked and fought on the farms and now our enemies came to be title settlers over us'.[121] The widespread hostility towards the African landlords prevented the immediate transfer of land.

The main focus of resistance to the new landowners was the Dundori low-density scheme. Intimidation and sabotage prevented most of the plot-holders from taking over their land until six months after independence. *The Daily Nation* reported that at 'Dundori, a group of Africans who recently bought a farm have also been threatened. They say that since their arrival on the farm they have been told repeatedly that they did wrong in buying it because the land should have been distributed among the labour when the European farmers left'.[122] At the same time, the Kenya press reported on the activities of a new group of ex-farm labourers operating in the Highlands: the *Kamau Muthori* or the 'Weeping Kamaus'.[123] The 'Weeping Kamaus' were formed as a response to the threat of outside moneyed landgrabbers. Like most activists they sought to discourage outsiders from moving on to low-density schemes.

The pressure that the landless Kikuyu exerted against the loyalists was sufficiently effective to lead to the postponement of 'landing the gentry' until after independence. Although a number of wealthy Africans obtained land in the Highlands during 1963, the establishment of an African middle class in Nakuru and Nyandarua districts took place mainly after independence.

Notes

1. Rothchild (1973).
2. In the Rift Valley the local administration actively encouraged and trained KADU politicians. See the very interesting memorandum, KADU and the Regional Boundary Commission, by the Provincial Commissioner in PC, RVP, Conf 22, Land and Settlement, 12 December 1962.
3. Rift Valley Province, Labour Department Annual Report, 1961.
4. See Naivasha District Annual Report, 1962, p. 9.
5. NLO, Lab 15/1, Annual Reports, 5.2.0. (RVP), 1963 Annual Report.
6. DC, NKU Adm. 15/3/8, Intelligence – Njoro Reports, no. 39, March 1961.
7. KNA, DC, NKU 2/154, Nakuru, Monthly Intelligence Reports, no. 81, April 1961.
8. *ibid.*, no. 82, May 1961.
9. DC, NKU, Adm 15/3/8, Intelligence – Njoro Reports, nos. 44 and 44A, June 1964.

10. *ibid.*, no. 45, July 1961.
11. KNA, DC, NKU 2/154, Nakuru Monthly Intelligence Reports, no. 84, July 1961.
12. *ibid.*, no. 85, August 1961.
13. *ibid.*, no. 86, September 1961.
14. Nakuru District Annual Report, 1961, p. 2.
15. Interview with Mark Mwithaga.
16. Laikipia District Annual Report, 1961, p. 2.
17. Nakuru District Annual Report, 1959.
18. Gertzel (1970), pp. 12–13.
19. KNA, DC, NKU 2/154, Nakuru, Monthly Intelligence Reports, no. 112, December 1962.
20. Laikipia District Annual Report, 1961.
21. KNA, DC, NKU 2/154, Nakuru, Monthly Intelligence Reports, no. 90, December 1961.
22. NLO, RVP Labour Department Annual Report, 1961.
23. NLO, C.I. vol. 2, Unemployment RVP and Resettlement Schemes, PC, RVP to Chief Commissioner, 16 October 1962.
24. KNA, DC, NKU 2/154, Nakuru, Monthly Intelligence Reports, no. 99/1, April 1962.
25. NLO, Lab/15/6, Monthly Reports, Labour Office, Thomson's Falls, May 1962.
26. An official reported: 'GAWU has been forced to take a tougher line over the eviction of unwanted labourers from farms'. See KNA, DC, NKU 2/154, Nakuru, Monthly Intelligence Reports, no. 102, May 1962.
27. Naivasha District Annual Report, 1962, p. 102.
28. Nakuru District Handing Over Report, July, 1962.
29. *ibid.*
30. KNA, DC, NKU 2/154, Nakuru, Monthly Intelligence Reports, nos. 109 and 110, September and October 1962.
31. NLO, C.I. vol. 2, Unemployment RVP and Settlement Schemes, PC, RVP to Chief Commissioner, 16 October 1962.
32. NLO, Lab 15/1, Annual Reports, S.L.O. (RVP), 1963 Annual Report.
33. NLO, Lab 15/6, Monthly Reports, Labour Office, Thomson's Falls, January 1963.
34. DC, NKU, Lab 27/3/3 vol. 1, Labour Reports, Naivasha, no. 3, June 1963.
35. NLO, Lab 15/1, Annual Reports, S.L.O. (RVP), 1963 Annual Report.
36. DC, NKU, Lab 27/3/2, Labour Office, Molo, Monthly Reports, no. 33, July 1963. One of the first African labour officers in the Rift Valley, a Mr. Wanjero, observed: 'The relations have been badly strained by "Uhuru" in the farming industry. Many farm workers believing that Uhuru means everything, have adopted bad tactics to acquire what does not belong to them . . . some have taken occupation of parts of their employers' land for cultivation and have ignored repeated warnings to stop doing so. Female employees, who are the worst offenders, have refused to accept discharge notices.' See *ibid.*, June 1963.
37. Cited in Anonymous (1982), pp. 14–20.
38. Nakuru District Handing Over Report, January 1962.
39. KNA, DC, NKU 2/10, District Monthly Report, Nanyuki, September–October 1962.
40. Wasserman (1973), p. 133.
41. KLO, L.O. 67545 vol. 1, Application to IBRD. Small Farm Settlement Scheme in the Scheduled Areas (no date).
42. Harbeson (1973), pp. 93–5.
43. See correspondence in NLO, C.I. vol. 2, Unemployment RVP and Settlement Schemes.
44. *ibid.*
45. Cited in Wasserman (1973), p. 139.

46. DC Nyandarua; Ol Kalou Salient. Situation Report, November 1963.
47. Wasserman (1973), p. 136.
48. NLO, Lab 15/1, Annual Reports, S.L.O. (RVP), 1963 Annual Report.
49. Nyandarua District Annual Report, 1964.
50. KNA, DC, NKU 2/174, KANU; and Interviews.
51. For example Kinanjui Mutegi, the chairman of the KANU branch in Elburgon, was a Mau Mau activist in the same area a decade previously.
52. Interview with C.A. Luckhurst, 12 May 1972.
53. DC, NKU Lab 27/3/2, Labour Office, Molo, Monthly Reports, August 1961.
54. *ibid.*, February 1961.
55. *ibid.*, January 1961.
56. NLO, RVP, Labour Department Annual Report, 1961.
57. One labour official enthused: 'To indicate the Union's policy of non-alliance with political parties . . . GAWU declined to assist about 20 employees who had been discharged from a farm in Solai for suspected political and subversive activities.' See NLO, Quarterly Report of the SLO RUP, January–February 1961.
58. NLO, Nakuru, Monthly Report, September 1962.
59. NLO, Naivasha, Inspectors' Reports, June 1962.
60. NLO, Lab 15/6, Monthly Reports, Labour Office, Thomson's Falls, January 1963.
61. NLO, GAWU I, no. 177, General Secretary, GAWU to General Secretary, KANU, 10 July 1962.
62. NLO, Lab 27/3/3 vol. 2, Labour Reports Naivasha, no. 3, June 1963.
63. *East African Standard (EAS)*, 12 October 1962.
64. *EAS*, 17 September 1962.
65. *Daily Nation*, 7 August 1963.
66. *ibid.*
67. *Daily Nation*, 8 March 1963.
68. *Daily Nation*, 13 August 1963.
69. DC Nyandarua, Confidential. Monthly Reports, November 1963.
70. Kilson (1966), p. 191.
71. *ibid.*, p. 192.
72. Weiss (1967).
73. Astrow (1983).
74. Interview with Christopher Wachira. 28 March 1972.
75. Carey Jones (1966), p. 159.
76. Interview with John Karibi, 25 March 1972.
77. KNA, P.O. 3/144, Bahati (Transit Settlements), no. 135/1, R.E. Wainwright to all Provincial Commissioners, 6 January 1963.
78. DC, NKU LND 16/8/1/3, Mpanda Settlement Scheme, no. 141, Civil Secretary, Rift Valley to Permanent Secretary, Minister, Home Affairs, 11 September 1963.
79. Naivasha District Annual Report, 1962, p. 2.
80. *EAS*, 7 September 1962.
81. *ibid.*, 19 October 1962.
82. *ibid.*, 14 September 1962.
83. *ibid.*, 26 September 1962.
84. *ibid.*, 5 October 1962.
85. *ibid.*, 21 September 1962.
86. KNA, DC, NKU 2/154, Nakuru Monthly Intelligence Reports, no. 110, October 1962.
87. NLO, Lab 15/6, Monthly Reports, Labour Office, Thomson's Falls, January 1963.
88. KNA, MAA 9/1026, Daily Crime and Incident Reports, 15 September 1962.
89. *ibid.*, 29 September 1962.
90. *EAS*, 15 March 1963.
91. *ibid.*

92. NLO, Lab 15/1, Annual Reports, S.L.O. (RVP), 1963 Annual Report.
93. NLO, Corr. 6, General Correspondence. Molo, no. 76, Labour Officer, Molo to Senior Labour Officer, RUP, 16 July 1963.
94. *ibid.*, no. 81, Labour Officer, Molo to Senior Labour Officer, RVP, 24 July 1963.
95. DC Nyandarua, Lab. 1/vol. 2, Labour Complaints and Evictions, no. 191, Wheeler, Regional Government Agent to Civil Secretary, Central Region, 16 July 1963.
96. KNA, DC, NKU 2/383, Nakuru Transit Farm, no. 5, Draft Proposals for Transit Farm, 7 July 1962.
97. *ibid.*
98. KNA, P.O. 3/114, Bahati (Transit Settlements), no. 55, Provincial Commissioner, RVP to Chief Commissioner, 19 November 1962.
99. KNA, DC, NKU 2/383, Nakuru Transit Farm, no. 275, D.C. Nakuru to all Division District Officers, 23 April 1963.
100. DC, NKU Lab. 27/1/7, vol. 2, Nakuru Transit Farm, no. 33, Regional Government Agent to Mr. James Maranitu, 28 January 1963.
101. KNA, P.O. 3/144, Bahati (Transit Settlements), no. 223/1, Divisional Special Branch, Nakuru to Regional Special Branch Office Nakuru.
102. KNA, DC, NKU 2/383, Nakuru Transit Farm, no. 536, F.P.D. Derrick, Ministry of Home Affairs to Civil Secretary, Rift Valley Region, 31 July 1963.
103. KNA, P.O. 3/144, Bahati (Transit Settlements), no. 220, Regional Secretariat, Rift Valley Region to The Permanent Secretary, Ministry of Home Affairs Nairobi, November 1963.
104. KNA, DC, NKU 2/383, Nakuru Transit Farm, no. 536 (cited in note 102).
105. DC, NKU Minutes of the First Combined Camps and Staff Meeting held at Nakuru Transit Farm Office on 31 July 1963.
106. KNA, P.O. 3/144, Bahati, no. 223/1 (cited in note 101).
107. *ibid.*, no. 220 (cited in note 103).
108. *ibid.*
109. *ibid.*, no. 223/1 (cited in note 101).
110. *ibid.*
111. *ibid.*, no. 220 (cited in note 103).
112. DC, NKU Lab 21/3/2, Labour Office, Molo Monthly Reports, no. 35, September 1963.
113. KNA, P.O. 2/1, Review of the Security Situation in the Rift Valley Region, Special Branch headquarters, Nairobi, 11 September 1963.
114. DC, Nyandarua, Incident Reports. Ol Kalou Salient, 5 May 1964.
115. Carey-Jones (1967), p. 168.
116. DC Nyandarua, Ol Kalou Salient: Background to Policies, M. Mercer, July 1965.
117. *EAS*, 11 October and 11 December 1963.
118. KNA, P.O. 3/121, Minutes of the LDSB, 22 August 1962.
119. DC, Nyandarua, Nyandarua District Annual Report 1964, p. 11.
120. Interview: Confidential.
121. Interview: Confidential.
122. *Daily Nation*, 15 October 1963.
123. Kamau is a common Kikuyu name. The term 'Weeping Kamaus' implies weeping Kikuyu or the dispossessed Kikuyu. Whether the Weeping Kamaus actually existed is open to question. During the period 1959 to 1964 there was a recurrent outburst of radical protest. However it is necessary to see these outbursts as a series of reactions rather than the product of organized resistance. We cannot agree with Kanogo's overemphasis on the organizational dimension of the KLFA. In particular Kanogo's claim that the 'KLFA was better organized, commanded stronger allegiance and had greater clarity of purpose than Mau Mau' represents an elementary misreading of the nature of this rural radicalism. See Kanogo (1987), p. 165. The limitation of this

final phase of rural radicalism was its lack of independent organization. The will to resist was there. Their pressure was instrumental in changing the scope of the settlement schemes. However lack of organization ensured that resistance was localized and fragmented allowing the KANU leadership to monopolize the political arena. Ironically, although Kanogo overestimates the organization of rural radicalism, she underestimates its achievement when she argues that in the 'early 1960s, the squatter's cause became submerged by other national interests'. See Kanogo (1987), p. 164. In fact until the late 1960s the squatters succeeded in keeping the land issue at the centre of Kenya's political agenda.

Eight

The Consolidation of Reaction

Controlled decolonization required the exclusion of the masses from political life. The defeat of Mau Mau and the containment of radical nationalists in the early 1960s were preconditions for the realization of this process. But the stabilization of capitalism in post-colonial Kenya also required the neutralization of grassroots aspirations towards social change. In the sphere of politics the main priority of the Kenyatta regime was to ensure that the urban and rural proletariat should be deprived of its own organizational and political voice.

As was the case with the nationalist movement during the period leading up to the Mau Mau split, post-colonial KANU represented an uneasy alliance between radical and moderate nationalists. However, this time it was the moderates who were in the ascendancy and the radicals who were on the defensive. In hindsight it is clear that individual radical leaders were tolerated inside KANU so as to strengthen the party's nationalist credentials. But it was only a matter of time before prominent KANU radicals came under fire. In June 1964, Bildad Kaggia, a former Mau Mau leader and a government minister critical of the conservative direction of the Kenyatta administration, was forced to resign. A year later Pio Pinto, a radical MP, was murdered. A more comprehensive purge took place at the KANU Reorganization Conference held at Limuru in March 1966. Through bureaucratic manipulation, the radical wing of KANU, led by Oginga Odinga and Kaggia, was ousted from positions of influence. Since 1966, with the exception of a brief episode during the 1968 elections, radical nationalism has been a marginal force in Kenyan politics.

The national pattern was reproduced in the Rift Valley, with the Kenyatta regime moving swiftly to impose its authority. The new African government was committed to the maintenance of the existing socio-economic structures, albeit in a modified form. Consequently, one of its first steps was to draw up plans for the elimination of social unrest in the

Rift Valley. As early as 3 April 1964, a meeting of civil servants organized under the auspices of the Ministry of Home Affairs drew up a plan for action.[1] Naivasha was selected as the first operational area for the drive against what were now termed illegal squatters.

It took nearly four years before the Kenyatta government was able to establish stability on the land. During this period, the conflict between the ex-squatters and the state took on a class character, as those without land tried to fight the new group of African capitalist farmers. By the end of 1968, this struggle had come to an end, with the new landlords clearly in ascendancy. A chapter in the struggle for land had come to an end. The emergence of protest in the late 1920s which matured into a mass movement in the 1940s and armed struggle in the early 1950s was finally destroyed by the Kenyan African ruling class in the late 1960s.

Demobilizing the mass movement

Although the transfer of power in the Rift Valley was relatively peaceful, many problems remained unresolved. The pre-emptive measures taken by the colonial administration provided a measure of security for the new political regime. Many activists associated with the agitation for free land were in detention. A loyal group of African collaborators were well placed in key positions in the civil service and the security forces. An aspiring group of African landlords and entrepreneurs provided an important social base for the new regime.

However, the situation in Nakuru and Nyandarua in particular was far from stable. Thousands of landless peasants were determined to acquire land, and they were joined by thousands of migrants, particularly from Central Province, who poured into the Rift Valley in search of land. These migrants, like those already in residence, looked upon European-held farms as their just reward for fighting for *Uhuru*.

KANU could not remain immune from the pressures for radical land reform. In Nakuru, Naivasha and Nyandarua, it became a battleground between those seeking free land and pro-government forces.[2] KANU could not but respond to popular opinions. Had it remained inactive on the issue of land it would have become isolated in the area. The local KANU leadership was forced to yield to pressure from below and articulated the demand for land of the squatters. As the national KANU leadership changed its course the radical elements came to dominate the local party organization. During the years 1964–68 a curious pattern emerged. Given the sensitive political climate the local KANU leadership postponed a showdown with the KLFA and the illegal squatters. A division of labour was established between the national KANU leadership and the lieutenants in Nakuru. In Nakuru, the local KANU spokesman put forward radical rhetoric of support for the illegal squatter movement, while in Parliament ministers denounced 'threats to property'. Personalities with past radical affiliations to Mau Mau, like Assistant Minister Fred Kubai, were despatched to Nakuru. Kubai's brief was to placate the squatters with promises of land in the future in exchange for common sense in the here and now.

KANU was thus able to act as the voice of the landless in Nakuru District. In the long run this would prove invaluable for the consolidation of the Kenyatta regime, but in the short run it meant that the local party became a permanent battlefield between conservatives and radicals. During the years 1964–68 the local branches of KANU were close to the rank and file and influenced by grassroots pressure. The response of the government was regularly to purge the local branches.[3] But no sooner was one group of radical officials purged than another arose to take its place.

The local KANU branches reflected the strength of feeling on the farms. Throughout 1964 demonstrations were held in the district demanding land from the government. Considerable hostility greeted Kenyatta's statement in September that the solution to unemployment was 'to go back to the land'.[4] 'What land?', was the reply. Civil disobedience became the norm as landless Africans organized to defend their interests. The report of the District Commissioner of Nakuru in 1965 gives a flavour of the period:

> The general outlook in the Molo division is not encouraging. Many so called freedom fighters are determined more than ever on the theme of free land and Government jobs; they are resolved to promote local support to obtain grievances for free lands. The DC held another baraza on the 10 February 1965 at Elburgon aimed at the drive to encourage active participation in the fight against illegal oath takers and subversive elements in the district.[5]

The growing class polarization created a political climate fraught with tensions. The African gentry formed the backbone of political support for the government. For the local peasants, these capitalist farmers were perceived as hostile carpetbaggers. Mass unrest could only be checked through regular police operations. But police raids on illegal squatter settlements could not solve the underlying problem: most landless Africans simply had nowhere to go.

To prevent the situation from getting out of hand the Kenyatta regime modified its policy of raids and evictions. A public relations exercise was launched to minimize the problem of landlessness. A circular from the Attorney General in September 1965 ordered that the term 'illegal squatter' be dropped in preference to the word 'squatter'. The Attorney General wrote: 'Please try to pass on to people this new application so that African squatters may not be made to look as if they are illegally residing in any part of Kenya'.[6] As a token gesture a few plots were made available to landless squatters in the District.[7]

These cosmetic exercises made little difference to the life of the landless peasants. The new African farmers tightened the screws on the squatters and life for the peasants deteriorated still further. The District Commissioner of Nakuru summed up the emerging pattern of class relations in 1969:

> The new African farmer forged ahead in his long road to self sufficiency with considerable credit on his part, despite a legion of difficulties. The Gordian Knot was still finance. Unfortunately this class of farmer has been very ruthless and inconsiderate in dealing with squatters whom they find on the farms after purchase. This might sow seeds of bitterness among the squatters when their fellow Africans treat them with impunity and contempt.[8]

This acknowledgement of class antagonism was rare within government circles. Most civil servants preferred to find outside troublemakers behind every outburst of protest.

Opposition to the policies of the Kenyatta regime took on an increasingly strident note in Nakuru District. Towards the middle of 1965 a ground swell of support for the radical wing of KANU became evident. Bildad Kaggia and Ochieng Oneko's denunciation of corruption and nepotism in Parliament found a strong response among the peasants. The police complained that KANU meetings in Nakuru District had become rallies 'for attacking the Government and its officials and supporting Mr Kaggia on the issue of free land.'[9]

When the radical wing of KANU split to form the Kenya People's Union (KPU) many local activists joined the new party. To the dismay of the local establishment the have-nots finally had an articulate and independent organizational structure. The administration swiftly moved to destroy the KPU in Nakuru. To this end they combined a subtle policy of divide and rule with out-and-out repression.

The government was not prepared to allow grassroots opposition to acquire a coherent political organization. KPU activists were harassed and their meetings were banned.[10] In 1967 the Special Branch devoted nearly its entire resources to the anti-KPU operation. One Special Branch officer drafted in from Nairobi remarked that one way or another 'subversion must be rooted out'.[11]

Repression was complemented by the tactic of divide and rule. The local establishment set out to split the KPU along tribal lines. In one case a group of Kikuyu KPU activists were approached and prevailed upon to have a private discussion with Kenyatta.[12] They were informed that the administration would assist the establishment of an association of ex-freedom fighters. They were told that this association would be given serious consideration for plots in settlement schemes and given assistance for purchasing land. These approaches had the desired results. The KPU could not compete against the newly formed Nakuru Ex-Freedom Fighters' Association and lost its influence among the local Kikuyu community. Since the Kikuyu constituted the majority of the population in the District it meant the irreversible decline of the KPU in Nakuru. The District Commissioner of Nakuru enthused about the new association: 'It is such a large number that they can claim to be a backbone to public opinion in the District'.[13] In his annual report for 1967, one district officer boasted: 'The KPU is only supported by a handful of Luos. The Kenya Land Freedom Army . . . (another name for the association FF) . . . which dominates the Elburgon area have been quiet since they have been officially licensed to collect money to buy a farm'.[14]

The destruction of the KPU was thorough. But although a small group of Kikuyu activists were pacified, the underlying agrarian problem continued to generate unrest. When Kenyatta visited neighbouring Naivasha in February 1968, hostility was barely kept under the surface. Local KANU officials pointedly ignored the ceremonies.[15]

Towards the end of 1968 the political climate in Nakuru became noticeably more stable. Years of economic insecurity had turned anger and determination into frustration and despair. There were still isolated cases of protest but those without land withdrew from protest activity. The local activists also lost much of their initial enthusiasm. Many of them turned towards the KANU establishment and sought political favours. Others attempted to turn their leadership qualities towards business and commerce.

The consolidation of reaction

The demobilization of the protest movement allowed the new African establishment to pursue its interests with vigour and confidence. Many squatters were rounded up and kicked off the land while others were forced to work for the new landlords for no pay. A report drawn up by the office of the Provincial Commissioner observed:

> Nearly all local employers now-a-days gave out shambas as a means of incentive scheme and surety for labour stability but in some cases the scheme is being wrongly applied by the new farmers, that is to say, some African farmers fail to pay their labour wages simply because the labour are provided with land to cultivate and grow foodstuff as subsistence.[16]

The new African landlords were undercapitalized. Many of them were absentee landlords who continued to reside in Nairobi or the Central Province. They utilized the availability of a large pool of landless squatters to their advantage. In most cases they cleared some of the squatters off their land and retained the rest as unpaid farm labourers with limited rights to a small plot.

Mass unemployment, estimated around 28 per cent had a demoralizing impact on the population. The intensity of economic insecurity among squatters in Nakuru may be gauged from the following report of the labour officer: 'with the construction of the Mount Margaret satellite tracking station getting under way, forty five people were taken on . . . Everyday more than 200 people turned out to try their luck some of whom were known to travel more than twenty miles everyday to the site.'[17]

The situation in the 1970s became worse. A demographic explosion combined with mass migration meant that between 1969 and 1979 the population of Nakuru District rose from 290,863 to 522,333.[18]

The polarization of class relations in Nakuru was particularly strikingly indicated by the unequal distribution of land. In 1974, of those Africans that owned land 91 per cent held only 21 per cent of the total – each holding less than three acres. At the other end of the social hierarchy, 2 per cent of the owners held 69 per cent of total land.[19] These manifest inequalities were widely resented, but a decade of poverty and repression had taken their toll. The peasantry lost interest in land agitation.

The consolidation of the new African establishment in Nakuru did not imply the end of political conflict. Only now it was a conflict among contending groups *within* the establishment for land, political influence and access to capital. A rich district, with a considerable amount of land available for sale, Nakuru was a much coveted prize. Virtually every group within the ruling class made a claim for Nakuru. Politicians and entrepreneurs from different parts of Kenya converged on the district to stake a claim. The Kenyatta family and its allies monopolized many of the best landholdings hitherto owned by European farmers. The then Vice-President, Daniel arap Moi, became the leading property-owner in Nakuru Town. Lower down the social hierarchy, fierce battles erupted over every acre of available land.[20]

During the past decade as the class struggle has become suspended so 'politics' has become nothing more than conflict within the elite. An amalgam of populist Kikuyu politicians and entrepreneurs constitutes the core of the Nakuru political establishment. The continuous process of shifting alignments between contending groups of politicians indicates that the fierce battles within KANU are devoid of any ideological significance. Branch officials and MPs come and go as one set of alliances breaks down in favour of another.

From Mau Mau to today

The neutralization and repression of the KPU has certain parallels with the containment of Mau Mau, but also important differences. In different ways and under different conditions Mau Mau and the KPU sought to give organizational expression to the grievances of the urban and landless proletariat. To be sure the KPU never achieved the mass support enjoyed by Mau Mau but, as the Nakuru example shows, it had the potential to connect with grassroots discontent. Both Mau Mau and the KPU faced state repression. Like its colonial predecessor, the Kenyatta regime used the state machine to deal with its political opponents.

Most KPU public rallies were banned under the Outlying and Special Districts Ordinance.[21] In June 1966, the Preservation of Public Security Act was amended to include preventive detention, and new powers designed to suppress political opposition were put on the statute book.[22] The civil service and the rest of the state apparatus were mobilized to crush the KPU. As Kenyatta told a group of provincial and district commissioners: 'civil servants are not impartial. They are KANU civil servants.'[23]

However it is important not to lose sight of the fundamental differences between the containment of Mau Mau and the suppression of the KPU. In contrast to the Mau Mau era, the Kenyan state after independence had a political organization, KANU, which could be used to mediate between itself and the masses. KANU relied not only on repression but also on its access to resources to buy off opponents and to reward supporters. When necessary, KANU could make use of nationalist rhetoric to win support. In Nakuru District it encouraged the newly formed Nakuru Ex-Freedom Fighers' Association to outflank the KPU. Concessions to this association were combined with a recognition of the role of 'freedom-fighters'. But with one crucial difference. KANU celebrated not so much Mau Mau as the ethnic ties that linked Kenyatta with the Kikuyu 'freedom-fighters'. This link, which promised material rewards, was understood in ethnic terms. In much the same way the KPU was dismissed as an ethnic threat to Kikuyu interests from the Luo. The isolation of the KPU in Nakuru District indicated that unlike the colonial regime, the Kenyatta government could develop significant social support against radical nationalism.

The vantage point of the late 1960s helps put Mau Mau into perspective. As indicated earlier, Mau Mau's greatest strength was its organizational independence. The split with moderate nationalists allowed radical activists to promote the aspirations of the masses and thus challenge the very foundations of the colonial order. The problem was that this challenge remained diffuse because Mau Mau did not develop its own independent ideology. The failure to evolve a coherent class-based social programme meant that Mau Mau was simply the militant wing of a nationalist movement. The fundamental conflict of interest between those who supported militant nationalism and those who advocated moderation was never clarified. As a result once the militants were suppressed the collaborators could take over the leadership of the nationalist movement.

The assistance of the colonial administration made possible the ascendency of Kenyatta over the nationalist movement. In reality Kenyatta and his class hated Mau Mau. As he argued in 1967: 'We are determined to have independence in peace, and we shall not allow hooligans to rule Kenya. We must have no hatred towards one another. Mau Mau was a disease which had been eradicated, and must never be remembered again.'[24] Yet such sentiment does not stop those who now rule Kenya from claiming the mantle of Mau Mau. Thus in 1969 leading colleagues of Kenyatta attempted to mobilize the Kikuyu masses against the Luo people through a campaign of oathing. This campaign was often justified on the grounds that it represented a renewal of the Mau Mau tradition.

In the post-Mau Mau era, radical nationalists lacked even organizational independence. Without organization or a political programme they could offer no alternative to Kenyatta. Imprisoned inside KANU, prominent radical leaders were nothing more than individuals with grievances. A recent radical assessment of this period notes that 'the militant nationalists' were left 'without an organizational base. They remained a minority faction within KANU, having failed to create their own sources of funds, their own propaganda organs, and institutionalized popular support'.[25] This failure of militant nationalism was no accident. Militants' involvement in KANU was a reflection of their isolation from mass politics. More to the point they felt more at home inside KANU than mobilizing the urban/landless proletariat.

Many individual radical leaders such as Bildad Kaggia, Oginga Odinga, Ochieng Oneko and J.M. Kariuki were courageous in their denunciation of the corruption and the elitism of the Kenyatta regime. But politically they lacked a coherent identity and an alternative. Their criticism centred on Kenyatta's failure to keep promises rather than taking a standpoint that was fundamentally different to that of the government. Such criticisms earned them imprisonment and, in the case of J.M. Kariuki, death. It is all the more ironic that these radical figures were indispensable in the consolidation of Kenyatta's influence. Their very presence in KANU and in the government endowed the new regime with credibility. Seen as friends of the people, radical leaders lent weight to the conviction that the Kenyatta government would do something for ordinary Kenyans. Putting up with radical KANU branches in the countryside was for the Kenyatta government a small price to pay for the legitimacy it bestowed on the party. Once the transition was made towards the stabilization of the new regime, Kenyatta could begin to rid his party of the troublemakers. Whereas in the early 1960s this would have constituted a dangerous course of action, by the mid-1960s the radicals were a spent force. They had become accomplices in their own political destruction.

The experience of the years 1945–69 in Kenya shows that an undifferentiated nationalist movement gives way to the triumph of reaction. It is an experience that has been confirmed time and again in post-war Africa. An undifferentiated nationalist movement contains within itself conflicts of interest which remain suppressed. Only the capitalist class and the petit-bourgeois can profit from leaving such conflicts of interests unresolved. That is why these social strata felt so ill at ease, even threatened by Mau Mau. Mau Mau brought the question of social change out into the open, forcing them to retreat. Once Mau Mau was defeated, an all-class nationalist party could be created, one that precisely because it was undifferentiated would be responsive only to the interests of the new African bourgeoisie. In this process the colonial regime played not an unimportant role. The establishment of such a collaborationist movement is the central strategic objective of controlled decolonization.

Decolonization in perspective

Writing in 1977, the Kenyan historian Ben Kipkorir noted that the Mau Mau Emergency was 'certainly responsible for the precise timing of the conclusion of British rule in Kenya but it must always be remembered that Kenya was the last of the East Africa territories to obtain formal Independence'.[26] Although this observation is in one sense unobjectionable, stated in this way it implies that Mau Mau was responsible for delaying the decolonization process. Aside from the dubious comparison of a settler-dominated colony with Uganda and Tanzania, Kipkorir misses the essential point. It was precisely because of the powerful dislocation caused by Mau Mau that the straightforward option of decolonization had to be ruled out. Special measures which could guarantee British interests had to be implemented before Kenya could achieve formal independence.

According to the perspective of Kipkorir, decolonization was speeded up by moderation and slowed down by militancy. Decolonization is thus seen as a reward for responsible behaviour. From this perspective Britain is portrayed as a bungling but essentially benevolent colonial power and resistance is depicted as an unnecessary irrelevance. One of the most influential historians of the British Empire, the late Jack Gallagher, actually denies the very existence of the struggle for freedom as a factor in the decolonization process. Gallagher writes: 'But where in all this are the freedom fighters? Not in West Africa, that is clear, for there was nothing to fight over except a time-table. But the places to look for them are in East and Central Africa. And there they were the white settlers.'[27] According to this tradition of mainstream imperial history with its emphasis on the 'official mind', the struggles of Kikuyu squatters is at best a minor detail on the canvas of history.

It is worth recalling that on the eve of the post-Second World War era, Britain had no intention of abandoning its empire in Africa. Tropical Africa in general and Kenya in particular were central to the calculations of the British Chiefs of Staff.[28] And with the decline of British power globally, Africa emerged as an important economic asset. As Sir Stafford Cripps, the Chancellor of the Exchequer, informed a Conference of African Governors in November 1947: 'the whole future of the sterling group and its ability to survive depends in my view upon a quick and extensive development of its African resources'.[29]

In August 1949, at a time when officials were reporting a breakdown in labour discipline on European farms in the Rift Valley, Arthur Creech Jones, the Labour Secretary of State for the Colonies, insisted on reaffirming the *status quo* in the White Highlands. He wrote to the Fabian Colonial Bureau:

> The Settled Area has been developed by European enterprise and, indeed, with African labour, contributes the major part to the economy and prosperity of the country. . . . I believe that if the Settled Area were declared to be generally available for African settlement it would have a most disturbing effect on relations between European and African.[30]

Six years later, the Report of the East Africa Royal Commission recognized that the *status quo* could not be sustained and that the Highlands had to be opened to African cultivators. This shift in the outlook of the 'official mind' was the direct product of Gallagher's invisible freedom fighters. The role of African resistance in the decolonization of the continent was decisive in forcing the hands of the Colonial Office. The February 1948 riots in Accra in the Gold Coast unleashed a chain of events that could not be contained within the framework of a colonial empire. As David Rooney, the biographer of Sir Charles Arden-Clarke, notes, the February 1948 events started a 'revolution which in a few years was to free two hundred million . . . Africans from the domination and control of Europeans'.[31] The actual process of decolonization was influenced by Whitehall's determination to limit the damage. Where the nationalist movement threatened to pursue a radical course, the schedule for decolonization was held up to gain time for the consolidation of reaction. There is more than a grain of truth in the 'generalization' cited by D. Goldsworthy, 'that Mau Mau hastened independence everywhere else in Africa but delayed it in Kenya'.[32]

The discussion on the process of decolonization tends to ignore the general pattern. The outbreak of resistance is often explained as a result of policy mistakes or the misrule of the governor concerned. From the perspective of the historiography of 'the official mind', it is the administrators that assume the central role. History is made by colonial officialdom and the role of resistance is of secondary importance. Thus great attention is devoted to the conflict of interest between field officers, colonial governors and Whitehall. These conflicts are often presented as key variables in the historical process. No doubt there were conflicts of interest within the colonial officialdom. But what significance are we to attach to them?

According to David Throup, local officials controlled the flow of information to London, thereby thwarting the Colonial Office's objectives in Kenya. Moreover, Throup suggests that Governor Sir Philip Mitchell was not suited to handle Mau Mau because of his lack of experience with radical nationalists.[33] In this scenario, Mitchell's failures bear responsibility for much of the crisis in Kenya. In the same vein, Rooney suggests that the Governor of the Gold Coast, Sir Gerald Creasy, failed to see the warning signs of the nationalist explosion. Following the criticisms levelled at the local administration by the Watson Report, Rooney writes of the 'inadequacy' and 'incompetence' of the colonial regime in the Gold Coast.[34] According to T.J. Spinner, the 1953 crisis in British Guiana was to a considerable extent due to the over-reaction of Governor Sir Alfred Savage to the situation.[35] It appears that Savage's previous tenure as governor of Barbados 'left him unprepared for the hectic, frantic political life of British Guiana'.[36] Our friends, the incompetent administrators, also make their appearance in Malaya in the period leading up to the outbreak of revolt. Throup's characterization of the Mitchell administration and Rooney's condemnation of the colonial rulers in the Gold Coast is echoed in R.F. Holland's criticism of the 'archaic bureaucracy' in Malaya. According to Holland, 'the local British authorities had failed to act decisively, in the face of an earlier accretion of incidents because the prospect of much greater metropolitan supervision was unpalatable for an entrenched and often archaic bureaucracy'.[37]

It is interesting to note that, despite the obsession of imperial historians with individual officials as the makers of history, the explanation for Britain's post-1945 colonial wars tends to hang on the recurrent theme of administrative incompetence. Can it be the case that a series of administrative errors provided the impetus behind the collapse of the Empire? Could a governor other than Mitchell have averted the Mau Mau rebellion, as Throup suggests?[38] From our consideration of Mau Mau and other colonial revolts it would appear that the incompetence of colonial officialdom has only a minor significance in the unfolding drama. What we have is not a series of over-reactions and mistakes but predictable courses of action. And instead of seeing each colonial emergency as part of a series of accidents it is possible to outline a common pattern.

Whatever the inclination of the colonial official concerned, the response to radical nationalism followed a common pattern consisting of four parts: these were first, a campaign of criminalization, secondly a pre-emptive blow, thirdly the construction of a group of collaborators and fourthly the encouragement of ethnic tensions through a policy of divide and rule. The recurrence of this pattern shows that whatever the motives of individual officials, they were mere agents of forces beyond their control.

The criminalization of Mau Mau has already been discussed. In the Gold Coast, the nationalist movement was labelled as part of the communist conspiracy. Alternatively it was suggested that the Convention People's Party used the 'Ju Ju' of 'darkest' Africa.[39] In response to the General Strike of 1950, Governor Arden-Clarke justified his call for a state of emergency in the following terms:

> the T.U.C. had no mandate for a general strike, and did not call a general strike . . . the strikes that have occurred have been engineered by certain members of the CPP . . . these are well known tactics advocated and practised by communists and others whose aim is to seize power for themselves by creating chaos and disrupting the life of the community.[40]

Lack of evidence for these accusations in no way inhibited Arden-Clarke from implementing a State of Emergency.

In British Guiana the Colonial Office was confronted with a democratically elected People's Progressive Party (PPP) government not to its liking. Unlike the interim governments of other colonies, the PPP ministers led by Cheddi Jagan refused to play the role of grateful natives. In October 1953 the British government suspended British Guiana's constitution, sent in troops and removed the PPP from office. The State of Emergency in British Guiana was justified on the grounds that it narrowly averted a communist takeover. The Colonial Secretary, Viscount Lyttelton, stated that there was irrefutable evidence of a 'deadly design' which aimed to 'turn British Guiana into a totalitarian state dominated by Communist ideas'.[41] Again, to this day Britain has deemed it unnecessary to publish its irrefutable evidence of the PPP's conspiracy.

In Malaya, the nationalist movement was indeed influenced by communists. This made the campaign of criminalization a straightforward matter. The colonial propaganda machinery simply alleged that Soviet instructions to revolt were transmitted to Malayan communists via a conference held in Calcutta in February 1948. Again all that is missing is the evidence.

The campaign of criminalization culminating in the declaration of a state of emergency provided the justification for a pre-emptive blow. Under special powers, militants were detained and organizations were banned. The objective was to remove the radical nationalists so as to gain a breathing space for the evolution of a moderate alternative. In the case of Kenya and Malaya, declarations of emergency acted as a catalyst for armed revolt. The events in Kenya have already been considered. In Malaya, the communist party faced a campaign of repression in the months leading up to the Emergency. Prevented from any access to legitimate political action, the communists were forced towards revolt. But like Mau Mau, the Malayan communist party was totally unprepared for the Emergency. If there was an instruction from Moscow, it certainly did not hear of it. According to M. Stenson its members were taken totally by surprise and their response was a 'panic scramble for the safety of the jungle'.[42]

The pre-emptive blow is often described as 'overreaction' in the studies of Britain's colonial wars. R.A. Burrowes' assessment of the British campaign of hysteria against Jagan in British Guiana is typical of the school of 'overreaction':

> The international press was also quite surprised, after the build up from Whitehall, to find that there was no civil war, no disorder in Guyana on their arrival. It became obvious to almost everyone concerned that the whole crisis was the result of an over reaction of the colonial civil servants stationed in Guyana and, in turn, of the British Government itself. In the context of the Cold War it is quite easy to see how such a muddle could come about.[43]

Far from being a muddle, the British *coup* which overthrew Jagan was an essential component of controlled decolonization. It was precisely the need to eliminate mass support for a radical nationalist movement that inspired the intervention. To achieve this objective London held up British Guiana independence until 1966, by which time the colony could be left in safe hands.

Moreover the suspension of British Guiana's constitution and the removal of its elected government had international repercussions. It served as an object lesson to other nationalist parties which might have considered an independent strategy. Nkrumah used Jagan's demise as an argument for his moderate policy of 'Tactical Action' and for ridding the CPP of radical personalities.[44]

Through the pre-emptive blow, the colonial administration gained time to construct a political alternative to the radical wing of the nationalist movement. Before Arden-Clarke was despatched to take over as Governor of the Gold Coast he was told by Creech Jones: 'I want you to go to the Gold Coast. The country is on the edge of revolution. We are in danger of losing it'.[45] Arden Clarke's reaction to this threat follows the predictable pattern. When he arrived, he asked one of the veteran officials: 'Can't you form a moderate party to keep these buggers out'?[46] At the time in 1949 the moderate option was still premature. But Arden-Clarke got his opportunity a year later. The Declaration of Emergency threw the CPP on the defensive and provided Arden-Clarke with an opportunity to educate Nkrumah in the realities of colonial politics.

In Malaya, British Guiana and Kenya, the colonial administration faced a more formidable problem. In these cases the radical nationalist movements had to be isolated or destroyed. In Malaya, counter-insurgency was only one side of the coin. The creation of a conservative nationalist movement was the political objective of the British military. Holland writes that 'through a combination of anti-insurgency techniques . . . deft political management, the British had made Malaya safe for Malay conservatives and Chinese businessmen'.[47] In British Guiana, during a period lasting more than a decade, the colonial administration succeeded in splitting the PPP and forging an alliance of moderate collaborators to whom power could be devolved.

One of the tactics used by British imperialism to weaken the power of the nationalist opposition was to provoke the ethnic dimension of political life. By the time independence arrived, the Gold Coast, British Guiana, Kenya and Malaya all suffered from the problem of ethnic tension. The success of divide-and-rule tactics was most striking in British Guiana. The PPP was a multiracial party with a strong class base among urban workers and the rural proletariat. After the 1953 Emergency the colonial administration systematically used every opportunity to exacerbate conflict between Afro-Caribbeans and Asians.[48] The Colonial Administration's efforts were well rewarded – by the end of the 1950s ethnic tension had become a key issue and the PPP was forced to become a party predominantly based on the Asian community.

The specific form of decolonization in Kenya follows the overall pattern. As in the Gold Coast, British Guiana or Malaya, the colonial government directly intervened in the shaping of the nationalist movement. The success of controlled decolonization was inseparable from the close links established by the colonial administration with a section of the nationalist leadership in the late 1950s and 1960s. The consolidation of a moderate nationalist movement around Kenyatta was the prerequisite for the displacement of the radical challenge. In this new circumstance, something like the Olenguruone factor could be easily contained. Thus the struggle of landless Kikuyu at Bahati Farm, discussed in Chapter 7, had all the makings of another Olenguruone. In the event it became a local affair with no external consequences – the KANU leadership could hold the centre stage unperturbed by events at Bahati.

The problem of national liberation

The defeat of Mau Mau and the destruction of the radical option in other ex-colonies by Britain must be taken account of in any balanced consideration of the subject. The demobilization of radical nationalism and the subsequent consolidation of reaction, a process repeated throughout much of Africa, raises important questions about the relationship of national liberation and decolonization. National liberation movements often represent alliances of conflicting social forces. These alliances are necessarily temporary groupings directed against colonial domination. Controlled decolonization aims to strengthen the conservative constituents of these alliances and always directs its blows against a movement's radical wing. Given a common stake in the perpetuation of capitalist social relations, conservative nationalists find the approaches of the colonial administration irresistible. There is now irrefutable evidence that at a certain stage in the transfer of power, the convergence of interests between the propertied elements and the colonial power far outweighs the national unity between the haves and the have-nots.

Marxist literature, with its emphasis on the primacy of class interests, anticipates the problem of alliances between different social forces fighting for national liberation. Marx and Engels warned about the fragile links that drew together conflicting interests around the struggle for freedom. In their writings they continually emphasized that it is often the propertyless masses that do all the fighting while the rich stand on the sidelines waiting to snatch the fruits of their victory:

> It is self-evident that in the impending bloody conflicts, as in all earlier ones, it is the workers who, in the main will have to win the victory by their courage, determination and self-sacrifice. As previously so also in this struggle, the mass of the petty bourgeois will as long as possible remain hesitant, undecided and inactive, and then, as soon as the issue has been decided, will seize the victory for themselves, will call upon the workers to maintain tranquility and return to their work, will guard against so-called excesses and bar the proletariat from the fruits of victory.[49]

The danger of obscuring the conflict of interest between those whose objective is merely *political change* and those who aspire to *social transformation* is a theme stressed in the writings of Marx, Engels and Lenin. The experience of *Uhuru* in Kenya and more broadly in Africa and the calls for a 'Second Independence' from radical quarters confirm the continued relevance of Marx's observations.

There is no a priori solution for the problem of national liberation. The conflict that inevitably erupts between those who fight for social change and those who have a stake in the perpetuation of the status quo is always resolved through the balance of class forces. Nevertheless from the experience of national liberation struggles this century it is possible to draw out two important lessons.

First, and this is amply illustrated by the experience of Mau Mau, the minimal guarantee of real change is the existence of a separate organization of plebeian or working-class elements. Without an independent organization led by and accountable to those without property, the KANU solution becomes inevitable. The experience of Africa shows that independence is always followed by an offensive of the propertied elements, and without an organized movement to counter-attack, the radical forces can become marginalized.

Secondly, the plebeian and working-class elements cannot wait until after independence to fight for their own separate interests. By the time independence arrives the balance usually shifts in favour of the propertied classes. Through controlling the state and the nation's resources the propertied classes are well placed to defeat their opponents. The separation of the movement for independence from the struggle for social transformation is always, without exception, resolved against the interests of the masses. Although the fight for national freedom takes a *logical* priority in that it represents an attack on the most immediate and the most tangible manifestation of domination it cannot be *chronologically* separated from the struggle for social liberation. To postpone the objective of social change to a distinct stage in the future invites a form of independence which is necessarily on the terms favouring vested interests.

It was in the course of the first modern anti-colonial struggle, that of the Irish national liberation movement, that the issues under discussion were raised in all their acuteness. The Irish nationalist movement represented a classical alliance of diverse social forces. It was to the merit of the Irish Marxist, James Connolly, to recognize that while national liberation required the support of different social strata, the working class had to organize itself independently to ensure that the struggle would not be degraded by the narrower concerns of the Irish capitalist classes.

For Britain the tensions in the Irish nationalist alliance provided an excellent opportunity for containing the threat it represented. Anticipating the strategy deployed in Africa four decades later, the British government took steps to bolster the conservative wing of Irish republicanism. In the crucial period following the 1916 Easter Rebellion the British clamped down on radical nationalists and released more moderate republicans from prison. The prominent republican Maire Corneford later claimed that as a result 'the counter-revolution within the republican movement began in October 1917'. Corneford observed: 'it could be argued that the British government moved with unerring instinct to benefit from a temporary confusion and help towards the most conservative sequence'.[50] It is this unerring instinct that stood Britain in good stead during the succeeding six decades.

The success of the Irish model of decolonization, leading to the marginalization of radical elements, is intimately linked to the moderates' domination of the nationalist movement. Connolly's address to the Citizen Army just before the Easter Rebellion retains its relevance to this day:

> If we win, we'll be great heroes; but if we lose we'll be the greatest scoundrels the country ever produced. In the event of victory, hold on to your rifles, as those with whom we are fighting may stop before our goal is reached. We are out for economic as well as political liberty. [51]

Connolly's warnings were to prove prophetic. Within six years the Irish nationalist struggle was transformed into a bitter civil war between moderates and radicals.

The absence of a clearly articulated social programme representing the interests of the masses ensured that differences inside the Irish Republican Movement were expressed as those between 'hard' men and moderates. Differences established on such subjective and arbitrary foundations ensure that the radical point of view remains without a clearly articulated perspective. This was also the central weakness of Mau Mau: radicals distinguished themselves from moderates primarily through the *means* they advocated for realizing an otherwise common goal. The failure to evolve a proletarian social programme for the national liberation movement means that conflicts of interests are expressed around narrow tactical questions, usually the means to be deployed in the struggle. Consequently disputes often acquire a generational foundation whereby the youth loses patience with the cautious elders. This phenomenon is paralleled throughout Africa, with the verandah boys and youth wings often in at the forefront of direct action against the colonial powers.

The experience of South Africa shows striking parallels with Mau Mau. There the African National Congress (ANC), founded in 1912 by a distinguished group of chiefs and sections of the educated elite, reflected the cautious approach of the KAU. Indeed the ANC sought reforms through arguing that if they were not granted, then the 'agitators' would prevail over the African population. The Reverend John L. Dube, the first President of the ANC, warned in 1926 that without change there would be:

> a fertile breeding ground for hot-headed agitators amongst us Natives, who might prove to be a bigger menace to this country than is generally realized today. Let us all labour to forestall them: that is my purpose in life, even if I have to labour single-handed . . . Race co-operation must be the watchword. [52]

This cautious conciliatory approach inevitably aroused the impatience of sections of the nationalist movement. At about the time of the emergence of the Kikuyu squatter movement the ANC leadership took steps to ensure that this impatience did not get out of hand. On Easter Sunday 1944, under the careful watch of the ANC leadership, the Congress

Youth League was launched. Many of the future leaders of the nationalist movement – Nelson Mandela, Walter Sisulu and Oliver Tambo –
were part of this new initiative.

In the succeeding five years the uneasy alliance discussed in relation to
the Kenyan nationalist movement was evident between the Youth
League and the ANC old guard. This tension crystallized in the boycott
controversy, leading to the adoption of the 1949 Programme of Action.
As in Kenya the debate was over tactics – the young militants took their
stand on promoting boycott and non-collaboration. In contrast to
Kenya, the Youth League succeeded in taking over the ANC leadership
– in 1949 Walter Sisulu became its Secretary General.

In contrast to Kenya, the Youth League was absorbed into the ANC
leadership. The ANC became a movement with influence over a broad
spectrum of social forces – well able to contain conflicts of interests.
To this day the question of what interests will prevail remains unresolved.
But without the emergence of an independent working-class movement,
with its own social programme for national liberation, the Kenya solution is inevitable. This is the inescapable conclusion drawn from the
experience of Ireland, Kenya and the rest of Africa.

Our aim is not to suggest that situations are the same the world over,
from Ireland to Kenya to South Africa. The specific conditions that
prevail in each case makes such comparisons facile. Rather it is possible
to point to the inherent instability of the boundaries that separate radical
from moderate nationalism. If conflicting social interests remain
unclarified, then such differences become merely differences in emphasis
with no long-term consequences. More to the point, under such circumstances reaction will always prevail. Radicalism and activism cannot be
long sustained without a coherent organizational expression. Although
there are exceptions, the general pattern is that the mood of defiance
gives way to caution. Thus even KANU, Kenyatta's nationalist party,
could live with a relatively radical youth wing. For without an organized
social base, radicalism becomes incoherent and ultimately an ineffective
point of view. The triumph of KANU over Mau Mau illustrates a
central problem of national liberation: if the questions of what Connolly
called economic liberty or of conflicting social interests remain
unresolved in the course of the struggle, the triumph of reaction is
guaranteed.

Notes

1. KNA, P.O. 3/315, Policy on Illegal Settlement, no. 11, Notes of meeting held in the
   office of the Permanent Secretary, Ministry of Home Affairs, on Friday 3rd April,

1964 regarding Illegal Squatters.

2. Interviews and *Daily Nation*, 12 September 1964.

3. DC, NKU L & O 17/17 vol. VII, Law and Order, KANU. See reports during the period under consideration.

4. Interviews.

5. DC, NKU Adm 15/3/4, Molo. Monthly Reports, no. 66.

6. DC, Nyandarua Lab 4/1/vol. 2, Unemployment, Illegal Squatters, no. 189, Special Commissioner, squatters, circular 14 September 1965, Legality of the Use of the term Squatter.

7. The small plots (4.5 acres) were insufficient to provide most of the recipients with their subsistence requirements.

8. DC, NKU Adm 15/3/3A vol. 2, Annual Intelligence Reports, Annual Report Year Ending 1969.

9. DC, NKU Adm 15/3/4, Molo, Monthly Reports, no. 67, April 1965.

10. DC, NKU See reports in *ibid.*, and Adm 15/3/5, Administration Monthly Reports.

11. DC, NKU Adm 15/4/4, DOs meeting, Incident Reports, December 1966.

12. Interviews.

13. DC, NKU Adm 15/32/3A, Administration. Intelligence. Annual Reports, no. 89, Nakuru Report (Annual) 1967.

14. *ibid.*

15. DC, NKU Adm 15/3/10, Administration. Monthly Reports. Naivasha, no. 36, Report for February.

16. PC, RVP Lab 27/3/1, vol. 3 (no file number), Report, September 1969.

17. DC, NKU, Lab 27/3/3, vol. 1, Labour Reports, Naivasha, no. 69, January 1969.

18. Senga (1980), p. 4.

19. Njonjo (1980), p. 39.

20. Land registration files for the period 1966 onwards were missing when the author visited the Land Office in Nairobi in 1972. When the author inquired about their whereabouts, he was told 'they are out on permanent loan'.

21. On the state offensive against the KPU see Mueller (1972), Chapter 4.

22. *ibid.*, p. 237.

23. Cited in *ibid.*, p. 237.

24. Kenyatta (1968), p. 189.

25. Anonymous (1982), p. 20.

26. Kipkorir (1977), p. 325.

27. Gallagher (1982), p. 148.

28. See Louis (1984), pp. 108–9.

29. Cited in Pearce (1982), p. 96.

30. Cited in Goldsworthy (1971), p. 142.

31. Rooney (1982), p. 82.

32. Goldsworthy (1971), p. 28.

33. Throup (1987), p. 237.

34. Rooney (1982), pp. 86–8.

35. Spinner (1984), p. 53.

36. *ibid.*, p. 35.

37. Holland (1985).

38. Throup (1987), p. 250.

39. Cited in Rooney (1982), p. 113.

40. *ibid.*, p. 104.

41. Cited in Spinner (1984), p. 50.

42. Stenson (1974), p. 145.

43. Burrowes (1984), p. 55.

44. Marable (1987), p. 114.

45. Rooney (1982), p. 88.

46. *ibid.*, p. 212.
47. Holland (1985), p. 111.
48. Spinner (1984), pp. 57–8.
49. Marx and Engels (1978), p. 282.
50. Cornford (1969), pp. 42, 44.
51. Cited in Greaves (1976), p. 403.
52. Cited in Gerhart (1978), p. 48.

Bibliography

Archival sources

During the course of research the following archives were consulted:

District Commissioner, Nakuru   (DC, Nakuru)
District Commissioner, Nyandarua   (DC, Nyandarua)
Kenya National Archives   (KNA)
Labour Officer, Molo   (Lab. Molo)
Kenya Land Office   (KLO)
Nakuru Labour Office   (NLO)
Provincial Commissioner, Nyeri   (PC, Nyeri)
Provincial Commissioner, Rift Valley Province (PC, RVP)
Public Record Office   (PRO)

Of these archives, that of D C, Nakuru, KNA and NLO were used most extensively. In addition Annual Reports and Handing Over Reports concerning Central Province and the Rift Valley Province were consulted on microfilm in the library of Loyola College, Montreal and in the Seeley Historical Library, Cambridge.

1. District Commissioner, Nakuru

A large number of files dealing with correspondence from the District Commissioner and higher officials at the provincial and the central administrative level were consulted. In addition monthly intelligence reports were examined. These include:

Land Deposit Sixteen
Labour Deposit Twenty Seven
Administrative Deposit Fifteen
Law and Order Deposit Seventeen
Trade and Customs Deposit Six
Education Deposit Twelve
Forest Deposit Sixteen
Forest Deposit Thirteen
Local Government Deposit Five
Community Development Deposit Twenty Six

2. District Commissioner, Nyandarua

A small number of files were consulted. This archive was mainly useful for the post-independence period, and contains monthly and annual reports on the period 1963–70. Files consulted include:

Labour Deposit One
Labour Deposit Four
Labour Deposit Twenty Seven
Trade and Commerce Deposit Six

3. Kenya National Archives
A large number of files pertaining to the Districts of the Rift Valley Province were consulted. In addition, files on Central Province and on Kikuyu living outside Central Province were perused. These include:
Attorney General Deposit Five
Chief Secretary Deposit Two
Chief Secretary Deposit Three
District Commissioner Fort Hall
District Commissioner Kakamega
District Commissioner Kiambu
District Commissioner Nakuru
District Commissioner Uasin Gishu
Government House Deposit Three
Labour Deposit Two
Labour Deposit Three
Labour Deposit Five
Labour Deposit Nine
Land and Settlement Deposit One
Judiciary Deposit One
Member for African Affairs Deposit Two
Member for African Affairs Deposit Seven
Member for African Affairs Deposit Eight
Member for African Affairs Deposit Nine
Provincial Commissioner Central Province
Provincial Commissioner Nakuru
Provincial Commissioner Rift Valley Province
President's Office Deposit Two
President's Office Deposit Three
President's Office Deposit One Hundred and Twenty Nine

4. Labour Officer, Molo
The deposits of the Labour Officer, Molo are located at the Nakuru Labour Office. Files cover the period 1953–70. Most relevant for our purposes were the following files:
Confidential Two
Confidential Three
Labour, District Security Minutes 1955–67

5. Kenya Land Office
Contains files on farms in the European settled areas. Particularly useful for the periods 1931–45 and 1954–59.

6. Nakuru Labour Office
Contains a file on every farm in Nakuru District. In addition it contains a valuable collection of monthly, quarterly and annual reports on all the districts of the Rift Valley Province. It also contains a complete set of files on the General and Agricultural Workers Union. The following files were particularly useful:
Confidential One
Confidential Twenty One

Bibliography

7. Provincial Commissioner, Nyeri
This archive was useful for obtaining information on the early period 1905-30. Most of the material remains unfiled. It also contains monthly reports on Nairobi during the period 1930-64.

8. Provincial Commissioner, Rift Valley Province
The office of the Provincial Commissioner in Nakuru contains useful files on all the districts of the province. The main files used were:
Land 16/2/2
Land 16/5
Labour 27/6/1
Labour 27/6/II
Labour 27/5/5
Labour 27/20/2
Law and Order 17/1/6
Law and Order 17/17
District Commissioner, Uasin Gishu
Confidential Twenty Two

9. Public Record Office
Series C.O. 533 Kenya Original Correspondence
Series C.O. 544 Kenya Sessional Papers

Interviews
Persons other than those who requested confidentiality are named in the footnotes.

Newspapers
East African Standard (EAS)
Kenya Weekly News (KWN)
Leader of British East Africa (LBEA)
These papers were consulted in the newspaper library of the British Museum, Colindale or in the Macmillan Library, Nairobi.

Unpublished theses

Mueller, S.D. (1972) 'Political parties in Kenya: patterns of opposition and dissent, 1919-1969' (PhD, Princeton).
Redley, M.G. (1976) 'The politics of a predicament, the white community in Kenya, 1918-1932' (PhD, Cambridge).
Spencer, J. (1977) 'The Kenya African Union, 1944-1953' (PhD, Columbia).
Throup, D.W. (1983) 'The governorship of Sir Philip Mitchell in Kenya, 1944-1952' (PhD, Cambridge).

Official publications

1. United Kingdom government: parliamentary papers and colonial reports

1934 Cmd. 4556 *Report of the Kenya Land Commission* (Chairman Sir Morris Carter).
1955 Cmd. 9475 *East Africa Royal Commission, 1953-55: Report* (Chairman Sir Hugh Dow).
1960 Cmd. 1030 *Historical Survey of the Origins and Growth of Mau Mau* (F.D. Corfield).

Bibliography

2. Kenya Government Publications

1913 *Native Labour Commission 1912-1913; Evidence and Report.*
1920 *Agricultural Census* (also 1921, 1923, 1928, 1930, 1931).
1927 *Report of the Local Government Commission, Volume 2, The Settled Areas.*
1939 *Settlement Committee Report.*
1947 *The Agrarian Problem in Kenya* (Sir Philip Mitchell).
1947 *The Problem of the Squatter; economic survey of resident labour in Kenya* (J.H. Martin).
1953 *Report of the Inquiry into the General Economy of Farming in the Highlands* (L.G. Troup).

Other publications

1. Books

Anonymous (1982), *Independent Kenya*, London.
Astrow, A. (1983), *Zimbabwe: The Revolution That Lost Its Way*, London.
Barnett, D.L. and Njama, K. (1966), *Mau Mau From Within*, New York.
Bloch, M. (1966), *French Rural History*, London.
Buijtenhuis, R. (1973), *Mau Mau – Twenty Years After: The Myth and the Survivors*, The Hague.
Buijtenhuis, R. (1982), *Essays on Mau Mau: Contributions to Mau Mau Historiography*, Leiden.
Burrowes, R.A. (1984), *The Wild Coast: An Account of Politics in Guyana*, Cambridge, Mass.
Carothers, J.C. (1954), *The Psychology of Mau Mau*, Nairobi.
Chandos, Viscount (1962), *Memoirs*, London.
Chesneaux, J. (1973), *Peasant Revolts in China 1840-1949*, London.
Clark, S. (1979), *Social Origins of the Irish Land War*, Princeton.
Clayton, A. and Savage, D.C. (1974), *Government and Labour in Kenya 1895-1963*, London.
Comeford, M. (1969), *The First Dail*, Dublin.
Cone, L.W. and Lipscomb, J.F. (1972), *The History of Kenya Agriculture*, Nairobi.
Gallagher, J.A. (1982) *The Decline, Revival and Fall of the British Empire: the Ford Lectures and Other Essays*, Cambridge.
Gerhart, G.M. (1979), *Black Power in South Africa*, Berkeley.
Gertzel, C. (1970), *The Politics of Independent Kenya*, London.
Goldsworthy, D. (1971), *Colonial Issues in British Politics 1945-61: From 'Colonial Development' to 'Winds of Change'*, Oxford.
Greaves, C. Desmond (1976), *The Life and Times of James Connolly*, London.
Harbeson, J.W. (1973), *Nation-Building in Kenya*, Evanston.
Harris, W. (1947) *A Discussion of the Problem of the Squatter*, Nairobi.
Holland, R.F. (1985), *European Decolonization 1918-1981*, London.
Horowitz, R. (1967), *The Political Economy of South Africa*, London.
Jones, N.S. Carey (1966), *The Anatomy of Uhuru*, Manchester.
Kaggia, B. (1975), *Roots of Freedom 1921-1963*, Nairobi.
Kanogo, T. (1987), *Squatters and the Roots of Mau Mau, 1905-63*, London.
Karimi, J. and Ochieng, P. (1980), *The Kenyatta Succession*, Nairobi.
Kenyatta, J. (1968), *Suffering Without Bitterness*, Nairobi.
Kilson, M. (1966), *Political Change in a West African State*, Cambridge.
Kitching, G. (1980), *Class and Economic Change in Kenya*, London.
Lamb, G. (1974), *Peasant Politics*, Brighton.
Leakey, L.S.B. (1954), *Defeating Mau Mau*, London.
Leo, C. (1984), *Land and Class in Kenya*, Toronto.
Leys, C. (1975), *Underdevelopment in Kenya: The Political Economy of Neo-Colonialism 1964-1971*, London.
Louis, W.R. (1984), *The British Empire in the Middle East 1945-51: Arab Nationalism, The United States and Post War Imperialism*, Oxford.
Marable, M. (1987), *African and Caribbean Politics: From Kwame Nkrumah to Maurice Bishop*, London.

Bibliography

Marx, K. (1973), *Grundrisse*, London.

Maughan-Brown, D. (1985), *Land, Freedom and Fiction: History and Ideology in Kenya*, London.

Mosley, P. (1983), *The Settler Economies: Studies in the Economic History of Kenya and Southern Rhodesia 1900-1963*, Cambridge.

Muriuki, G. (1974), *A History of the Kikuyu, 1500-1900*, Nairobi.

Murray-Brown, J. (1972), *Kenyatta*, London.

Odingo, R.S. (1971), *The Kenyan Highlands: Land Use and Agricultural Development*, Nairobi.

Pearce, R.D. (1982), *The Turning Point in Africa: British Colonial Policy, 1938-1948*, London.

Ranger, T.O. (1985), *Peasant Consciousness and Guerrilla War in Zimbabwe*, London.

Rooney, D. (1982), *Sir Charles Arden-Clarke*, London.

Rosberg, C.G. and Nottingham, J. (1966), *The Myth of 'Mau Mau': Nationalism in Kenya*, New York.

Rothchild, D.R. (1973), *Racial Bargaining in Independent Kenya*, Oxford.

Rudé, G. (1970), *Paris and London in the 18th Century*, London.

Senga, W. et al. (1980), *Population Growth and Agricultural Development in Kenya*, Nairobi.

Skocpol, T. (1979), *States and Social Revolutions: A Comparative Analysis of France, Russia and China*, Cambridge.

Sorrenson, M.P.K. (1967), *Land Reform in the Kikuyu Country*, Nairobi.

Sorrenson, M.P.K. (1968), *Origins of European Settlement in Kenya*, London.

Spinner, T.J. (1984), *A Political and Social History of Guyana 1945-1983*, Boulder.

Stichter, S.B. (1982), *Migrant Labour in Kenya: Capitalism and African Response, 1895-1975*, London.

Throup, D.W. (1987), *Economic and Social Origins of Mau Mau 1945-53*, London.

Tignor, R.L. (1976), *The Colonial Transformation of Kenya*, Princeton.

Tilly, C. (1978), *From Mobilization to Revolution*, Reading, Mass.

Townshend, C. (1983), *Political Violence in Ireland*, Oxford.

Van Zwanenberg, R.M.A. (1975), *Colonial Capitalism and Labour in Kenya 1914-1939*, Nairobi.

Wassermann, G. (1976), *Politics of Decolonization: Kenya Europeans and the Land Issue, 1960-1965*, Cambridge.

Weiss, H. (1967), *Political Protest in the Congo*, Princeton.

Wipper, A. (1977), *Rural Rebels*, Nairobi.

Wolf, E.R. (1969), *Peasant Wars of the Twentieth Century*, New York.

2. Articles

Alavi, H. (1965), 'Peasants and revolution', in R. Miliband and J. Saville (eds), *The Socialist Register*, London, pp. 241-77.

Arden-Clarke, C. (1958), 'Eight years in the Gold Coast', *African Affairs*, January.

Arrighi, G. (1970), 'Labour supplies in historical perspective: a study of the proletarianization of the African peasantry in Rhodesia', *Journal of Development Studies*, vol. 6, no. 3, pp. 197-234.

Berman, B.J. (1976), 'Bureaucracy and incumbent violence: colonial administration and the origins of the "Mau Mau" Emergency', *British Journal of Political Science*, vol. 6, pp. 143-75.

Bundy, C. (1972), 'The emergence and decline of a South African peasantry', *African Affairs*, vol. 71, no. 285, pp. 369-88.

Bundy, C. (1985), 'Land and liberation: the South African national liberation movements and the agrarian question, 1920s-1960s', *Review of African Political Economy*.

Ferguson, D.F. (1976), 'Rural/urban relations and peasant radicalism: a preliminary statement', *Comparative Studies in Society and History*, January.

Furedi, F. (1973), 'The African crowd in Nairobi; popular movements and elite politics', *Journal of African History*, vol. 14, no. 2, pp. 275-90.

Furedi, F. (1974a), 'The social composition of the Mau Mau movement in the White

229

Bibliography

Highlands', *Journal of Peasant Studies*, vol. 1, no. 4, pp. 486–505.

Furedi, F. (1974b), 'The development of anti-Asian opinion among Africans in Nakuru District, Kenya', *African Affairs*, vol. 73, no. 292, pp. 347–58.

Furedi, F. (1975), 'The Kikuyu squatters in the Rift Valley, 1918–1928', in B.A. Ogot (ed.), *Hadith, 5: Economic and Social History of East Africa*, Nairobi; pp. 177–94.

Gough, K. (1968–69), 'Peasant resistance and revolution in South India', *Pacific Affairs*, vol. 41.

Grossman, H. (1948), 'The evolutionist revolt against classical economics', *Journal of Political Economy*, vol. 51, nos. 5 and 6.

Kanogo, T.M.J. (1977), 'Rift Valley Squatters and Mau Mau', *Kenya Historical Review*, vol. 5, no. 2, pp. 243–52.

Keller, E.J. (1973), 'A twentieth century model: the Mau Mau transformation from social banditry to social rebellion', *Kenya Historical Review*, vol. 1, no. 2, pp. 189–206.

Kipkorir, B.E. (1977), 'Mau Mau and the politics of the transfer of power in Kenya, 1957–1960', *Kenya Historical Review*, vol. 5, no. 2, pp. 313–28.

Landsberger, H.A. (1974), 'Peasant unrest: themes and variations' in H.A. Landsberger (ed.), *Rural Protest: Peasant Movements and Social Change*, London.

Lukacs, G. (1971), 'What is orthodox Marxism?', in G. Lukacs, *History and Class Consciousness*, London.

Maina wa Kinyatti (1977), 'Mau Mau: the peak of African political organization in colonial Kenya', *Kenya Historical Review*, vol. 5, no. 2, pp. 287–311.

Marx, K. and Engels, F. (1978), 'Address to the Central Authority of the League', in Marx and Engels: *Collected Works*, vol. 10, 1978.

Njonjo, A.L.N. (1980), 'The Kenya peasantry: a reassessment', *Review of African Political Economy*, no. 20, pp. 27–40.

Ochieng, W. (1976), 'Review of *Roots of Freedom 1921–1963*', *Kenya Historical Review*, vol. 4, no. 1.

Ogot, B.A. (1977), 'Politics, culture and music in central Kenya: a study of Mau Mau 'hymns 1951–1956', *Kenya Historical Review*, vol. 5, no. 2, pp. 275–86.

Omosule, M. (1974), 'Kiama Kia Mungi: Kikuyu reaction to land consolidation in Kenya', *Transafrican Journal of History*, vol. 4, nos. 1–2, pp. 115–34.

Rennie, J.K. (1978), 'White farmers, black tenants and landlord legislation: Southern Rhodesia 1890–1930', *Journal of Southern African Studies*, vol. 5, no. 1, pp. 86–98.

Shanin, T. (1971), 'Peasantry as a political factor', in T. Shanin (ed.), *Peasants and Peasant Societies*, Harmondsworth.

Stenson, M. (1974), 'The ethnic and urban bases of communist revolt in Malaya', in J.W. Lewis (ed.), *Peasant Rebellion and Communist Revolution in Asia*, Stanford.

Tamarkin, M. (1977), 'Mau Mau in Nakuru', *Kenya Historical Review*, vol. 5, no. 2, pp. 225–41.

Wasserman, G. (1973), 'Continuity and counter-insurgency: the role of land reform in decolonizing Kenya, 1962–1971', *Canadian Journal of African Studies*, vol. 7, no. 1, pp. 133–48.

Yankwich, R. (1977), 'Continuity in Kenya history: negative unity and the legitimacy of the Mau Mau rebellion', *Kenya Historical Review*, vol. 5, no. 2, pp. 349–63.

Index

35, 36, 37n; underdeveloped land, 30

unemployment, 158–61, 166, 210; *see also* labour

Vidal, M.,45

wage–labour, 11, 25, 27
Wainana, Duncan, 132
Wambugu, Kingori, 95
Waruhiu, Cheif, 54, 85, 116
Wasserman, G., 182, 184
Watson Report, 215
Waweru, Michael, 96
Waweru, Njugune, 94
Watu wa Mungu (God's people), 69–70
Webster, J., 158
'Weeping Kamaus' *see Kamau Muthori*
Weiss, H., 190
wheat production, 25, 28, 32; Laikipia District, 28; Nakuru District, 28
White Highlands, 4, 5, 9, 11, 13,

19, 23–37, 43, 46; African ownership of land in, 162–3, 171n, 183–5; decolonization, 172–204; economic hardship (1961), 174; land reform, 182–5, millenarian sects, 70; *see also* Rift Valley

women: Bahati Transit Farm, 196; compulsory labour, 91; Limuru, 89, workers, 26
Women and Youth Wing (Kenya African National Union), 169
World War I, 42
World War II, 26–7, 31, 78

Yankwich, R.,16
Yatta, 82
Yeoman land settlement schemes, 183
Young Kikuyu Association, 76
Youth League (African National Congress), 222

Zaire, 190
Zimbabwe, 3, 6, 131, 190; *see also* Southern Rhodesia